Designing a World-Class Architecture Firm

Designing a World-Class Architecture Firm

The People, Stories, and Strategies Behind HOK

Patrick MacLeamy, FAIA

WILEY

Cover image: Courtesy of HOK
Cover design: Wiley

This book is printed on acid-free paper.

Copyright © 2020 by John Wiley & Sons, Inc. All rights reserved.

Published by John Wiley & Sons, Inc., Hoboken, New Jersey.

Published simultaneously in Canada.

No part of this publication may be reproduced, stored in a retrieval system, or transmitted in any form or by any means, electronic, mechanical, photocopying, recording, scanning, or otherwise, except as permitted under Section 107 or 108 of the 1976 United States Copyright Act, without either the prior written permission of the Publisher, or authorization through payment of the appropriate per-copy fee to the Copyright Clearance Center, 222 Rosewood Drive, Danvers, MA 01923, (978) 750-8400, fax (978) 646-8600, or on the web at www.copyright.com. Requests to the Publisher for permission should be addressed to the Permissions Department, John Wiley & Sons, Inc., 111 River Street, Hoboken, NJ 07030, (201) 748-6011, fax (201) 748-6008, or online at www.wiley.com/go/permissions.

Limit of Liability/Disclaimer of Warranty: While the publisher and author have used their best efforts in preparing this book, they make no representations or warranties with respect to the accuracy or completeness of the contents of this book and specifically disclaim any implied warranties of merchantability or fitness for a particular purpose. No warranty may be created or extended by sales representatives or written sales materials. The advice and strategies contained herein may not be suitable for your situation. You should consult with a professional where appropriate. Neither the publisher nor the author shall be liable for damages arising herefrom.

For general information about our other products and services, please contact our Customer Care Department within the United States at (800) 762-2974, outside the United States at (317) 572-3993 or fax (317) 572-4002.

Wiley publishes in a variety of print and electronic formats and by print-on-demand. Some material included with standard print versions of this book may not be included in e-books or in print-on-demand. If this book refers to media such as a CD or DVD that is not included in the version you purchased, you may download this material at http://booksupport.wiley.com. For more information about Wiley products, visit www.wiley.com.

Library of Congress Cataloging-in-Publication Data

Name: MacLeamy, Patrick Edward, 1942– author.
Title: Designing a world-class architecture firm: the people, stories, and strategies behind HOK / Patrick Edward MacLeamy, FAIA.
Description: Hoboken, New Jersey: Wiley, [2020] | Includes index.
Identifiers: LCCN 2019053600 (print) | LCCN 2019053601 (ebook) | ISBN 9781119685302 (hardback) | ISBN 9781119685456 (adobe pdf) | ISBN 9781119685432 (epub)
Subjects: LCSH: Hellmuth, Obata & Kassabaum. | Hellmuth, Obata & Kassabaum—Employees.
Classification: LCC NA737.H385 M33 2020 (print) | LCC NA737.H385 (ebook) | DDC 720.92—dc23
LC record available at https://lccn.loc.gov/2019053600
LC ebook record available at https://lccn.loc.gov/2019053601

ISBN 9781119685302 (cloth); ISBN 9781119685456 (ePDF); ISBN 9781119685432 (ePub); 9781119685463 (obook)

Printed in the United States of America

VF7BF435B-1EBF-4183-A7FC-7EEAD14E6D16_031220

For Jeanne . . .
the love of my life and HOK's greatest gift.

Contents

Introduction ... xiii

Coming to HOK ... xvii
Looking for My Place ... xvii
Closer to Home ... xvii
The Interview ... xix
Big Dreams ... xix
Impressions of HOK ... xx
My First Assignment ... xxi

SECTION ONE   The Founders, 1955–1982 ... 1

CHAPTER 1   The Problem with Traditional Firms ... 3
Why St. Louis? ... 3
Hellmuth & Hellmuth ... 4
George Francis Hellmuth ... 5
The Depression-Proof Firm ... 6

CHAPTER 2   A New Kind of Architecture Firm ... 9
Starting HYL/LHY ... 10
Gyo Obata ... 11
George Kassabaum ... 13
Forming HOK ... 15
HOK's Early Years ... 17

CHAPTER 3   Innovate Early and Often ... 21
Marketing Innovation ... 21
Design Innovation ... 23
Production Innovation ... 25
Start-to-Finish Innovation ... 28
Core Boards Innovation ... 29
Staffing Innovation ... 29
Ownership Innovation ... 30

CHAPTER 4	**Company Culture Is Crucial**	33
	Mutual Respect	33
	Considerate Communication	34
	Taking Care of Employees	34
	Family Atmosphere	35
	Storytelling	36
	The HOK Name	37
	St. Louis Office Fire	38
CHAPTER 5	**Growth: Project Offices**	41
	Planting a Flag in San Francisco	41
	Launching in Washington, DC	43
	Landing in Dallas	44
CHAPTER 6	**Many Jobs, One Firm**	47
	Going to Pittsburgh	47
	Settling in San Francisco	48
	Working in Alaska	50
	San Francisco Projects	53
CHAPTER 7	**Managing Versus Leading**	57
	Becoming a Project Manager	57
	Managing Versus Leading	58
	Case Study: Moscone Center	60
	HOK as Matchmaker	63
CHAPTER 8	**Transitions: Succession Planning**	67
	Naming Successors	67
	Adding HOK New York	72
	George Hellmuth Triumphs	73
	George Kassabaum Dies	74

SECTION TWO   The Obata Era, 1982–1993 — 77

CHAPTER 9	**A Designer Leads the Firm**	79
	Building Buildings Again	79
	Rise of Project Specialists	80
	The New Marketing	80
	The HOK Matrix	81
	Growing Pains	82
	Signs of Trouble	83
	Bringing in the Pros	84

CHAPTER 10   Run Toward Trouble — 87
- Becoming Managing Principal — 87
- Run Toward Trouble — 88
- Collecting Money — 89
- Working in the Middle East — 90

CHAPTER 11   Growth: Project Specialists — 93
- Lessons of Los Angeles — 93
- Sports Design Specialty — 94
- Team Member in Tampa — 96
- Retail Design Specialty — 97
- Opening in Hong Kong — 98
- Launching in London — 99

CHAPTER 12   Selling Stock to Investors — 101
- Kajima Invests — 101
- Expanding in Europe and Asia — 103
- Traveling to Tokyo — 103
- HOK Tokyo — 106
- Sustainable Design — 107

CHAPTER 13   Transitions: Hiring Family — 109
- Bob Stauder Resigns — 109
- Clark Davis Helms St. Louis — 110
- Bill Hellmuth Joins HOK — 110
- Gyo Obata Consults — 112

SECTION THREE   The Sincoff Era, 1993–2002 — 115

CHAPTER 14   Get Bigger or Get Better? — 117
- The Sincoff Strategy — 117
- Sharing the Strategy — 120
- Offices Push Back — 124

CHAPTER 15   A Firm-Wide Role — 127
- Innovating in Silicon Valley — 127
- Doubling Your Reach — 129
- Overseas Adventures — 130
- Joining the ExCom — 133

Contents

CHAPTER 16 Embracing Technology — 135
    Computer-Aided Design — 135
    Tech 2000 — 136
    Going Paperless — 139
    buildingSMART — 140

CHAPTER 17 Growth: Buying Firms — 145
    CRS, Houston — 145
    Eduardo Terrazas y Asociados, Mexico City — 147
    HOK Chicago — 148
    Cecil Denny Highton, London — 148
    Urbana Architects, Toronto — 149
    Lobb Partnership, London — 150
    Expansion in Europe — 150
    HOK Dubai — 151

CHAPTER 18 Enforcing Financial Metrics — 153
    Charm School — 153
    The 50 Percent Rule — 155
    The 90-Day Rule — 155
    The 10-Month Rule — 156
    Simplified Accounting — 157
    Expanding the Board — 158

CHAPTER 19 Transitions: The Second Generation — 161
    King Graf Retires — 161
    George Hellmuth Dies — 161
    Paul Watson Steps Aside — 162
    Mahon and Pratzel Join the ExCom — 163
    Jerry Sincoff Retires — 163

CHAPTER 20 Confronting Crisis — 165
    The Kajima Crisis — 165
    The Bank of America Crisis — 166
    The HOK Sport Crisis — 166
    Becoming CEO — 167

SECTION FOUR — The MacLeamy Era, 2003–2016 — 169

CHAPTER 21 Communicating Your Vision — 171
    A Company in Crisis — 171
    The Election — 173
    The Pyramid Strategy — 174

CHAPTER 22 Empowering Firm Leadership — 179
- Invigorating the ExCom — 179
- Expanding the ExCom — 180
- Naming a Design Successor — 181
- Finding an Operations Leader — 182
- Removing Office Leaders — 183
- Empowering the Board of Directors — 185
- Positive Peer Pressure — 186
- Replacing Board Members — 186

CHAPTER 23 The Effort Curve — 189
- The CURT Summons — 189
- The Effort Curve — 190
- Smart Effort Curve — 192
- The Effort Curve at HOK — 193
- Case Study: KAUST — 194
- The MacLeamy Curve — 196

CHAPTER 24 Fixing Offices — 197
- Finding New Leaders — 197
- The Fixer — 198
- The Recruit — 200
- Case Study: HOK New York — 201
- Tweaking the Bonus Program — 202

CHAPTER 25 Fixing Central Services — 205
- Consolidating Accounting — 205
- Fixing Advance Technology — 206
- Streamlining Human Resources — 207

CHAPTER 26 Reclaiming Company Culture — 209
- Visiting the Offices — 209
- Explaining HOK Stock — 210
- Posting Staff Photos — 212
- Reviving Core Boards — 213
- Celebrating 50 Years — 214
- A Different Kind of Retreat — 215

CHAPTER 27 Buying Your Freedom — 219
- Paying Off the Bank — 219
- Buying Out Kajima — 221
- Spinning Off HOK Sport — 222

CHAPTER 28 — Transitions: The Third Generation — 225
- Susan Williams Joins the OpsCom, ExCom — 225
- General Counsel Promotion — 226
- Human Resources Changes — 227
- Riccardo Mascia Heads Home — 228
- Bill Valentine Retires — 228
- Financial Team Changes — 229
- Carl Galioto Joins the ExCom — 229
- Consolidating Offices — 230

CHAPTER 29 — The Right to Dream — 231
- Pressing Sustainable Design — 231
- Case Study: Abu Dhabi National Oil Company — 232
- HOK Product Design — 234
- Expanding Again — 235
- Back in the Game — 236
- Finding the Next CEO — 238
- My "Repurposing" — 240

Afterword: HOK Today — 241
- The State of HOK — 241
- Looking to the Future — 242
- The Hellmuth Strategy — 243

Acknowledgments — 245

About the Author — 247

Index — 249

Introduction

When I became CEO of HOK, people would often ask me, "Now that you're an executive, do you miss designing buildings?" I would always reply, "No, because now I'm designing a firm." That answer, so often repeated, became the inspiration for the title of this book: *Designing a World-Class Architecture Firm*. Of course, I was not HOK's original designer.

HOK's founders—George Hellmuth, Gyo Obata, and George Kassabaum—were visionaries who set out to establish a new kind of architecture firm that would outlast them all. They succeeded—and then some. Today, 65 years later, HOK is one of the largest architecture and engineering firms in the world.[1] This book tells the inside story of how they did it. However, it's not just a history of HOK, even if that history is fascinating—and often funny. Instead, I have used HOK's story as a vehicle for sharing lessons we learned along the way that will be beneficial to other architects, designers—and really anyone in a creative or service business.

Most architecture books are about a firm's design work, but not this one. I have included some significant projects to illustrate milestones in HOK's growth and development, but that is not the main thrust of the book. Instead, as the subtitle says, I have written about the people, stories, and strategies behind HOK because they are stories worth sharing with lessons worth learning.

People. Let's start with the people. Founder George Hellmuth watched his father's architecture practice repeatedly go boom and bust throughout his childhood. How did that inform his efforts to build a "depression-proof" firm? George Kassabaum drafted the atomic bomb rack for the *Enola Gay* aircraft. Did that have anything to do with his unofficial motto? He often told us: "Do the right thing, always." Gyo Obata served in the U.S. Army, even though his Japanese-American family was interned during World War II. Perhaps, that character-building experience helped him set aside his own ego, listen carefully to each client, and come up with the best design solution just for them—a hallmark of HOK's work.

Stories. HOK's stories were my original inspiration for writing this book. Whenever HOK people would gather for a bull session swapping our firm's very own folklore, someone would always say, "We should write down these stories. They're funny and insightful at the same time." There were humorous stories, like the time one of our early leaders was mistaken for royalty in Saudi Arabia. There were inspiring stories, such as the weekend HOK's St. Louis office went up in flames and devoted employees managed to set up a new office and re-create crucial lost work by Monday morning. And there were harrowing

---
[1] "ENR 2018 Top 500 Design Firms," *Engineering News Record*.

stories, like the double crisis when our investors threatened to pull their funding and our bank threatened to call our loan—both on the same day—either of which would have bankrupted HOK.

Strategies. The founders were children of the Great Depression and deployed multiple strategies to help HOK not only thrive during good times but also survive during bad times. Later leaders layered on their own insightful strategies for success. Of course, sometimes we improvised emergency tactics on the fly, in response to mistakes or even disasters. I share all the lessons we learned along the way, whether from our successes or our failures. Those lessons apply if your firm wants to get bigger—or just better. There is relatable, actionable advice in every chapter, such as:

- Expand into multiple cities, diversify into multiple services, and embrace multiple building types to recession- and depression-proof your firm.
- Organize your practice around specialized leaders—like design, technical, marketing and management—because it's more efficient than if every leader does everything.
- Lead, don't manage, your people. Think of it like leading them into battle rather than cracking the whip from behind.
- Reshape your compensation program to reward not just profitability, but other factors important to your company culture, such as collaboration, quality of design, and client service.
- "Run toward trouble," rather than avoiding it, because small problems become big problems and big problems become disasters if you allow them to fester.
- Shift your efforts earlier in the design process so you catch mistakes when they are still just drawings, rather than when they are already under construction, and you will save time, money—and your reputation.
- Enforce financial metrics—yes, creative professionals need them too—and this book contains clear, simple ones you can adapt.

I spent 50 years at HOK, working my way up from junior designer to CEO—where else can you do that?—so this book also contains a dash of memoir and opinion. I observed the transition from drawing on paper to designing by computer and from one Midwestern office to a global practice of many offices. I was there for the evolution from a pure architecture firm to a highly diversified practice spanning architecture, engineering, interior design, graphics, consulting, and more. I watched as HOK architects went from being generalists—who could and would design anything—to specialists focused on health care, hospitality, aviation, sports, justice, and more. In other words, I witnessed the majority of the firm's history and learned most of its lessons directly.

However, despite being there, rest assured that I did not just rely on my own memory to write this book. I spent two years and interviewed more than 40 HOK colleagues to gather material. I accessed reams of internal documents and scores of external articles about HOK. I put in the time because I appreciate all that HOK did for me and because I believe that what I learned is worth sharing with others. If, after all this effort, there are any errors in the book, they are mine and mine alone.

This book is best read from start to finish, rather than as a reference book. After all, it's a story, and each chapter builds upon the last. That said, as I recount pivotal moments in HOK's history, I make a point of calling out the business lessons we learned that others can benefit from. At times, I may overexplain terminology an architect would already know, but have done so in hopes other creative and service professionals can get something out of the book. To reinforce information that may be helpful to readers, at the end of each chapter you will find a section called "To Design a World-Class Firm" with bullet points recapping the takeaways found in that chapter.

Architecture is a passion, not just a profession, and my own passion for the field extends to the business side. Just as designers delight in finding elegant solutions to design challenges, I came to love finding elegant solutions to business challenges. I hope that what HOK and I learned can help you design your own world-class firm.

Coming to HOK

In the spring of 1967, I was finishing graduate school in architecture at the University of Illinois at Champaign–Urbana. Graduation was approaching in June, and my fellowship was running out. I was excited to get out into the world and see what I could do, and I needed a job right away. I was born and grew up in Alton, Illinois, located on the Mississippi River a few miles upriver from St. Louis. Having grown up near St. Louis, I was eager to go somewhere else to begin my career.

Looking for My Place

Determined to find a firm that felt like a good fit, I drove my Volkswagen Bug—the car of choice for college students of the mid-1960s—to Chicago, for an interview at Skidmore, Owings & Merrill (SOM). Their offices were in the iconic Inland Steel Building at 30 Monroe Street. Designed by Walter Netsch of SOM in the 1950s, the building featured perimeter columns and a side core for stairs and elevators, leaving the interior floors open. The SOM office was completely modular, in the international style, with long rows of drafting tables lined up under banks of fluorescent lights. I received a job offer at SOM, but the cold, rigid look of the place didn't feel right, and I declined. It may sound crazy to turn down a job offer, at what was perhaps the most prestigious architecture firm in the United States, because of the sterile look of its offices, but I was a budding architect looking for the right place to learn and grow. My search continued.

On spring break, I loaded my portfolio into the Bug and drove to Boston because design magazines regularly featured Boston firms. I interviewed with a lower-level staffer at a firm called Cambridge 7, who said my work was good but that they couldn't hire me that day. "Would you like to become an unpaid intern until we have an opening?" he asked. I needed a job *now*—and turned him down.

Closer to Home

I began to think about interviewing with Hellmuth, Obata & Kassabaum (HOK), a young firm in St. Louis. In architecture school my professors required me to select and critique a modern building, and I chose the James S. McDonnell Planetarium in St. Louis, designed by Gyo Obata of HOK and completed in 1963. I had visited the planetarium several times and was fascinated by the elegance of the design.

xvii

The defining form of any planetarium is the dome under which images of the night sky are projected. However, in most planetariums, the dome is almost invisible after adding the lobby, restrooms, exhibition spaces, and offices. Instead, Obata placed the McDonnell Planetarium dome as a freestanding element inside a thin-shelled concrete hyperboloid, a graceful curved shape that tapers in from the base to a narrow waist before increasing toward the top. The hyperboloid is light, elegant, and appears to float above its prominent site in a corner of Forest Park.

Inside, an open lobby and exhibit space surround the planetarium, allowing unobstructed views of the dome. A working observatory is located within the open top of the hyperboloid shielded from city lights, making live observations of the sky possible. As I reflected on the brilliance of the McDonnell Planetarium design, I began to think it would be a great experience to work with Gyo Obata.

James S. McDonnell Planetarium, St. Louis, Missouri.
Source: Photo by Robert Pettus. Photo Courtesy of HOK.

Bill Voelker, one of my friends from my undergraduate days at Illinois, was working at HOK as a designer under Obata, and I called him for advice. "How did you get to HOK?" I asked Bill. "What's it like?" "HOK is a great place, like a big family, and we're doing dynamic work," said Bill. "I can get you an interview with Obata." By now it was May, and I was on the verge of graduating. I got back in the VW and this time drove the short distance to the HOK office in St. Louis.

The Interview

The receptionist took me to meet Gyo Obata for my interview. He was in his mid-40s, slight of build, with a graying crewcut and dressed in a white shirt with a narrow black tie. Obata was filled with energy. His first question was "What are your ambitions?"

"I love architecture and feel I may have some gifts. I want to do great work," I said.

Although he looked through my portfolio, Obata seemed more interested in who I was as a person. After some conversation, he looked me in the eye and said, "This firm is *going places*. We just won the largest high school project in the country to design five new high schools in Pittsburgh, Pennsylvania to replace all the high schools in the city. It's a big, challenging project and you can get in at the beginning. I will oversee that project and want you to work *directly* with me. How about $650 per month?"

My father had schooled me in how to handle this question. "Always say you were hoping to get more," he had told me. "I was hoping for more," I said. "Okay, we'll make it $700," said Obata. I was immensely impressed with my dad's advice: I'd been hired one minute and the next had successfully negotiated my first raise—$700 a month would be . . . $8,400 a year! "If I can get up to $10,000 a year, I'll be rolling in clover," I thought.

"When can you start?" asked Obata. I explained that my last class was in 10 days, then I would attend graduation and come to St. Louis. "Forget that," he said. "No one remembers their graduation. You start the Monday after your last class." And it was settled.

Big Dreams

St. Louis still was not my first choice as the city to begin my career, but I had a plan. I would work at HOK for a few years, then leverage that experience to land a position in a more exotic locale, maybe San Francisco. In just a few years I could be opening my own firm on the West Coast. But first, I needed to work under a licensed architect for three years, then sit for two days of grueling licensing exams at the state capital in Jefferson City. After those three years, I'd have a good portfolio to show. Then I could go west and really do something, I thought.

Why did I dream about the West Coast? Maybe because it seemed like the greatest possible contrast to industrial Alton, where I'd grown up. The surrounding area is open prairie and farmland, but Alton is situated where farmland gives way to the Mississippi floodplain, a flat area where steel mills, oil refineries, glassworks, and other heavy industries sprang up to utilize the river for shipping.

I found a place to rent at the Plaza Square Apartments directly across the street from the HOK office. The day of my last class came. I loaded up my Volkswagen in Champaign-Urbana, tied my mattress on the roof with binder twine, and drove three hours down to St. Louis. When I got there, the front of the mattress was covered with bugs. It was an inauspicious beginning to what would turn out to be a 50-year journey.

Impressions of HOK

It was June 1967. The HOK office occupied the second floor of a six-story building at the intersection of Olive and 14th Streets, 14 blocks from the Mississippi River. It was a bustling, exciting place. Two receptionists were busy answering the phones and receiving a steady stream of visitors. In those days, no one had telephones at their desks. Instead, there was a central switchboard with six or eight lines and a few phones scattered at stations around the office. Staff members were constantly being paged for calls: "Jerry Sincoff, you have a call on line two." It looked vibrant and impressive to someone just getting out of college.

Obata's corner office had glass walls, which allowed him to see his design team—but also allowed *them* to see *him*. It struck me as very democratic. HOK's offices were flooded with natural light from south-facing windows. Every project had a design leader and these leaders occupied semi-enclosed spaces in the center of the room, up against the elevator core. Their design teams worked at drafting tables on the perimeter of the room, closer to the windows. Yes, the grunts got the best light! So many companies place their executives' offices around the perimeter of the building, and as a result, lower-level employees never see the sun. HOK was different.

The department contained multiple design teams working on different projects. A small team was drawing up Obata's first concepts for a new graduate library for Stanford University. Another team was at work designing a new academic building for the University of Wisconsin. Not long after I started, Obata reassigned my old friend Bill Voelker to a team designing a new airport located midway between Dallas and Fort Worth, Texas. This just reinforced my impression that HOK was a young firm on the move.

Obata's department hummed with energy and purpose. Designers discussed their projects constantly, so the department was filled with conversation. Teams held more formal meetings with clients or engineering consultants in one of the busy conference rooms. The youngest, least experienced team members—like me—made lots of models and did drawing revisions as requested by the design leader or by Obata.

The design department was made up of almost all men, and everyone wore a white or blue dress shirt with a tie. Many of the designers took their cue from Obata and wore slacks and sport coats.

George Hellmuth was HOK's marketing principal. When I joined HOK in 1967, it was growing rapidly, all because Hellmuth had figured out you could use an airplane to expand your marketing, even if you only had one office in St. Louis. At the time, the average architecture firm was made up of eight people. That is still the case today. There's been no movement. Not every firm wants to grow, but HOK wanted to—and was—thanks to Hellmuth.

The first time I met Hellmuth, he was wearing a conservative dark suit with a white shirt and red tie. He tilted his head up and down to view me through the different lenses in his bifocals. He seemed to have a good sense of humor, and his assessment of me was, "Well, you look like you belong in Obata's department." He was referring to the tiny length of hair that covered the tops of my ears at a time when older men wore a short hairstyle. This was a sign to Hellmuth that I might best belong among the designers.

Hellmuth's office—like his haircut—was more traditional, with wood paneling, elegant drapes, and a heavy desk with a blotter. His secretary and his marketing team sat nearby. Just the fact that he had a full-time marketing team was revolutionary. Clients often came to Hellmuth's area for meetings in a well-appointed conference room. The trappings were intentional. Hellmuth was sort of the "grown up in the room," the respectable, second-generation St. Louis architect, who put prospective clients at ease, then reeled them in.

George Kassabaum led production, the largest department in the firm, with more people than marketing and design combined. Bustling teams of production architects made sure HOK's designs would work in the real world, keeping the rain out and the heat in. The versatile Kassabaum really held two jobs, because he was also responsible for firm-wide administration, with a team of accountants on hand to help.

My first meeting with Kassabaum did not take place immediately, as he was soon to become the national American Institute of Architects (AIA) president and was often away fulfilling this role. I learned that Hellmuth and Obata supported his AIA work since it helped the profession and enhanced HOK's reputation. Kassabaum was president of the American Institute of Architects from 1968 to 1969. This was another positive HOK characteristic I came to admire as time passed. The founders and the firm encouraged and supported people who had the desire to be involved with outside academic, professional, civic, or charitable activities.

I wondered how Kassabaum could afford to be away so much, especially since his responsibilities were large and demanding. After a few months, I finally had the opportunity to meet him between his frequent trips to AIA headquarters. He was distinguished-looking, fit, and impeccably dressed in a well-tailored suit, white shirt, and conservative tie. Handsome, with a full head of hair graying around the temples, he struck me as a true professional, someone to instill confidence in others.

Kassabaum brought me into his orderly office, offered me a chair, and said, "Tell me about yourself." He really *listened* as I began to talk, making me feel like the most important person in the world at that moment. He asked a few questions, then said, "This firm is built on people—talented, dedicated people. If you want to build a career here, it's up to you. If you decide to leave to find opportunity somewhere else, it's up to you. If you leave and discover you made a mistake, you are welcome to return to HOK—*one* time." I never forgot his words, and never left HOK. Over the years, other HOK people left to find opportunity elsewhere, but many returned after they were disappointed by what they found.

My First Assignment

Obata assigned me a space in the section of the design department occupied by the newly formed Pittsburgh *Great High Schools* team. Why that name? HOK certainly hoped the design would be great, but it was called the Great High Schools project because the city planned to consolidate all of Pittsburgh's existing high schools into five larger campuses.

My team was the largest in the office, with five or six designers. Our team leader, Bill Valentine, was on vacation my first two weeks at HOK, and I asked my teammates what he was like. They said he was enthusiastic, energetic, and smart—and one of Obata's favorite designers. When Bill returned from vacation to take responsibility for our team, it was as if a whirlwind had arrived. He seemed to be everywhere at once, visiting each team member, reviewing design progress, and leading us in new directions.

Bill was slim, with a head of curly hair and eyes that crinkled when he smiled. Instead of a suit and tie, Bill wore jeans and a white or blue dress shirt open at the neck—no tie. Sometimes he was so absorbed in his work that he did not seem to notice that his shirttail was hanging out. When Bill sat in his chair talking to someone, he had a way of drawing his feet up on the front of the seat so that he was talking over his knees. In later years, Bill gave up on dress shirts and began to wear black collarless shirts—long before Steve Jobs.

Bill liked to study the Great High Schools in cross-section to see how they fit with the hilly topography of Pittsburgh. I helped him draw the sections, then began to make study models of critical parts of each school. Bill often sent me across the street to the HOK model shop to make even larger study models of foam. He made frequent visits to the model shop to review my progress, and would often say, "Let's try something different." When Bill was satisfied, we brought the model across the street for Obata's review.

One day, when I was still basically brand new, as I sat at my drafting table working on another big cross-section, Obata's secretary came by and handed me an envelope. "You're going to Pittsburgh next week with Bill Valentine to meet the local architects," she told me. "Here's your plane ticket and hotel reservation." Although it seems quaint now, the idea that someone would pay me to get on an airplane and fly somewhere, then put me up at a hotel so I could go to a meeting, seemed like a dream.

My overwhelming impression as a young architect was that great things were happening at HOK. It was an exciting time to be there. In 1967, HOK had 150 people, and even though it was only 12 years old, had grown to become the largest firm in the state and one of the largest in the nation. The energy and ambition of the founders and the culture of teamwork and mutual accountability struck me as something very special. I began to wonder how these three brilliant men had come together to create this extraordinary firm.

> **M**y overwhelming impression as a young architect was that great things were happening at HOK.

SECTION ONE

THE FOUNDERS, 1955–1982

CHAPTER 1

The Problem with Traditional Firms

George Hellmuth, Gyo Obata, and George Kassabaum wanted to design a world-class architecture firm. But before they could establish HOK, they needed to come together in the same city. George Kassabaum's family moved around a bit during his childhood, and he ended up going to college in St. Louis, because it was not far from their latest hometown. Gyo Obata was from far away, in Berkeley, California, and also came to St. Louis for college. Both Kassabaum and Obata would leave and come back, before finally meeting Hellmuth in St. Louis. Hellmuth was the only one of the founders to grow up in the River City, where he had the formative experience of watching his father and uncle struggle to keep their own small architecture firm afloat. St. Louis may seem like an improbable place for one of the world's largest design firms to form, yet it has a significant history.

Why St. Louis?

St. Louis was a bustling French trading settlement that became part of the United States with the Louisiana Purchase, negotiated between President Thomas Jefferson and Napoleon Bonaparte in 1803. During the winter of 1803–1804, the Lewis and Clark expedition assembled men and supplies at Camp Dubois a few miles upstream from St. Louis. That spring, Lewis and Clark crossed the Mississippi and began their epic journey up the Missouri to explore the West. As a boy, I played at Camp Dubois Historic Site just a few miles from my home.

As the nation grew west, the need to move goods and people across the Mississippi, and St. Louis's central geographic position, combined to bring the city to prominence. In late 1874, a team of visionaries, including bridge designer James B. Eads, and a young entrepreneur named Andrew Carnegie, opened a combined roadway and railway bridge across the Mississippi. Named the Eads Bridge for its creator, it was the world's first all-steel arch bridge, the first bridge to exclusively use cantilever support, and one of the first to make use of pneumatic caissons. John A. Roebling, designer of the more-famous

Brooklyn Bridge, visited the construction site in St. Louis to learn how Eads managed to sink the caissons so deep. St. Louis had long been a city dependent on the Mississippi river for transport north and south. Now railroads connected St. Louis to the east and west, making it a hub of American commerce.

By 1903, St. Louis had grown to become the fourth largest city in the country and hosted a World's Fair to celebrate the centennial of the Lewis and Clark Expedition and the city's role in the settlement of the West. Inventors introduced the ice cream cone at that fair, and a firm called Hellmuth & Hellmuth was practicing architecture in St. Louis at that time.

Hellmuth & Hellmuth

George Hellmuth—father of HOK's George Hellmuth—and his brother, Harry Hellmuth, were partners in the firm. Naturally, they called their company Hellmuth & Hellmuth, and it had its heyday in the early 1900s, when St. Louis was at its peak. The practice was typical of that time, with the two partners and some draftsmen. Hellmuth & Hellmuth specialized in designing commercial buildings, projects for the Catholic Church, and grand mansions for wealthy St. Louis business leaders.

Hellmuth & Hellmuth's best-known work was the International Fur Exchange Building, completed in 1919, with office spaces for buyers and a large room for fur auctions. At that time, trade in beaver hides and other pelts was still significant and would continue into the 1950s. However, by 1997 the building was vacant and set to be torn down. Hotel developer Charles Drury stepped in to halt demolition and save the building, which he renovated, along with two adjoining properties, to become a hotel and restaurants. The International Fur Exchange Building is now listed on the National Register of Historic Places.

When Hellmuth & Hellmuth secured a commission for a project, George and Harry hired draftsmen to help with the work. During the course of the project, the partners trained them to do the work properly, and gradually a more effective operation would emerge. When the project ended, often there was no new work to take its place, so Hellmuth & Hellmuth would lay those people off, with the firm effectively losing the positive effects of the training.

The partners would begin again to find new work, then hire another fresh team, often bringing in brand new people who they once again needed to train. The end of every project meant the firm was starting over again, and it lost good, seasoned people when the work ran out. Without knowing where the next project was coming from or who might be needed for the work, the firm was never able to plan its own future. Hellmuth & Hellmuth lurched from crisis to crisis.

The second—and fatal—flaw in a traditional practice like Hellmuth & Hellmuth became apparent when the partners wished to retire, and no provision had been made to buy them out. The firm had to close its doors and the partners were left with little to show for their work. Succession planning was overlooked and underappreciated in the world of architecture.

FIGURE 1.1 International Fur Exchange Building, St. Louis, Missouri, designed by Hellmuth & Hellmuth. Source: Photo courtesy of HOK.

George Francis Hellmuth

But years before that, in 1907, George and his wife had a son. They named him after his father, but with a different middle name. Young George Francis Hellmuth also grew up wanting to become an architect. I have noticed that architecture often runs in families, and the Hellmuths are just one example. However, young George didn't want to emulate his father in all ways. He was distressed by the ups and downs he observed at the traditional firm run by his father and uncle. Architectural practice seemed like a roller coaster, and he wondered if the disheartening boom and bust cycles were inevitable.

The younger George Hellmuth graduated from Washington University with a Master of Architecture degree in 1931, then traveled to France for a year of touring and study at the École des Beaux-Arts in Fontainebleau. He returned to St. Louis in 1932, eager to begin work at Hellmuth & Hellmuth. However, the country, St. Louis, and the firm were in the grip of the Great Depression and his dad and uncle could not afford to hire him.

Instead, Hellmuth landed a job with the City of St. Louis as a junior architect designing bus stops and comfort stations. He worked for the city for seven years, then approached his father again about joining Hellmuth & Hellmuth. "No one in St. Louis knows how to practice architecture successfully," his father told him, "and that includes me. If you want to learn how, go to a big city, find a big office, and get them to take you on."[1] That's not bad advice for anyone following in a family member's footsteps.

Hellmuth took his father's suggestion and, in 1939, moved to Detroit, which was then flourishing as an auto manufacturing city and a rival to Chicago for dominance in the Midwest. He found work with Smith, Hinchman & Grylls (SHG), a regional firm with a reputation for good design and steady work serving the growing auto industry.

Hellmuth began as a junior designer at SHG, but his marketing skills soon became evident to the firm's leadership. They transferred him to the solicitation department to help SHG look for new projects. As Hellmuth served in this role, he began to understand how critical marketing for new work was for the long-term success of SHG—or any firm. On the strength of his marketing skills, he quickly rose to be an SHG vice president.

However, Hellmuth knew that no architecture firm could succeed on marketing alone. He was convinced that SHG could build an even stronger practice through better design. He persuaded the firm to hire Minoru Yamasaki, a talented young designer from the East Coast, for $10,000 a year—a good salary for that time.

The Depression-Proof Firm

Hellmuth continued to think about how to create the ideal architecture practice, one that didn't fall into crisis and lose most of its staff and knowledge every time a project ended. He developed a series of insights about how to design a world-class architecture firm and was determined to bring them to the attention of SHG leadership.

Hellmuth was a visionary and, over time, these revelations would have a major impact on his own fortunes—and on the design industry. Here they are:

FIGURE 1.2 George Hellmuth. Source: Photo courtesy of HOK.

   Talented People. Hellmuth's first insight was that talented people are the key to a successful architecture

---

[1] Walter McQuade and Paul Grotz, *Architecture in the Real World: The Work of HOK*. New York: H.N. Abrams, 1985.

practice. Without talented people, no firm can plan for the future. Architecture firms should attract talented people, then keep them long-term to leverage their growing skills and abilities. Of course, keeping talented people long-term meant having steady work, and that led to the next key insight.

Full-time Marketing. Hellmuth's second insight was that full-time marketing was essential to replace the current work before it was finished. Marketing to obtain a worthwhile new project took time—as much as five years. Hellmuth often described marketing as farming. "First you till the ground, then plant the seeds, then tend the fields. Only after that effort can you harvest the results," he liked to say. In addition, full-time marketing could be even more successful if supported by an effective, professional public relations program to cultivate awareness of the firm's abilities and build relationships with potential clients.

> *Hellmuth's first insight was that talented people are the key to a successful architecture practice. Without talented people, no firm can plan for the future.*

Diverse Work/Cities/Services. Hellmuth's third insight was to diversify the work of the firm to the maximum extent possible. He believed a diversified workload was superior to a focus on one type of building. For example, most architects kept busy during the post—World War II baby boom by designing schools. Hellmuth understood that abundant school projects would dry up one day soon, and that other work was necessary before the baby boom went bust. His diversity insight also extended to geographic diversity. If work in one city was slow, work in another city could well keep a talented staff busy. Finally, he understood that diversified professional services were important to bring more work from each project in-house, rather than farming out much of that work to other firms. Some clients need landscape architecture, or engineering services, or interior design. A diversified firm would develop the capacity to serve those needs, in addition to building design.

Specialized Leaders: Hellmuth's fourth insight concerned specialized leaders. He proposed that each partner focus on a separate responsibility—marketing, design, and production—for maximum efficiency. Partners in traditional firms did everything—sell, design, and produce the work. Hellmuth believed that, by specializing, each partner could become an expert in his area of responsibility. This would also help avoid power struggles, since the partners would oversee separate domains.

In summary, George Hellmuth reinvented the modern practice of architecture with four savvy ideas:

1. Attract and keep talented people.
2. Build a steady workload through full-time marketing and active public relations.
3. Strive for diversity of work, geography, and services for long-term workload stability.
4. Have specialized leaders run the firm, with separate focuses on marketing, design, and production.

In 1944, Hellmuth wrote "The Depression-Proof Firm,"[2] a 23-page paper detailing these ideas. He was determined to put it into action. He approached SHG leadership with his paper, but they only seemed interested in winning the next job—not his long-term firm-building strategy.

Chapter 1: To Design a World-Class Firm

1. Hire and keep talented people long term. Otherwise, the time and money you invest in training them is a waste. Service businesses, like architecture, are only as good as their people.
2. Consider carefully before you lay people off, because you lose not only staff members, but also their reservoir of knowledge.
3. Secure your next commission before your current project ends, so that you can plan your firm's future and stop the stressful boom and bust pattern.
4. Assign one leader to full-time marketing to win new work so other leaders can focus on designing and delivering the work.
5. Don't rely on marketing alone. Good design must be in place too and is the key that will sustain the practice.
6. Develop a professional public relations program to bolster your reputation—and your marketing.
7. Diversify your practice by expanding into multiple cities, developing multiple services, and embracing multiple building types to recession-proof your firm.
8. Organize your practice around specialized leaders—such as design, production, marketing, and management—because it's more efficient than if every leader does everything.

---

[2] "HOK's George Hellmuth 1987 Interview," YouTube, December 14, 2009. Accessed April 18, 2019. https://youtu.be/uXXAf0ujFL4.

CHAPTER 2

A New Kind of Architecture Firm

Hellmuth began to dream of founding his own firm where he could devote himself to finding a steady stream of projects and his partners could devote themselves to getting the work done. Hellmuth's son, Nick, also an architect, told me, "My dad had two outstanding gifts. The first was selling. The second was identifying people with talent." Hellmuth's gift for identifying talented people led him to two SHG colleagues. Minoru Yamasaki was the well-regarded designer he had helped recruit to SHG. Joe Leinweber, another SHG vice president, was a top production architect who had been with the firm since 1924. When Hellmuth approached them with his ideas for a new kind of architecture practice, they agreed to form their own firm.

FIGURE 2.1 Minoru Yamasaki and George Hellmuth c. 1949.
Source: Photo courtesy of HOK.

Starting HYL/LHY

In 1949, the three partners opened Leinweber, Hellmuth & Yamasaki (LHY) in Detroit. In accordance with his depression-proof strategy, Hellmuth became a full-time marketer with the responsibility to bring in new work, allowing Yamasaki to concentrate on design and Leinweber on production.

Remember, Hellmuth was convinced the new firm needed geographic diversity. He retained many contacts from his work for the City of St. Louis and believed he could win more new work there. Deep connections like this can make a big difference. If work was slow in Detroit, maybe St. Louis could keep the firm's talented people busy. Hellmuth persuaded his new partners to open a second office in St. Louis—but with his name first, a savvy move. Hellmuth, Yamasaki & Leinweber, or HYL, opened in St. Louis not long after LHY opened in Detroit. Hellmuth divided his time between Detroit and St. Louis in pursuit of new projects, while Yamasaki and Leinweber spent most of their time in the Detroit office.

The young St. Louis office began to grow, requiring more talent. Hellmuth's St. Louis contacts eventually led to the largest commission for the young firm, a new terminal for Lambert Airport. While Detroit-based Yamasaki would be the designer, the St. Louis HYL office needed to expand to handle production for such a large project. In 1951, HYL hired George Kassabaum, a member of the Washington University faculty, as Leinweber's St. Louis assistant for production.

Yamasaki soon needed an assistant too, to help with the growing design workload. His architect friend John Dinkeloo recommended Gyo Obata, a bright young designer

FIGURE 2.2 Minoru Yamasaki talking to Gyo Obata, c. 1952.
Source: Photo courtesy of HOK.

working for rival SOM in Chicago. When Yamasaki and Obata met, they discovered a special connection. Both were *nisei,* born in the United States to Japanese immigrants. Yamasaki had found the perfect design assistant.

Gyo Obata

Gyo Obata was born in San Francisco in 1923. His father, Chiura Obata, came from a distinguished line of Japanese artists in Sendai, Japan. He emigrated to the United States in 1903, at age 17, and settled in the Bay Area. He soon became a successful artist and eventually joined the art faculty at the University of California, Berkeley. His wife, Haruko, was a noted *Ikebana* artist who introduced the art of Japanese flower arranging to the West Coast.

FIGURE 2.3 Gyo Obata.
Source: Photo courtesy of HOK.

Obata's father traveled often to the Sierra Nevada Mountains to paint, and Yosemite was his favorite location, so the Obata family camped in Yosemite every summer. Chiura Obata met and became good friends with famed photographer Ansel Adams, who spent a lifetime photographing Yosemite and the Sierras. The Adams family lived in Yosemite Valley and operated Best's Studio, a small gallery featuring his photographic prints. Adams invited Chiura Obata to exhibit his Yosemite paintings there, and both men taught summer classes through the gallery. Obata remembers his father and Ansel Adams often spent summer evenings together discussing art.

Obata grew up in Berkeley, and his parents were sure he would become an artist like them. However, Obata also enjoyed science and, with his mother's encouragement, decided to pursue architecture. He enrolled at UC Berkeley to study architecture in September 1941. However, after Japan bombed Pearl Harbor just three months later, the U.S. government interned most Japanese-Americans in camps for the duration of World War II. It was a close call for Obata. "I left Berkeley the night before my whole family was interned," Obata recalled later.[1]

Though he would have to leave his family while they were held in an internment camp, regulations permitted Obata to continue his education—just not in California, Oregon, or Washington, the three states bordering the Pacific Ocean. "Washington University in St. Louis was one of the few colleges that accepted Japanese-Americans," Obata explained. He added that if the telegram announcing his acceptance had arrived just one day later, "I'd have been sent to the camps, too."[2] Sometimes you have to seize the moment. Obata traveled by train to St. Louis where he was befriended—he would say adopted—by the university faculty and students.

---

[1] Liam Otten, "A Challenge to Democracy Explores Legacy of Japanese Internment Camps | The Source | Washington University in St. Louis." *The Source,* May 16, 2017. Accessed April 18, 2019. https://source.wustl.edu/2009/09/a-challenge-to-democracy-explores-legacy-of-japanese-internment-camps.
[2] Ibid.

FIGURE 2.4 Gyo Obata with sister Yuri, mother Haruko, and father Chiura Obata, c. 1939. Public domain. Larger copy of photo courtesy of Kiku Obata.

Obata's wartime experience made a deep impression. He was determined to overcome the barriers placed in his way during the war. He was a naturally shy, soft-spoken student, but developed a strong, resilient, competitive nature that served him well his entire life. Obata also developed a deep affection for the people of Washington University and his adopted city of St. Louis.

After graduating from Washington University in 1945, Obata received a scholarship to study under Finnish master architect Eliel Saarinen at Cranbrook Academy in Bloomfield Hills, Michigan. Cranbrook offered a diverse education in arts and crafts, as well as architecture, and attracted faculty and students from around the world. While there, Obata made many friends and gained an international perspective on design. Like his father before him, he formed a lifelong friendship with visionaries who would become famous: Charles and Ray Eames, the internationally acclaimed designers who made significant contributions to modern architecture, furniture design, graphic art, and film.

"When I went to Cranbrook to study with Eliel Saarinen, he was interested in students working on city planning, so I worked on a master plan for the St. Louis region," Obata recalled, later in life. "He taught me not to be afraid of large projects, of the planning involved." That's good advice for all architects. "Learning about community, urban planning and the relationship of buildings to each other was a very important part of my learning and an important inspiration to me,"[3] Obata said. He received a Master of Architecture and Urban Design degree from Cranbrook in 1946.

In an ironic twist, Obata spent two years in the U.S. Army, after graduating from Cranbrook, serving the same government that had interned his family. The army ordered him to report for duty at a remote base on Adak Island, part of the Aleutian Chain of islands stretching from Alaska toward Asia. Before shipping out, he asked one of his army friends what it was like and the guy told him, "You'll love it—there's a girl behind every tree!" When Obata arrived, he discovered there were no trees on Adak Island.

In 1947, Obata received his army discharge and found his first architecture job at the Chicago office of Skidmore, Owings, and Merrill. Just two years later, he received the important call from Minoru Yamasaki, asking him to join the newly formed Leinweber, Hellmuth, and Yamasaki office in Detroit. As Obata recalls, "I started at Mr. Yamasaki's Detroit office, but was soon spending most of my time working on the new international airport in St. Louis."[4]

After only a short time in Detroit, Obata relocated to the HYL office in St. Louis to work directly with the airport team, where he was reunited with a Washington University colleague, George Kassabaum.

George Kassabaum

George Edward Kassabaum was born in 1920 in Atchison, Kansas, the only child of George Alexander Kassabaum and Dorothy Gaston Kassabaum. His father worked as General Secretary for the Young Men's Christian Association (YMCA). When George was five years old, the YMCA transferred his father to Fort Scott, Kansas, so the family relocated. This move was to have a long-term impact on George, as his daughter Karen Kassabaum Ivory recalled from a family story: "When George was a schoolboy of about 10 years old in Fort Scott, he passed a Presbyterian church every day on his way to school. He thought it was the most beautiful building he had ever seen and announced that he wanted to become an architect and design beautiful buildings."

FIGURE 2.5 George Kassabaum. Source: Photo courtesy of HOK.

---

[3] Cathy Sivek, "An Interview with Gyo Obata, FAIA, Founding Partner of Global Architectural Firm HOK," ArchitectureSchools.com, February 2, 2006. Accessed April 21, 2019. http://architectureschools.com/resources/an-interview-with-Obata-obata-faia-founding-partner-of-global-architectural-firm-hok.
[4] Ibid.

The family moved again due to his father's YMCA work, this time to Oklahoma City, where young George Kassabaum attended high school. While many children's career interests vary over time, he still wanted to become an architect. His mother helped him research universities that offered architecture degrees. They decided Washington University in St. Louis was the best choice: It had a good reputation in architectural education, and it was in the Midwest, not too far from home.

Kassabaum enrolled at Washington University in the late 1930s. He made many friends among the students and faculty and developed a deep bond with the university which was to continue his entire life. Kassabaum was a good student. Because of his natural inclination to be well-organized, he gravitated toward production, the portion of a project where architects transform a good design into working drawings, then work with the contractor during construction until the building is finished. There's a lesson here: Some architects yearn to be designers, because that's where the glory is, but if your true talents lie elsewhere, you can have a wonderful career as a project architect or project manager. Kassabaum did both.

World War II interrupted Kassabaum's studies. From 1944 to 1945, he worked for Boeing Aircraft and served in the U.S. Army Air Corps. He applied drafting skills he learned in architecture school to his work at Wright-Patterson Air Force Base in Dayton, Ohio. Although his Air Force superiors would not confirm this, Kassabaum was quite sure he drew up the bomb rack for the *Enola Gay,* the plane that dropped the first atomic bomb on Hiroshima, Japan, in 1945.

> **K**assabaum was quite sure he drew up the bomb rack for the Enola Gay, the plane that dropped the first atomic bomb on Hiroshima, Japan.

Kassabaum returned to Washington University after the war and received his Bachelor of Architecture degree in 1947. After graduation, he got his first job with Murphy and Mackey, a St. Louis architecture practice led by two Washington University faculty members. Joseph Murphy was dean of the School of Architecture, and Eugene Mackey also taught at the school. Kassabaum himself later joined the architecture faculty at Washington University.

During his teaching career, Kassabaum was fixed up on a blind date with Marjory Verser, who had also graduated from the university and was working in the Business School. Marjory was a natural extrovert, lively and talkative, and Kassabaum was quieter, but a great listener. Marjory often said of that first date, "I had a touch of laryngitis that evening, so George thought he had found a nice, quiet woman to spend a lifetime with. Was he wrong!" After a whirlwind romance, they got married in early 1949. Throughout his life, Kassabaum continued to be somewhat quiet and a great listener, qualities essential to his success as the production leader of HOK.

In 1950, Kassabaum joined HYL as Leinweber's top assistant for production. George Hellmuth was already in the office, and Gyo Obata had recently transferred there from Detroit. The three men who would cofound HOK were now working together at the same firm. The stage was set.

By 1955, the St. Louis HYL office had become very busy, requiring more of Yamasaki's attention. But he was frail after a stomach ulcer operation and found frequent travel to St. Louis a burden. Yamasaki had also become unhappy with the broad variety of projects Hellmuth brought to the office. He wanted to design signature projects—prominent, important, and notable buildings—not ordinary buildings like schools.

Lambert Airport was the only "signature project" to come from the HYL St. Louis office, and Yamasaki believed Detroit offered more opportunities. On one of his visits to St. Louis, he invited Hellmuth to lunch at the Statler Hotel. During lunch, Yamasaki proposed closing the HYL St. Louis office and relocating Hellmuth to Detroit to look for signature projects. Hellmuth reacted negatively to Yamasaki's proposal. He still believed success came from a diversity of work, not just signature projects. There's a saying that comes to mind: "There are no bad projects. Only bad architects." Yamasaki was a good architect, but the point is that truly great architects will find the potential and do wonderful things even with ordinary buildings.

Hellmuth was proud of the HYL St. Louis office and believed it was on the path to success. His reaction to Yamasaki's proposal was so strong, that after lunch he sought out Gyo Obata and George Kassabaum and proposed a new partnership. As Hellmuth recalled later, "The entire conversation took about two minutes."[5] Hellmuth needed extraordinary partners and had approached the two best leaders in the HYL St. Louis office to join him in forming a new architecture practice.

The two firms parted ways amicably. Hellmuth took over the St. Louis office, staff, and workload. Yamasaki did the same with the Detroit office, which he renamed Minoru Yamasaki and Associates. Joe Leinweber remained with Yamasaki in the Detroit office for many years and eventually became a freelance production architect available for hire by other firms. Yamasaki designed many of his beloved signature projects in the Detroit area and elsewhere over a long career. He is best known for his design of the twin towers of the World Trade Center in New York City, completed in 1973, and the tallest buildings in the world at the time.

Some years later, I was on a marketing visit to New York with George Hellmuth. As we were driving to an appointment, the World Trade Center came into view. Hellmuth looked at the Twin Towers and said, "My old partner, Yama, designed those towers, and I'm proud of him. But, I had to stamp the drawings on his first project because he wasn't a registered architect yet!" Yamasaki died in 1986, before terrorists destroyed the Twin Towers in the September 11, 2001 attacks.

Forming HOK

George Hellmuth was 48 years old when he and Yamasaki divided HYL. At an age when many people have lost the spark of ambition, he was just getting started. Hellmuth, who had watched his German-American father and uncle repeatedly build up and tear down

---

[5] Frank Peters, "Art and Politics in the Dawn of Architectural Stardom," *St. Louis Post-Dispatch*, February 23, 1986.

FIGURE 2.6 George Hellmuth, Gyo Obata, and George Kassabaum ca 1955.
Source: Photo courtesy of HOK.

their own firm, reprised his role as the full-time marketing principal, responsible for bringing new work to HOK. He was determined to fulfill his depression-proof-firm strategy and win a diverse portfolio of work for the new partnership.

Gyo Obata, just 32 years old and the son of Japanese immigrant artists, became the design principal. He brought intensity, innovation, and modernist passion to his role. Obata's goal was to find interesting design opportunities in every commission Hellmuth brought to the firm, whether they were "signature" buildings or more modest ones.

George Kassabaum, 35 years old and the prairie-raised descendant of German-Americans, was the principal in charge of production, a position ideally suited to the organizational talents he had honed at Washington University. His role was to carry Obata's designs through to successful bidding and construction, on time and on budget.

In summary, Hellmuth brought in the work, Obata designed the work, and Kassabaum saw the work through. They were different men, with different backgrounds, and decided their differences were strengths, not weaknesses—a smart outlook. On the other hand, all three founders shared certain traits that would prove critical to HOK's success half a century later:

Ambitious: All three founders had outsize ambitions. They wanted to build a national—or better yet international—design practice. They wanted to design not just buildings but a firm unlike any other. And they were long-term thinkers, with the audacity to set strategic goals that required decades to see to fruition.

Innovative: All were innovators. They wanted to reinvent the practice of architecture. Hellmuth wanted to follow his depression-proof-firm strategy and build the most diversified practice possible. Obata wanted to tap into the best people and best consultants to change how architects practiced design. And Kassabaum was driven to create ever-more clear, unambiguous drawings and specifications delivered on budget and on schedule.

Honest: The founders set out to build a reputation for honesty and integrity as a foundation for future growth. "Do the right thing, always." was Kassabaum's saying and the young firm quickly adopted it as an unofficial motto.

Unified: Finally, the founders wanted a unified firm where things were harmonious on the inside. There was plenty of challenge on the outside. As part of this, they believed in seeking out the very best ideas, no matter who they came from. They wanted people to leave their egos at the door and work together as a team. They knew teams win through teamwork, not because of individual stars.

All the new firm needed was a name. Hellmuth suggested that they follow architecture tradition by listing the last name of each partner. They created a logo with the H, O, and K printed in orange, in lower case characters, around a plus sign. It was simple and clean. Hellmuth, Obata & Kassabaum—HOK—was in business, and the great adventure had begun!

FIGURE 2.7 Original HOK logo. Source: Courtesy of HOK.

HOK's Early Years

The founders retained 26 HYL staff members as new HOK employees. The new firm had a ready-made backlog of work, thanks to existing HYL projects, giving Hellmuth time to cultivate future clients. The most notable project HYL turned over to HOK was completion of the new terminal complex for Lambert St. Louis Airport. At a time when most airports were imitations of railway stations, Lambert's terminal was seminal, a gently curving space that conveyed a feeling of lightness that was a fitting transition for passengers about to travel by air.

FIGURE 2.8 Lambert Airport terminal, St. Louis, Missouri.
Source: Photo by Ezra Stoller/Esto. Photo courtesy of HOK.

St. Louis Magazine would later say of Lambert, "When the main terminal was completed in 1956, it instantly became what architectural historian Michael Allen called 'a landmark that really set the standard.'" The magazine went on to say, "The terminals at New York's John F. Kennedy International Airport, the District of Columbia's Dulles International Airport, and Paris's Charles de Gaulle Airport—all built in a sweeping midcentury style—are said to have been inspired by Lambert's elegant lines."[6]

A tricky issue arose. Who would take credit for design of the Lambert Airport terminal complex? Yamasaki listed the project as his creation since he led conceptual design while at HYL. Obata had assisted Yamasaki with the design at HYL and completed the project at HOK, so he also took credit. There's an old-but-true saying in architecture: Poorly designed projects are orphans, but successful designs have many parents!

One of the earliest commissions Hellmuth won for the newly minted HOK was to design the chapel at Priory School in suburban St. Louis, which was run by the Benedictine Order of monks. He had a bit of an advantage. Hellmuth's four sons attended Priory School and he knew everyone there. The chapel had unique requirements. Each monk was obliged to say mass every morning, so the Benedictines needed a chapel with many altars. Of course, they also needed enough space to accommodate the congregation at Sunday mass.

---

[6] Tim Woodcock, "The History of Lambert Airport," *St. Louis Magazine*, August 22, 2014. Accessed April 21, 2019. https://www.stlmag.com/news/jet-age-design.

FIGURE 2.9 Priory Chapel, St. Louis Missouri.
Source: Photo by George Silk. Photo courtesy of HOK.

Obata's unique design concept emerged as a round chapel with altars all around the perimeter. He worked in collaboration with famed engineer Pier Luigi Nervi to develop an iconic façade featuring three tiers of whitewashed, thin-shell concrete parabolic arches. The first tier of 20 arches contains altars for the monks to say mass in the mornings before school. The second tier of arches steps back from the first tier and contains high windows bringing light to the chapel interior. The third tier of arches steps back from the second tier to form a bell tower. The main altar is in the center of the chapel for Sunday mass. The Benedictine Order was delighted with the completed chapel and Obata had established himself as a new force in the world of design. Other projects followed, including McDonnell Planetarium, the building that attracted me to HOK.

HOK landed its first substantial commission in 1961, a new campus for Southern Illinois University in Edwardsville, Illinois, across the Mississippi River from St. Louis. The project required establishment of an Illinois office, and the firm's first, modest attempt at geographic diversification was underway.

Chapter 2: To Design a World-Class Firm

1. Open shop in a location where you have deep connections. Then, emphasize the name of the founder who has the most local contacts in that area.
2. Don't be afraid of large projects, including urban planning of entire towns.
3. Find and follow your own true talents, which may mean becoming a project manager or project architect instead of a designer.
4. Look for the potential to do great work even when designing ordinary buildings.
5. Contemplate how differences among you and your partners can be strengths, not weaknesses.
6. Be ambitious even if it means setting strategic goals that will take decades to come to fruition.
7. Do the right thing, always.
8. Remember that teams win through teamwork, not because of individual stars.

CHAPTER 3

Innovate Early and Often

HOK was just 12 years old when I joined in 1967, with 150 people in two offices and a growing list of varied design commissions in St. Louis and elsewhere. Innovation had become a core value at HOK, and I could see it everywhere.

I had never worked in a large, innovative firm before. The six-man practice in the Alton area, where I had spent summers, was a typical small firm. For example, when the firm won a new school project, the junior partner came up with a design. But when it came time to add details to the design—things like how the windows, doors, and lobby should look—the chief draftsman pulled drawings of the last school project from a drawer and assigned other draftsmen, including me, to trace over the old details to make details for the new school. The result was that most schools looked much the same. Innovation was absent at the firm and in its work.

Small firms followed the methods of the past, practicing an ongoing craft that carried forward from one project to the next. They drew everything by hand, in pencil, on vellum—a translucent paper used for drafting. The only machines in the typical small architecture office were telephones, a coffee machine, a typewriter for the secretary, and a printer for large drawings.

By contrast, when I arrived at HOK, innovation was encouraged—and expected—of everyone.

Marketing Innovation

George Hellmuth loved marketing—and loved winning even more. He was a natural salesman—earthy, flamboyant, and fearless, especially when reaching out to top client leaders. He organized HOK's marketing operation around his personal style. He once said, "I know a lot about design; I've won prizes in it. But I never pleased myself with what

I designed. I would rather use what I know to hire a damned good designer, then go out and land jobs for him."[1]

Prospecting for leads and finding potential new projects came first. Hellmuth subscribed to numerous clipping services, gathering bits of material from newspapers and magazines around the country. He and his long-time secretary, Dorothy Forrest, sifted through clippings every week, deciding which clients or projects were most likely to bear fruit. Then he wrote a letter to each, asking for an introductory meeting.

Hellmuth also maintained contacts with past clients, calling them on the phone or taking them to lunch. This is worth emulating. After all, if you've done your job right, past clients already like you and your work. Hellmuth would pepper them with questions: "What do you need? How can we help? Who from your company should I see? Can you introduce me?" He was happiest when on the hunt for a new project and took full advantage of the new age of air travel, flying to meet clients in other cities. Hellmuth made regular trips to Washington, DC to meet members of Congress and federal agencies. Sometimes he impressed faraway clients by just showing up at their offices. In this age of email, showing up in person makes even more of an impression.

Many architects thought meetings with potential clients were opportunities to talk about themselves and show off their work. Hellmuth was different. He believed the secret to winning work was being sincerely interested in the client—understanding the project from their point of view. Clients understood their own businesses, but little about the process of designing and building. By listening carefully, Hellmuth gained an understanding of what was most important to a client, and only then would he respond with how HOK could help their project be successful. Know this: Great marketers listen before they talk.

Hellmuth had another weapon in his sales arsenal—he was not above using flattery. When talking with a potential client, he was always complimentary, and once remarked, "Never underestimate the effect of flattery on even very important people."[2]

Some large government and corporate clients leave selection of the architect to committees of midlevel officials whose careers often depend on making the right choice. What if they pick the wrong architect and the building ends up overbudget? What if the finished building is not functional? What if the design is viewed unfavorably by their superiors? Hellmuth understood the pressures these officials faced, and spent time reassuring them, staying in touch as new concerns surfaced. He became their friend and advisor, gaining their trust as they made the final choice of an architecture firm—ideally HOK.

How do you convince a client you can design a type of building you have not designed before? This is the most difficult selling job in architecture and Hellmuth loved the challenge. He cultivated sincere friendships with clients, and sometimes the bond of friendship became a substitute for prior experience. Sometimes Hellmuth won over clients by emphasizing the opportunity for a fresh look from the imagination of his design partner Obata. Sometimes Hellmuth brought Obata along, and Obata would impress clients with his careful, listening approach. At other times, Hellmuth emphasized the large size of HOK, and the people and resources he could bring to the work. By the time I joined, in

---

[1] Walter McQuade and Paul Grotz, *Architecture in the Real World: The Work of HOK* (New York: H.N. Abrams, 1985), p. 27.
[2] Ibid., 28.

1967, HOK had become one of the largest design firms in the country, with a deep pool of talented people ready to take on particularly challenging projects.

Another hurdle Hellmuth faced was winning work outside of St. Louis in cities where HOK had no exposure. For architects, geographic expansion is *hard*. Clients naturally favor local architects—public clients, especially, when local tax money is involved. Local clients need compelling reasons to hire an architect from out of town, reasons strong enough to overcome their preference for spreading the wealth to local businesses. Sometimes a strong design reputation was enough to win the job. At other times, depth of experience in the building type was necessary.

Even with a good reputation and experience, winning the project often required Hellmuth to partner with local architects to share the work. This provided public officials with a ready answer for criticisms about spending local tax money on an outside architect. Sometimes it was necessary to establish a project office, where HOK and local architects worked together, keeping local tax money at home. For example, my first HOK project, the Great High Schools project in Pittsburgh, required a project office—and not one, but four, local architects.

Fortunately, Hellmuth loved the hunt for new work across the United States, and, eventually, around the world. He kept a big map of the country on the wall in his office and delighted in placing red pins in locations where HOK was awarded a new project. The map was his way of measuring progress. As HOK added offices in other cities, he used black pins to mark those locations, marking the achievement of another goal in his depression-proof-firm strategy.

By deploying all these strategies—and his own salty charm—Hellmuth was often successful in bringing a new contract back to the office, like a successful hunter bringing food to the family table. On the occasions when another firm was selected, he would return to the office and say, "I'll get 'em next time." Sometimes another well-entrenched firm would be selected several times in a row, and Hellmuth would say, "If I can't beat 'em, I'll outlive the bastards!"

Eventually, HOK grew too big for Hellmuth to do all the marketing by himself, so he began to assemble a marketing team. King Graf became his first assistant, followed by Dan Gale and Jerry Gilmore. Hellmuth taught his marketing techniques to these successors. Their collective success set HOK on the path to becoming the most diversified design firm in the world.

Design Innovation

Gyo Obata brought a passion for design to HOK and was determined to do great work. More specifically, he wanted to design beautiful—but also highly functional—buildings. Believe it or not, this was a novel approach at the time—and sometimes still is. Obata's childhood as a Japanese American, and the challenges he faced during World War II, motivated him to overcome obstacles to success. Obata believed in Hellmuth's diversification strategy and was interested in the design challenges presented by new building types, even if switching among types made his job harder. He embraced the challenge and learned that he could translate his experience designing one type of building to other

> *...Obata never developed a personal style, instead allowing each building to evolve based on a thoughtful search for the best solution.*

types. It's significant that Obata never developed a personal style, instead allowing each building to evolve based on a thoughtful search for the best solution. So many famous twentieth-century architects made it all about them. Not Obata. He put the needs of the projects and clients first, before his own needs—and ego. Twenty-first-century architects can benefit from his example.

When Hellmuth won a new building type, Obata took great care to assign the right designer and project team to the work, and then that team stayed together for the duration of the job for continuity. Team members were told to keep an open mind about what the client wanted, to avoid preconceptions. When describing this process, Obata had a way of pausing . . . to gather attention. Then he said the next word with emphasis: "The most important thing is to really . . . *listen* . . . to the client."

He had learned that the best, most innovative designs came from actively listening to clients and applying their thoughts to the design from the beginning of a project through to the end. After all, clients know best how their own organization works and how it utilizes a building. Often Obata developed unique insights about a building type that architects with deep experience had overlooked. His practice of active listening built a bond of trust with clients, often leading to friendship. Many of those clients returned to Obata for new projects. Over many years Obata—and HOK—learned that the best projects result from listening to the client.

An important part of Obata's design innovation came from his reliance on three-dimensional models. Most architects did not make models during design and might only make a display model after design was complete. Obata was different. He insisted on using quick, "study models" to better understand the design. He might come by, look at the current version of a design, and say, "That's interesting, make a study model." The design team built the models from stiff paper, pinned or taped together right at their desks, to see how an idea looked in the round. "There is a hard-wired connection between the hand and the brain," Obata explained. "You look with your eyes, but it deepens your understanding when you make a model with your hands." HOK was an early adopter of Styrofoam for study models, which were cut by hand and held together with T-pins. I had learned model-making at school, but never this way, or so quickly. Even after computers came into the office, Obata insisted designers continue making models because deeper understanding comes from that hand-eye connection.

In addition to the quickie models we built at our desks, HOK maintained a model shop across the street from the office. A staff of three helped designers make the largest study models and built formal presentation models to show to clients. The shop contained up-to-date tools for working with wood, plastic, and foam. I built many models in that shop, and learned that, if I was well-behaved, I would be allowed to borrow the shop's woodworking equipment. Over several weekends I made a bookcase for my largely empty apartment.

Obata also contributed two-dimensional innovations to HOK. All designers worked by sketching successive design ideas on new layers of tracing paper placed directly over the old layers. Obata required designers to keep their tracing paper layers in order, in a pile, so that he could review the development of a design idea. He might dig down through a pile to find an earlier version of the design that he liked better, then make his own sketch to lead the design in his preferred direction. Today, architects can do the same thing by making sure to save and review various versions of their computer-aided design (CAD) drawings.

Sometimes we found it helpful to enlarge a drawing to study a portion in more detail. At most firms, enlarging a drawing required laborious redrafting by hand. The HOK design department contained a large Xerox machine that accepted a drawing at one side and produced an enlarged drawing on the other side in a few seconds. It sounds obvious today, but at that time it was a giant step up in efficiency.

In addition, Obata pushed the boundaries in his collaboration with engineers. Most firms relied on engineers in their home cities, and frequently waited until design was complete before bringing them into the project. By contrast, Obata searched from coast to coast to find the best engineers for each project and engaged them early, when design was just beginning. This practice of hiring the best engineers early bore fruit at HOK right away. For example, Obata's design for Priory Chapel would never have become an elegant, light structure without the help of structural engineer Pier Luigi Nervi. Their collaboration established Obata as a design innovator and HOK as a force to be reckoned with.

When designing the Great High Schools project, Obata reached out to Bill LeMessurier, a highly-regarded structural engineer from Boston. I got to know him personally during that project and remember him as passionate about his work and determined to help Obata take his design to new levels. LeMessurier later gained fame for his innovative structure for the Citicorp headquarters in Manhattan. After that building was completed and occupied, questions from a student led him to discover a serious structural flaw. He had the integrity to approach Citicorp about the problem and offer a solution that was implemented floor-by-floor while the building remained occupied.

Production Innovation

George Kassabaum set high standards for production, the process of making sure designs are feasible, preparing documents for bidding, and working with the contractor during construction. He believed clients deserved buildings completed on time and on budget. He also believed contractors deserved well-organized and complete information to construct the buildings. Kassabaum understood the natural tension between quality and schedule, and once quipped at a conference, "There are two types of clients, those who want it right and those who want it Tuesday."[3]

Kassabaum's department was the largest in the office, with dedicated teams to shepherd each project through to bidding and construction. Each team was led by a *project manager,* who was responsible for organizing, wrangling, and then delivering each

---

[3] Roger Friedland and John W. Mohr, *Matters of Culture: Cultural Sociology in Practice* (Cambridge: Cambridge University Press, 2006).

project through to completion—by the deadline and within the budget. Each team also had a *project architect,* who was responsible for preparing the technical drawings and specifications necessary for construction.

For those not familiar with this process, architects make drawings to describe items best represented visually, such as floor plans, details, and elevations, which are drawings of the facades of buildings. They write specifications to describe items best represented by words, like what color paint the contractor should use and how to mix and apply it—information not easily conveyed in a drawing.

Just as Obata and his designers innovated in how they drew and refined their designs, Kassabaum encouraged his production architects to find better, more flexible ways to translate design into a completed building. HOK production architects made innovative use of *Mylar,* synthetic plastic drafting sheets, instead of traditional drafting paper. Mylar was semitransparent, had the right texture to accept pencil drafting, and was easy to erase without damage—a great improvement over paper.

Kassabaum's department was also an early adopter of the pin-bar drafting system for architectural drawings. A metal bar attached to the top of each drafting table contained pins matching pre-punched holes in the Mylar drafting sheets. Production architects could place several Mylar sheets containing different information over the pins, aligning them exactly. That made it easy to coordinate architectural and mechanical plans, for example, by layering them over each other.

Detail drawings are critical to describe how parts of a building fit together, such as how a window fits into a wall. Common practice for most architects was to draft many different details on a large sheet, starting at the top and proceeding to the bottom. Detail sheets tended to be crowded, messy, and disorganized. Details were often drawn out of a logical sequence. Architects frequently drew details too small to be clearly understood by the contractor or squeezed too many details onto a sheet. These shortcomings required the contractor to hunt through the detail sheets to find needed information, slowing construction. Every moment lost during construction costs money, and since a project may last for years, the accumulation of small inefficiencies can have a big impact.

Kassabaum recognized that this practice was seriously flawed and encouraged his production architects to find a better solution. Two of his top people, Bob Stauder and Herb Koopman, began to experiment with drawing details freehand—without drafting tools. It sounds counterintuitive in this technological age, but this was refreshingly efficient. They learned they could place a sheet of Mylar over an earlier detail and make a freehand sketch, adapting or improving an old detail for a new or changed condition. The process was quick and flexible. If a detail needed to be changed, it only took a few moments. Better yet, the freehand technique worked best if the detail was drawn larger than usual, providing the benefit of extra clarity for both the architect and the contractor.

Finally, Stauder and Koopman innovated how details were organized on detail sheets. They started drawing all freehand details on 8-1/2 × 11 or 11 × 17 sheets of Mylar and storing them in a drawer until the drawings were nearing completion. Then the project architect arranged the details in a logical order on large Mylar sheets and fastened them with clear tape. The HOK print shop used a photographic process to create a clean, new Mylar sheet with all the details shown in sequence. This process of freehand detailing followed by organized sequencing was well-suited to the evolving process of architecture.

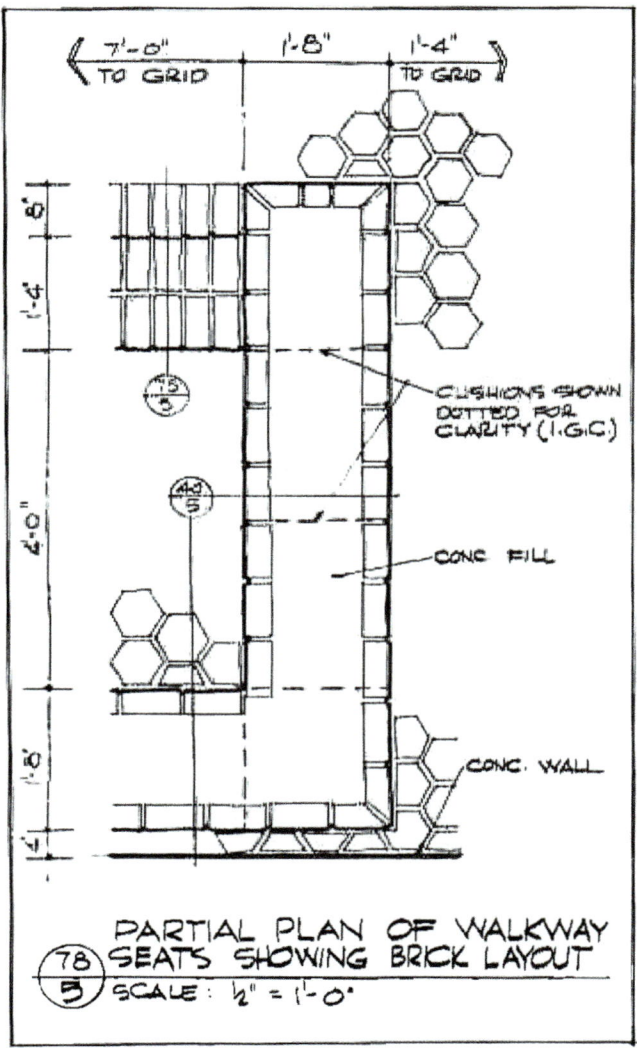

FIGURE 3.1 Example of a freehand detail, c. 1969.
Source: Image courtesy of HOK.

Xerox machines, pin bars, Mylar, and the rest, were all tools of that time. Of course, they are totally obsolete today, so why mention them? Because innovation never goes out of style. The point is that HOK people were finding new ways to use the tools available to them. Architects today should look around at the tools of *this* time—Building Information Modeling (BIM), virtual reality, and more—and dream up new ways to use them. Organization never gets old either. Arranging details for the contractor in a logical sequence is just as helpful today as it was then. You'll just use new tools to do so.

Kassabaum also set high standards for personal integrity inside and outside of the office. Remember, his motto was "Do the right thing, always." It was especially important when genuine problems arose. A good example was Our Lady of the Snows, a Catholic shrine and retreat center in Belleville, Illinois designed for The Missionary Oblates of Mary Immaculate. Shortly after completion, the client complained that the roof was leaking. Kassabaum discovered the leaks originated in a flawed HOK detail and called the client. "It's our fault. We'll take care of it," he told them. HOK oversaw and paid for repairs. Rather than being angered by the mistake, the clients were impressed with Kassabaum's integrity, and became lifelong friends and supporters.

Kassabaum was also responsible for firm-wide administration, including accounting and legal support. He was the ideal man for the job. Despite his workload, he always left his office on time, and rarely worked weekends—unlike Obata and his design team. Sometimes people would chide him about not working overtime, but he always said, "If you organize your work properly, you can leave on time, and have more time for family and other activities." It sounds idyllic in this age of overwork. Two Kassabaum traits helped him manage his workload: personal organization and an ability to delegate responsibility.

Start-to-Finish Innovation

Another HOK innovation was the firm's emphasis on getting involved in projects at the very beginning and then assigning teams that stuck with those projects until the very end.

It started with Kassabaum, who observed that architects tended to disengage from society to concentrate on their work, and who believed the profession suffered as a result. When he became AIA president, he said, "Architects shouldn't wait around for politicians, economists and sociologists to come to us. Too often they decide where a building is to be built, how much it will cost, and then call in an architect. By that time, too many important decisions have been made."[4]

Kassabaum believed that instead architects should be civic-minded, get out into the world, and engage with decision makers to help make good choices early. Today we call this "predesign services," where architects do things like help a client choose the ideal site, decide how many stories a building should be, and so on. Intervening early came to be a core belief of my own. More on that later. As for Kassabaum, he practiced what he preached. He was a latter-day renaissance man, fully immersed in civic, professional, and academic life. In addition to his lifelong work with the AIA, he remained connected with Washington University as a faculty member, fundraiser, and trustee. HOK benefited early and often from his deep ties to the community and profession.

Gyo Obata also contributed to HOK's beginning-to-end innovation. In many firms, designers only actively participated during the design phase. Then, they turned over responsibility to a production team led by a project architect. Gyo understood that design was a *process*—not a *phase*—and must continue from the beginning of design through the end of construction. Thus, another innovation was that Gyo or his designated designer remained with each project throughout production, as the technical

---
[4] "Top Architect Advises Involvement Beyond Duties," *The Oregonian*, June 24, 1968.

team prepared drawings and specifications. HOK designers reviewed details, materials, and anything else that would affect the final design of the building. Design involvement even continued during construction, when designers reviewed contractor shop drawings, material samples and, finally, colors. Even after construction was complete, one step remained for the designer: touring the finished building with the owner to assess the finished design.

But it wasn't just the design department that followed projects from beginning to end. HOK assigned one person from each of the firm's disciplines to go after a job, and then the same team saw the project through. Believe it or not, many firms at the time assigned staff to a project on an as-needed basis, with people coming and going when they needed to put out fires for some other client. Instead, at HOK, the founders would identify the designer, project manager, and project architect for each project, and make those people part of the pitch. If HOK landed the contract, that same designer would conceive the building, the project architect would make sure the design worked, and the project manager would follow up to see that everything happened on time and on budget. The insight here is that designers are creative, but less grounded. It helps to pair them with a project architect who oversees the technical design and a project manager who keeps things on track. Then, by keeping the entire team together, they develop a kind of institutional memory for the details of the project that is invaluable.

Core Boards Innovation

Speaking of HOK's different disciplines, the founders encouraged people with similar roles to meet together to share their knowledge and help each other to succeed. Hellmuth's marketers met together in this fashion, as did Obata's designers and Kassabaum's people too. In fact, two groups formed In Kassabaum's department—one for project managers and another for project architects—since Kassabaum wore two hats at HOK and had teams for each. These groups were open to people in each department, regardless of their seniority, and encouraged a free flow of ideas. HOK eventually named them "core boards" because they represented the four core competencies of the firm: marketing, design, management, and production.

Staffing Innovation

In addition to architects, HOK employed other design professionals who worked with the architects, as well as on their own projects. The first landscape architect HOK hired, Neil Porterfield, was a University of Pennsylvania graduate with a passion for planning. In conversations with me, he described large-scale planning as essential for saving the planet from wasteful, unplanned development. I, too, came to believe in the power of good planning to improve the world and this would play a big role in my later career.

Chip Reay, the first graphic designer at HOK, was engaged in multiple projects including designing museum displays and environmental graphics. He also helped Obata with presentations for his latest designs. Chip's office was crammed with magazines, drawings, and reports—on the walls, on his worktable, and stacked on the floor. He was a fluid, creative thinker, and Obata often relied on him to help brainstorm design ideas for challenging projects.

Interior design was not yet a recognized profession, but several architects in the department were focused on designing the interiors of buildings, including the furniture. Most architecture firms had small sample rooms next to a library of building product catalogs, but, at HOK, the samples filled a big room, and included furniture in addition to architectural products. Looking back, it was a sign that HOK already understood that design was the entire building, inside, and out, not just a pretty façade.

Since Hellmuth believed public relations was important for building an architecture firm's name recognition, he hired Bill Remington as a public relations specialist, one of the first in-house PR people in architecture. Remington's job was to get HOK published in newspapers and magazines, especially in the architectural press. Hellmuth often used reprints from magazine articles as persuasive props during meetings with prospective clients.

Paul Watson, the HOK in-house lawyer tasked with reviewing all owner-architect contracts, occupied his own office a few steps away from George Kassabaum. I was to learn later that HOK was probably the first design firm to employ an attorney full time instead of relying on legal advice from a local law firm. HOK's founders were interested not just in designing great buildings, but also in designing a great firm. That included bringing nonarchitects on board to help build the business. What nondesign professionals could you bring in house to enhance your own company?

Ownership Innovation

When Hellmuth, Obata, and Kassabaum founded HOK in 1955, Hellmuth was determined to avoid the shortcomings he had observed at traditional partnerships. Remember, the first flaw was that most partnerships distributed all cash profit to the partners at the end of each year, leaving little to no cash for operating the firm the following year. Of course, it's better to take a portion of your capital and invest it back into growing or improving your firm. The second defect was that when the partners were ready to retire, no one working in the firm could afford to buy them out. The partners were left with the choice of selling the firm to outsiders or closing it down.

Hellmuth had seen this pattern with his own father and uncle and wanted to avoid it. That's why he and the other founders established HOK as a corporation instead of a partnership. This was highly unusual for an architecture firm at that time and meant that HOK's ownership would be in the form of stock. Hellmuth, as the senior founder, received 50% of the shares, whereas Obata and Kassabaum each received 25%. Seven years later, Obata and Kassabaum both bought some of Hellmuth's stock so that each owned an equal third of HOK.

The founders wanted to design a world-class architecture firm and adopted some farsighted stock-ownership restrictions to support their vision. These included ideas that could be valuable to other designers as well:

HOK Stock Rules
1. **HOK stock is for active employees only**
   Stock ownership was limited to active employees, including the founders. When someone retired or left the company for any reason, they were required to sell their HOK stock back to the company and the company was required to buy it at the current month's price.
2. **HOK stock may not be part of an inheritance**
   If an active employee dies, heirs receive the cash value from the employee's stock, not shares. This provision was designed to prevent surviving spouses or children of employees from having a say in the operation of the firm.
3. **The founders' stock ownership is age-limited**
   The founders were required to sell their stock back to the company at age 65. They could continue working at HOK but could no longer be an owner. This provision prevented a weakness of many firms, where the owners stay on too long and leave the staff with no ability to buy them out. This provision only applied to the founders.
4. **Stock ownership will be in a parent company**
   The founders were confident HOK would open offices in other cities, and a number of separate companies would need to be formed to allow for that to happen. However, they wanted stock to be issued from only one company, which eventually became HOK's parent company.

This ownership relationship required HOK to operate in a more businesslike way. The founders never took all the money out of the firm at the end of the year as a partnership might, instead reinvesting some of each year's profit back into the company. They made good livings, but never became fabulously wealthy, because they chose to put money back into the company. They had a bigger mission in mind than just dollars—they were investing in the long-term future of the firm.

The founders developed a plan to offer stock to key employees as a method of expanding ownership to the next generation of leaders. Their goal was to create a virtuous cycle. As senior leaders retired, upcoming leaders would become owners. They also invited a handful of those next-generation leaders to serve as HOK board members. Board members did not have much power, which stayed with the small committee of founders running the firm, but they got a chance to learn and brought in their own fresh ideas and new perspectives. Board membership would become so important later that we would restructure the firm to create more opportunities for future leaders.

Another advantage of offering employees stock was that the additional stock sold to younger employees consisted of newly issued shares, not the original stock held by the founders. By selling stock to employees rather than giving it to them, the value of HOK increased by the amount of money the new owners put into the firm. Thus, HOK stock was not diluted, and retained its value. The founders began to offer HOK stock to younger people well before any of the three approached the mandatory age when they had to sell their stock back to the company. In the years before I joined the firm, the founders offered stock to only a few key employees. But in 1968, they conducted the first large-scale stock sale to about 20 selected employees. I was fortunate to be included in that group.

It's important to note that HOK did not *give* stock to its employees. Rather, the firm *sold* stock to us—just like any corporation would—and we had to come up with the money to buy it. HOK made this process almost painless by arranging with Boatmen's Bank, HOK's corporate bank at that time, to extend an automatic loan to any employee buying stock. HOK received the loan proceeds in exchange for the stock, and the employee paid off the loan over the course of a few years, with an automatic payroll deduction.

When HOK offered me this ownership opportunity, I was still wondering if I should stay with the firm. Having a piece of the ownership gave me a seat at the annual shareholders meeting and made me feel like part of something bigger. It cemented me to HOK in ways I didn't entirely understand at the time. Buying that stock was one of the smartest things I ever did. Later, I would use stock ownership to reunify HOK, after we had lost our way.

Chapter 3: To Design a World-Class Firm

1. Listen to potential clients before you talk, to learn what they really want and need, and you will be an outstanding marketer.
2. Listen to clients before you design, and you will be a better designer who comes up with the most innovative solutions.
3. Prioritize designing beautiful but functional buildings that really work for your clients over developing a recognizable personal style.
4. Balance the natural tension between quality and schedule to get the best buildings completed on time and on budget.
5. Innovate with the tools of your time. Discover new ways to use them—whether to be more organized or to create better designs.
6. Get out into the world and help your city or client make good decisions about their building needs before design even starts.
7. Assign the designer, project manager, and technical architect to a job at the start and have them see it all the way through.
8. Bring other professions—from graphics to interiors, from PR to law—in house for closer collaboration.
9. Invest some cash back into your firm every year, rather than distributing all of it to the partners, so you can grow or improve your practice.
10. Consider setting up your firm as a corporation, meant to outlive you, rather than as a partnership that dies with the partners.
11. Restrict stock ownership to active employees, so you can control your company and its destiny.
12. Create a virtuous cycle by offering to sell newly issued shares of stock to younger employees, as the company grows. This will build loyalty—and your firm's value.

CHAPTER 4

Company Culture Is Crucial

George Hellmuth, Gyo Obata, and George Kassabaum were different people with different personalities, but they shared a powerful vision of a firm where people treated each other as teammates and helped each other to succeed. They valued harmony. Plenty of rivalry existed outside the firm for projects, but inside, the founders insisted that teamwork was the best way for HOK to compete. To simplify this thought, which would work well at any company, the idea was:

Collaboration inside is the best way to compete outside.

My friend Bill Voelker had described the atmosphere as that of "a big family," and I came to think of it as HOK culture. People at the firm really did do their utmost to help each other succeed. When I came to HOK, the firm had such a unified culture that everyone shared a common frame of reference. I heard many HOK leaders say, "If you don't fit into the HOK culture, you are going to leave sooner or later, and you might as well leave sooner!"

Mutual Respect

HOK was remarkably egalitarian, with a sense of mutual respect between everyone from file clerk to founder. This was most important in the quest for new and better ways to do things. The founders actively encouraged people to seek out the very best ideas and solutions, regardless of who they came from—an enlightened approach any firm could adopt. We were encouraged to innovate and take risks, even if it didn't always work out. If a junior employee dreamt up the best idea, senior people set their egos aside and went with it. Period. This was a real novelty at a time when most companies took a top-down approach. Architecture has at times suffered from a cult of personality, where so-called "black cape" architects demanded total obedience from their apprentices. HOK was different.

The founders also demonstrated mutual respect by using first names around the office. People called Kassabaum "George K." and Hellmuth "George H." Later, people started calling George H. "Papa George," when his son—also an architect and named George Hellmuth—came to work at HOK. I called Gyo Obata "Mr. Obata" during my interview, but he soon corrected me, and he was always "Gyo" after that. It was a first-name-basis kind of place. In fact, as I write this book, it makes me faintly uncomfortable to refer to the founders by their last names, but with so many Georges and Bills and Bobs, I have done so for clarity. (I have called later leaders by their first names.)

Part of mutual respect at HOK was self-responsibility. The firm relied on everyone to do the right thing. In fact, no one filled out a time sheet. Staff members were mostly salaried, and each person was expected to be diligent in his or her work. Obata himself always came in on Saturdays, so his team did, too. People worked, as needed, until a job was finished. It was also normal to see people working at night. In return, HOK respected our efforts and made it possible to do this with the least amount of stress. If people had to work late, HOK fed them and the founders lauded their work at the next staff meeting. It was part of the family feel. People treated each other with respect, were patient with each other's shortcomings, and celebrated both personal and firm growth.

Considerate Communication

The founders had a soft-spoken way of conveying what they wanted that I came to think of as "Suggest, Don't Tell." They would make something sound like a request—"Why don't we do it this way"—but we all understood that it wasn't really a suggestion, it was an order. However, couched the way it was, it sure sounded a lot nicer. Maybe it was a midwestern characteristic, but in speaking like this, they were again demonstrating mutual respect for employees. When the leaders spoke, they didn't have to issue commands and edicts. Everyone knew what was expected. None of the founders had to raise his voice to be understood, and I never heard any of them shout in anger. This communication style trickled down to the staff in the way we addressed each other.

Another aspect of the founders' considerate communication was how they drew a line between public and private discussions. They praised excellent efforts and good teamwork publicly but corrected substandard work or lack of teamwork in private. If necessary, they let us know that we had disappointed them, but didn't harp on it, instead challenging us to do better next time. I have since heard a workplace saying for this: "If you're not happy with my work, tell me. If you are happy with my work, tell everybody." Publicly humiliating people just makes them resentful. It doesn't help them improve, a concept many managers don't get.

Taking Care of Employees

When I was a young architect, I walked around with a copy of Ayn Rand's book *The Fountainhead*, in which the main character Howard Roark had great personal integrity—and was an architect! After much sacrifice, he ultimately achieved success and fame through the patronage of a powerful newspaper owner. I had also learned about the patronage system used during the Renaissance, when wealthy clients like the Medici family supported artists like Michelangelo. Even though HOK was my employer, I began to think of the firm as my patron, nurturing me in my career, so that I, in turn, could take care of HOK clients. This is more than nice—it's smart—since employees are the most important asset of any service business.

A good example of HOK taking care of its people occurred about a year after I joined the firm. I was working at my desk when Hellmuth came through the design department followed by one of the accountants, pushing a little cart filled with envelopes. Hellmuth gave each person an envelope and said a few words. When Hellmuth reached my desk, he retrieved an envelope from the cart and gave it to me. It was personalized with my name. He shook my hand and said, "Here's a gift of appreciation for your hard work. Thank you." The envelope contained a bonus check made out to me, and I was thrilled! The founders understood that treating people well and giving them opportunities to grow were two keys to building a great firm.

Family Atmosphere

Hellmuth also had a more down-home way of thanking the staff. Every summer, he invited us to his farm in the Ozark Mountains of southern Missouri for a weekend of fun. The land was not suitable for traditional farming as the soil is thin and rocky with many caves, springs, and streams. Hellmuth's farm was called "The Sinks" for the stream that ran alongside the farmhouse before "sinking" directly into a hill nearby, forming a cave.

When I arrived in my VW Beetle on a typically hot, muggy Missouri summer day, HOK men were everywhere. Yes, it was mostly men then. In fact, Hellmuth called us "my boys." Employees were sitting in the shade, lounging on the grass or swimming in the stream. Several had climbed on a ledge and were cannonballing into the stream, spraying everyone nearby with cool Ozark water. Good, clean fun was the order of the day.

When evening came, a station wagon pulled up and the tailgate opened to reveal every type of soft drink, beer, "adult beverage," and mixer imaginable. Everyone had a drink or two and told HOK stories. Dinner was simple: steak and salad. One group made salads, but Hellmuth grilled all the steaks himself. He said, "A steak isn't good enough for my boys if it doesn't hang off both sides of the plate," so these were enormous slabs of beef! Everyone lined up to get a plate, loaded up some salad, then stopped at the grill to get a steak from Hellmuth.

When it was my turn, he looked me in the eye and said, "Thank you, Patrick," and he meant it sincerely. This was another way Hellmuth personally acknowledged each person's hard work. Everyone sat at picnic tables, or on rocks, or at big tables indoors. It was a great time, with lots of laughter. When it came time to sleep, everyone found a flat spot, took out a sleeping bag or an air mattress, and slept right where they were.

On Sunday morning, Hellmuth rang an old-fashioned school bell to get everyone moving. He organized groups to go to church, having mapped out directions to a church for every denomination. "It's okay to have a good time Saturday night, but by damn you're going to go to church on Sunday," he insisted. Hellmuth established a wholesome code of conduct by his example. In fact, when an opportunity came to design the St. Louis Playboy Club, he turned it down. It didn't fit in with HOK culture.

These weekends—Hellmuth opening his home and inviting everyone in for a feast—were one more embodiment of HOK culture. The time spent swimming, horsing around, eating, and laughing helped everyone feel like family. He gave us a place to bond. Actually, he gave us two.

HOK's annual party was held in Hellmuth's backyard in St. Louis, where he also welcomed our spouses and friends. His mother lived next door and the two backyards were connected, so he used both for the party. A committee decorated the yard, and arranged live music, so it was a noisy event. People gave little speeches, and someone was usually pushed into the pool. Every year one of the neighbors would complain about the noise and end up calling the police, but Hellmuth always invited the officers in and gave them dessert. The police would warn the crowd to hold the noise level down, then depart.

> **O**ne of the biggest challenges HOK would face in the future was how to maintain that family culture when the firm was spread all over...

These occasions were very personal and permeated with the wholesomeness of the Midwest. After only a short time at the firm, I felt like part of something larger—a team and a family. One of the biggest challenges HOK would face in the future was how to maintain that family culture when the firm was spread all over the country—and then the world.

Storytelling

Storytelling was another important part of HOK culture and can strengthen any company. Just as tribes have told existential stories around the fire for centuries, HOK people told stories as a way of connecting. The senior staff especially loved to tell humorous stories about clients and projects. King Graf, Hellmuth's senior assistant, was one of my favorite storytellers. He told and retold a tale about traveling with Hellmuth to an interview for a new grade school in a little town in Missouri. The interview was held in one of the classrooms. As they approached the classroom door, they heard the school officials interviewing another team, so they sat in the hallway on a couple of tiny chairs, holding their giant portfolios and waiting with their knees up under their chins.

The HOK interview was scheduled for 7:00 p.m. Hellmuth was not a patient person and kept checking his watch. At 7:00 p.m. the other team was still in the classroom, so he went to the door and knocked. Conversation in the classroom stopped for a second, then resumed. Hellmuth waited a moment for someone to come to the door, and then —Blam! Blam! Blam!—pounded on the door. A man from the school district cracked the door open and Hellmuth said, "Our time started five minutes ago." "Well, please wait," the man replied, only to be pushed out of the way. Hellmuth suspected the project was wired for another firm, so he strode into the room and declared, "I'm George Hellmuth of HOK and I'm here for an interview. I know we're the best, you know we're the best, so just give us the damned job!" Then he turned and left. At the end of King's story someone always asked if HOK got the job. King would smile and say, "Hellmuth was right—we didn't win that one!"

Hellmuth loved to travel in pursuit of work around the world and loved to tell stories about his adventures. St. Louis was a TWA hub, and he always flew first class on TWA. He was one of their biggest customers and got to know all the flight attendants, then called stewardesses. One day Hellmuth went to TWA and said, "I fly with you all the time, and I want to set it up so that whenever I make a reservation, I always get seat 5B." The TWA representative said it would wreck their reservation system, but finally agreed that on flights originating in St. Louis, he could reserve seat 5B. As he was leaving, Hellmuth quipped, "And one more thing: make sure it's always on the shady side of the plane." He was kidding, of course, but was totally serious about hopping on an airplane at a moment's notice to pursue work for HOK.

One Saturday morning in 1968, several of us were working in the St. Louis office when the building began to shake. Most people don't think about the fact that St. Louis is near the New Madrid fault zone, which has produced three of the largest earthquakes in U.S. history. Suddenly, the whole room was in motion and everyone stopped what they were doing—except Chi Chen Jen, an HOK designer who was originally from Taiwan. He knew about earthquakes and was through the door, down the stairs, and outside the building before the rest of us realized it was an earthquake. By the time I looked out the window to see what was going on, he was down on the street, no doubt wondering where we all were. King Graf had been in a bathroom stall when the earthquake hit, and the lights went out. He came out of that bathroom like a shot—trying to pull his pants up!

George Hellmuth and King Graf were not the only storytellers. Paul Watson, the first HOK attorney, liked to tell a story about his first day at HOK. George Kassabaum hired Paul, and, while showing him around, introduced him to Obata, saying, "Gyo, meet Paul Watson, our new in-house lawyer." Obata looked at Paul, then said, "Lawyer? We don't need a lawyer." Kassabaum was surprised, and said, "I told you we were going to hire a lawyer and you agreed." Obata replied, "I'm not sure I'm going to like him, so let's make him temporary." Paul turned to Obata and said, "Good, I'm not sure I'm going to like you either!" Obata and Watson became good friends after that exchange and worked together for years.

These stories and many others reflect HOK Culture, who we are as people. Lots of them poke a bit of fun in a mild-mannered way. Hearing—and telling—stories like this when we were working late, or on the road, or at the annual barbecue was one more thing that made me feel like part of the family. Even the firm's name became the stuff of stories.

The HOK Name

The founders' last names were difficult to spell, so the firm became best known by the initials H-O-K. Years later, we shortened the name to just the initials for simplicity. But for now, people around the firm loved to poke gentle fun at the challenge of the founders' names.

Here's a Kassabaum story that took place in an era when HOK had established several offices, but receptionists still wrote phone messages by hand. The receptionists were all trained to answer the phone by saying, "Good morning, Hellmuth, Obata, and Kassabaum. How may I direct your call?" George Kassabaum called the Dallas office and asked to speak with King Graf. The receptionist replied, "I'm sorry, Mr. Graf is out of the office. Would you like to leave a message?" Kassabaum said, "Please have him call George Kassabaum when he returns." The receptionist said, "How do you spell Kassabaum?" Kassabaum replied, "Young lady, look on your paycheck!"

King could tell and retell funny stories about Kassabaum—and Hellmuth and Obata—because he held a unique position of trust with all three founders. He never boasted about his special role. Instead, he made yet another joke about the firm name, saying "If Kassabaum retired and I became his replacement, the firm would be called Hellmuth, Obata & Graf, or HOG—and that would never do!"

Much later, in the 1980s, we all enjoyed another good laugh about the HOK name. Vernon Geisel, one of our architects, had previously worked in Moscow for the U.S. Embassy and wrote and spoke fluent Russian. Vernon subscribed to some Soviet magazines and brought one to the office. It contained an article about HOK, including our logo and pictures of some of our buildings. The article was titled "HOK: A Hawk in the Skies of Architecture." The author claimed it was no mistake that the HOK initials sounded, phonetically, like "hawk," because we were a big capitalist company intent on gobbling up our smaller competitors! It was still the Cold War era, and Soviet apparatchiks regularly instructed state journalists to slant stories against the United States and Western companies. We were oddly flattered, figuring we had really made it, if HOK was the subject of Soviet propaganda.

The HOK name was misconstrued—and misspelled. Over the years Chip Reay, the graphic designer in St. Louis, collected misspellings from mail that came into the HOK mailroom. When the office relocated to new space in downtown St. Louis, Chip created a humorous announcement containing the many misspellings of the firm name. Everyone had a good laugh over it, including the founders. My personal favorite is the last name on the list.

St. Louis Office Fire

HOK culture played a part in serious times, too. A fire swept through the St. Louis office on Friday evening, November 8, 1974. HOK occupied several floors in the Syndicate Trust Building, a downtown landmark that had formerly been a department store. It took 110 firefighters to bring the fire under control. Finally, at about midnight, officials allowed tenants into the building for a first look at the damage. After wading through the water and burned debris, George Kassabaum told the *St. Louis Post Dispatch* that he expected most—possibly all—work on current projects would be completely lost.

How would HOK survive? How would HOK respond? Employees heard about the fire from news reports and spontaneously began to call each other. They agreed to

Chapter 4 Company Culture Is Crucial

```
            Elmo O. Kassbarn
       Hellmuthoobata & Kassabuam
        Egelmuth, Obhatta & Kosselboum
        Hillmieth, Obafa & Rassabaum
       Hellmoth, Obatate, Lassa, Bovy Inc.
        HELLMUTH OBEY,KOSSOBAUM
         Hellmuth, Obata, Haussa & Baum
  Hillmuth-Obrata-Kassenbaum Inc. Architects
         Kelmuth O Bauer & Kronbaum
         Hellmjth, Ovata and Jassevam
             Pnata & Massabaum, Inc.
        Hellmuth-Rossabaum and Ober
        HELLMUTH CABATA & KASSABAUM, INC.
          Hellmuth, O'bata & Kasseoaum
          Hillmuth-Oboto & Kasselbaum
             Mr. Hellmuth Ogata
               Mr. Caooobata, AIA
       Orch, Helmugh, Obata and Kassabaum
           Helmouth-Obate-Kassbaum
         George E. Kassabaum & Associates
        Hallmuth, Cpato & Kauabaum, Architects
               Kassabaum Engineers
        Hellmuth, Ofata and Kassabauna, Inc.
         Hellmurt, Obata, & Kassabourn
          Hellmutts Obata Kassabaum
              Judge Kassabaum
          Hellmuth, Obara, Kassabaum
           Helmouth-Obate-Kassbaum
             Miss Helen Cossoboun
          HELLMUTH, ABADA & KASSABAUM
      Heelmuth-Obala-Karrabaum, Architects
                Hillmuth OBath
         Hillmuth, Abata & Kassaburn
          Hulmuth, Obata & Cosabel
          Hellmuth, Obata & Kassabauni
        Hellsmouth, Abato, & Kassablum
             Obata & Kassaeaun
       Messrs. Helmith, Obata & Kassaburm
          Halgrath & K.A. Saboon
         Kelmuth O Bauer & Kronbaum
            HELLMUTH OBARAOKABILM
         Hellmuth Obata Kosshaun
         Hellmuth O'Barta Mfg. Co.
         Mr. Hellmuth O. Kassabaum
                 HOK Ass.
```

FIGURE 4.1 Humorous announcement listing misspellings of HOK founders' names. c. 1970.
Source: Image courtesy of HOK.

meet the next morning at a nearby restaurant and make a plan of attack. Everyone went to the unburned portion of the office on the tenth floor and began to organize. One team went to visit a nearby building, where two floors were empty, and found enough space was available to reestablish an office. By midmorning, the phone company was installing telephones as the team blocked out areas for each department to occupy.

A second team surveyed the staff to find out who had drafting tables and specialized tools at home to replace the ones destroyed by the fire. Other architecture firms pitched in as well, and HOK sent a trucking service around to collect everything. Someone noticed that the old, unused department store cafeteria was still full of oak captain's chairs, and these became temporary desk chairs.

As employees began picking through the charred mess, a minor miracle: someone opened a large, specialized filing cabinet, called a "flat file" used for storing architectural drawings. Their find? The drawings inside were charred at the edges, but salvageable. Only the drawings on the drafting boards were a complete loss. That meant the very latest versions of various projects were gone forever, but HOK would survive. A hum of relief, excitement, and renewed activity surged through the group.

By 11 a.m. Monday morning, HOK employees were back to work. One design team, working on a new Duke University Hospital project, was preparing a presentation they were to make the very next day. Team member Larry Sauer, told the newspaper,

"We never considered telling the client not to fly here for the presentation."[1] Another presentation, for Community Federal Bank, was due that Friday, but the fire had incinerated the model the team planned to show the client. It had taken two weeks to build the elaborate model. The team constructed a new one, complete with miniature landscaping, in four days.

No one ever questioned whether this was part of the job or whether the company would pay them overtime. Staff arrived on their own and did what was needed. HOK was open for business the following Monday morning, and client meetings already on the calendar proceeded without a hitch. "No management people called anyone. No one was asked. They just came," Obata told the *St. Louis Post-Dispatch*.[2]

The fire was an unexpected challenge—piled on top of all the expected ones—but the response by HOK people was a testament to the strength of HOK Culture.

Chapter 4: To Design a World-Class Firm

1. Encourage collaboration inside as the best way to compete outside.
2. Respect your employees, and they will return the favor.
3. Set egos aside to seek out the very best ideas and solutions, no matter who they come from.
4. Develop your own form of considerate communication.
5. Praise good work publicly; deal with problems privately.
6. Take good care of your employees and they will take good care of your clients.
7. Tell and retell the stories of your own firm to share your values and pull people together.

---

[1] Patricia Rose, "A Phoenix Rose at HOK," *St. Louis Post-Dispatch*, November 27, 1974. Accessed April 21, 2019. https://www.newspapers.com/image/140699320.
[2] Ibid.

CHAPTER 5

Growth: Project Offices

The three founders were united around the goal of geographic expansion beyond their St. Louis roots in accordance with Hellmuth's depression-proof-firm strategy. After all, if they were going to design a world-class architecture firm, they needed to get out into the world. But each founder had a different idea about *where*, and *how*, to expand.

Hellmuth told his partners, "You simply have to establish a real presence in New York and Washington. Too much significant work is going on there to be among the missing."[1] He was in a hurry and proposed buying a firm with an established reputation in each city. The advantage of his approach was instant local credibility, but the disadvantage was the high initial purchase price.

Obata had a special interest in San Francisco; He wanted to plant the HOK flag where he had been "kicked out" many years earlier. Kassabaum favored Los Angeles, which was emerging as the dominant West Coast city. Both Obata and Kassabaum liked the idea of winning major new commissions in other cities, establishing project offices there, and then marketing for new work as the project was underway. The advantage of their approach was low initial cost, but the disadvantage was establishing local credibility, which could take years.

So, they agreed to disagree—and did both. It was expedient for HOK and is not a bad idea for any firm to grow opportunistically, depending on which opportunity presents itself in different markets. Sometimes HOK expanded by growing from a project office and sometimes by buying another firm, depending on the opportunity. In the early years, most new offices grew out of project offices.

Planting a Flag in San Francisco

In 1966, HOK won the commission to design a new graduate library for Stanford University. Obata led design from St. Louis, and HOK assembled a small team in San Francisco to

---
[1] Walter McQuade and Paul Grotz, *Architecture in the Real World: The Work of HOK* (New York: H.N. Abrams, 1985), p. 34.

coordinate and complete the project. "Stanford University said they'd give us their Graduate Library project if we opened an office in the Bay Area, so we opened a small office," Obata recalled later. "I was familiar with it since I was born there."[2]

Temporary project offices like this one supported specific projects, and often included staff from local firms that partnered with HOK to do the work. Hellmuth was convinced HOK could get more Bay Area work if a good marketer could look for new clients while the Stanford project was underway. He remembered Dan Gale, who had impressed Hellmuth as a natural marketer when he worked for HOK in St. Louis. After several years, Dan had left HOK and relocated to the clear air of Aspen, Colorado to alleviate his daughter's asthma. Hellmuth called Dan and persuaded him to relocate to California as the new HOK San Francisco marketing principal. Dan accepted, one of many to return to HOK—once—and began a search for work. But the work he found was not in San Francisco. It was in Alaska. HOK's project locations were about to get way more exotic.

One of the ways architects find projects is by networking with contractors, engineers, and other consultants. In San Francisco, Dan met Richard Flambert of Flambert & Flambert, a kitchen consultant that specialized in designing large, institutional kitchens for hotels, universities, and hospitals. Flambert traveled extensively in his practice, including to Alaska, which was booming after the discovery of North Slope oil and the construction of the Trans-Alaska pipeline.

Flambert had consulted for Crittenden, Cassetta, Wirum & Cannon (CCWC), an architecture firm in Anchorage, and knew they were swamped with design jobs and struggling to handle larger and more challenging projects. In 1969, he offered to introduce Dan to CCWC senior partner Ed Crittenden, and the two traveled to Anchorage for a meeting. It was a perfect fit. CCWC had more contracts than it could handle and HOK San Francisco needed work. HOK immediately began to provide design and production leadership for the largest and most challenging Alaska projects while assisting CCWC with smaller work. The two firms began marketing to Alaska clients together as CCWC & HOK, winning more commissions around the state, including a high school on Kodiak Island, student housing for the University of Alaska Fairbanks campus, and a major addition to Providence Hospital in Anchorage.

By late 1969, Alaska work was so substantial that Obata asked Bill Valentine, his most trusted designer, to move to San Francisco as the first design principal outside of St Louis, effectively turning the little project office into the first permanent satellite HOK office. Bill recalls that when he agreed to move to San Francisco, Obata said, "That's good . . . could you fly to Anchorage in the morning?" Things were moving that fast. Sometimes you just have to seize the moment, even if it's a stretch.

HOK opened the San Francisco office just 11 years after its founding. Over the next seven years, HOK created three more offices—in Washington, DC, Dallas, and New York. The founders discovered opening new offices was difficult and would learn many sobering new lessons.

---

[2] Cathy Sivek, "An Interview with Gyo Obata, FAIA, Founding Partner of Global Architectural Firm HOK," p. 2, ArchitectureSchools.com, February 2, 2006. Accessed April 21, 2019. http://architectureschools.com/resources/an-interview-with-Obata-obata-faia-founding-partner-of-global-architectural-firm-hok.

Launching in Washington, DC

As the San Francisco office grew, Hellmuth established a marketing office in Washington, DC to support his regular trips there to market to federal agencies. Setting up a marketing-only office is another way of growing and makes sense in a target-rich environment like Washington, where Hellmuth called regularly upon the General Services Administration (GSA), the State Department, the Army Corps of Engineers, and the Smithsonian. His early efforts led to a State Department commission to design the U.S. Embassy in San Salvador.

Hellmuth visited Smithsonian officials often, and in 1965 secured the commission for a major new museum on the National Mall, the park connecting the Capitol building and the Lincoln Memorial. The space race was well underway, and Congress had appropriated money for a national air and space museum to house the nation's expanding collection of airplane and rocket artifacts.

The Smithsonian required a local associate architect for the work, and Hellmuth selected Petticord and Mills, successful Washington architects with previous experience on the National Museum of American History. The two firms worked together on the museum project, then merged, in 1975, creating a full service HOK office in Washington, DC. This works well as long as the two firms share a similar company culture. Obata designed the Air and Space Museum from St. Louis, making frequent trips to Washington to meet with Smithsonian officials.

Fatefully, by the time the design wound its way through the bureaucratic process and got approved, inflation had driven the construction cost well beyond the original congressional appropriation. The Smithsonian asked HOK to redesign the museum to fit within the original budget. Sometimes the best design solution comes from second chances. And sometimes it comes from an underling. This was one of those situations where HOK's unique belief in finding the very best solution—regardless of who it comes from—paid off. Chi Chen Jen, the Taiwanese-born designer who had evacuated so fast in that St. Louis earthquake, had an idea. He proposed an elegant assemblage of three large, skylit glass galleries for the display of aircraft and space memorabilia separated by four marble cubes for smaller exhibits. It was brilliantly simple, and Obata went with it.

Sometimes the best design solution comes from second chances. And sometimes it comes from an underling.

The Smithsonian dedicated the redesigned museum on July 1, 1976, at the height of the United States Bicentennial festivities, under the leadership of Director Michael Collins, the former astronaut who had journeyed to the moon on Apollo 11, in 1969. The National Air and Space Museum quickly became the most popular museum on the National Mall and earned praise in the architectural press, establishing a much-needed national reputation for both Obata and HOK. Any design firm that can nab a prominent commission early in its corporate life—then design an elegant solution—will benefit, as HOK did. It remains the most-visited museum in the United States, with 7.5 million visitors in 2016, for example.

FIGURE 5.1 National Air and Space Museum, Washington, DC.
Source: Photo by George Silk. Photo courtesy of HOK.

Landing in Dallas

Dallas, Texas was not on the minds of the founders when they first considered adding offices. That would soon change with the advent of a major project opportunity. This time, Obata's burgeoning design reputation, more than Hellmuth's clever marketing ability, led to the establishment of another new office. It happened in a mad rush of opportunity and action.

The twin Texas cities of Dallas and Fort Worth are only 31 miles apart, and both maintained competing airports until 1966. After prodding by the Federal Aviation Administration (FAA), the cities agreed to jointly build and operate a new airport on a large tract of land midway between their two city centers. They recruited Thomas Sullivan, former head of Kennedy Airport in New York, as director of the new airport to be called Dallas-Fort Worth International Airport (DFW). Acting on the advice of friends in the aviation industry, Sullivan invited Gyo Obata to Dallas for a preliminary interview and was impressed with his ability to listen and absorb ideas for the new airport. A few days later, Sullivan asked Obata for information about HOK and examples of recent work. Sullivan explained that he wanted to brief the airport board—and that the meeting was the next morning!

Frantic, Gerry Gilmore of the marketing department worked all day to assemble the requested material. Then—in a classic move inspired by Hellmuth, his mentor—he flew to Dallas and hand-delivered the package to Sullivan late in the evening. Sullivan looked through it but was not satisfied, and asked Gilmore for more supporting detail. At 1 a.m.,

Gilmore called King Graf in St. Louis, rousting him from bed. King put on his clothes, drove downtown to the office, and assembled yet more material for Sullivan. Then he arranged for a chartered plane to fly it to Dallas! Gilmore met the plane, rushed to Sullivan's office, and hand-delivered the new material to him just as the board meeting was beginning.

Gilmore waited nervously outside Sullivan's office to learn the outcome. Finally, Sullivan called Gilmore into his office, telephoned Obata, and said, "Obata, I just finished the presentation to the airport board. I'm sitting here with your guy, Gilmore, and I'm afraid I've got some bad news for you." A big grin spread over his face. "The bad news is that I sold you to the board this morning, and now you're going to have to design this damned thing."[3]

HOK was required to establish a Dallas project office as a condition of the contract. As with San Francisco, the founders believed the project office was an opportunity for a permanent HOK office. Maybe it was because King Graf had performed so admirably, half-asleep, in the middle of the night, to help land the DFW Airport job, that Hellmuth asked him to relocate from St. Louis to Dallas and look for more commissions. King would remain in Dallas for a decade and was successful in winning many more contracts, establishing Dallas as a major HOK office.

Dallas-Fort Worth International Airport began operations in 1973, and today serves over 60 million passengers annually, with five terminals and 165 gates. In 2017, Airports

FIGURE 5.2 Dallas-Fort Worth International Airport under construction.
Source: Photo by George Silk. Photo courtesy of HOK.

---

[3] McQuade and Grotz, 44.

Council International named DFW the best large airport in North America for passenger satisfaction.

These three offices, opened at such an early point in the firm's history and within seven years of each other, established the pattern HOK would follow in the future: seek out major design contracts, which sometimes required opening a local project office; grow promising project offices into major branches; acquire firms when necessary to gain entry to a market. It was risky to open new offices so quickly, but, for now, the firm appeared to be up to the challenge.

Chapter 5: To Design a World-Class Firm

1. Expand by buying other firms when you have the money and need instant credibility.
2. Expand by growing project offices into branch offices, when you don't have the money, but have plenty of time to establish credibility.
3. Establish just a marketing office in a new city, when you don't have the money—or a project—to break in there.
4. Remember that sometimes the best design solution comes from second chances—or comes from an underling.
5. Work to win a high profile commission early in your company's development, for the good press and national reputation it can spark.

CHAPTER 6

Many Jobs, One Firm

It was time for a vacation before my next design assignment, and I headed west in my trusty VW Beetle to tour the Rocky Mountains. I fell in love with the city of Boulder, Colorado, where the plains end abruptly at the eastern flank of the Rocky Mountains. It was a beautiful place, with clear air and a dramatic mountain setting. Maybe I could live here? I went to a phone booth with a huge phone book dangling from a metal chain, and found the yellow pages listing for architecture firms. I ripped the pages out and took them back with me, thinking I'd write to these firms and see if any had an opening.

But before I got around to writing to Boulder architects, HOK gave me a big opportunity. It was the first of many times that I got a brand new job without ever leaving the firm. Attracting, training, and then keeping talented people was one of George Hellmuth's best ideas and a central tenet of his depression-proof-firm strategy. Yes, you are giving employees the opportunity to build careers, but you are also giving your company an opportunity to deepen its reservoir of experience and knowledge. I didn't know it then, but I was part of the grand experiment.

Going to Pittsburgh

Schematic design of the Great High Schools was nearing completion. The work would soon move to a project office in Pittsburgh staffed by HOK and four local Pittsburgh firms. Bill Valentine needed a designer in Pittsburgh to ensure that the integrity of the design would be carried out at the project office. He asked for me. It was a huge responsibility. At that moment, I could not have imagined in my biggest, wildest dreams the journey that would unfold for me—all at one firm. Boulder might have been a good life, but nothing like what awaited me at HOK.

The Pittsburgh project office was located on the north side of town and held 25 architects, including half a dozen people I knew from HOK. Every so often, King Graf or Bill Valentine flew to Pittsburgh to review our progress. King focused on our relationships with the client and our associate architects, while Bill immersed himself in the design work. When Bill and King were in town we would sometimes go for dinner at Klein's, a family-owned seafood restaurant first opened in 1900. Oddly enough, in land-locked Pittsburgh it was famous for fresh seafood flown in daily from the coast. As a born and bred Midwesterner, I experienced lobster for the first time there, not knowing it was just one of many delicious experiences HOK would bring into my life.

One of my favorite opportunities, while living in Pittsburgh, was the chance to visit Fallingwater. Frank Lloyd Wright designed this masterpiece as a summer home for retailer Edgar Kaufman and his family in a beautiful, wooded site a short drive east of town. It is a marvel of design, dramatic yet intimate, appearing to grow from the rocks of Bear Run Creek. It is uniquely designed just for this special setting and the idea that buildings should be designed to fit into their specific surroundings became one of my enduring beliefs, one I think all architects should adopt. I loved Fallingwater and visited every few months to experience Wright's showpiece as the seasons changed.

Pittsburgh had a better climate than my hometown, with beautiful fall colors and friendly, industrious people. I worked there for a year and continued to report to Bill Valentine and Obata. I did all kinds of work for them, and they came to rely on me for difficult design challenges. I loved the lifestyle in Pittsburgh and was tempted to remain, but HOK had other plans for me.

Settling in San Francisco

Bill Valentine and I loved to play racquetball, and during his visits to Pittsburgh we often played at the downtown YMCA after work. During one of Bill's visits we played at the Y, as usual. As we were standing in the locker room after the game, soaked in sweat, Bill said, "We just got a bunch of Alaska work, and it's being done out of San Francisco. Obata asked me to move there to head up design, and I've been traveling back and forth from St Louis to San Francisco to Alaska to Pittsburgh. It's more than I can handle, and I need help. How would you like to move to San Francisco?"

I had never been to San Francisco, but, remember, it was one of the cities I had dreamed of when I vowed to get out of St. Louis someday. I said, "It sounds wonderful. Sign me up!" Bill replied, "Well . . . I have to ask Obata first." I expected this would be a straightforward request, but Bill wanted to wait for the right moment and put it off for weeks. Yes, seizing the moment can be key, but so can waiting for the right moment. Obata was worried that HOK was taking too many talented people away from the St. Louis office to supply new offices in other locations. When Bill finally thought the moment was right, he approached Obata with the idea of my relocation to San Francisco. On cue, Obata said, "We are giving up too much design talent in St. Louis, so I don't think it's a good idea." Bill had already thought of a good reason and said, "But Gyo, he's already out of the St. Louis office at the project office in Pittsburgh, so doesn't that make it okay?" Obata thought about it for a few moments, then said, "I guess it's okay." Those few moments of reconsideration changed my life.

Bill told me San Francisco had beautiful white buildings—architects always focus on the buildings—that were surrounded by the sparkling blue water of San Francisco Bay. "Fly out and rent a car," he told me. "You need to find a place to live. I just rented a house in Mill Valley, a great town just north of San Francisco. Get off at Blithedale Avenue and there's a little corner store where you can pick up a weekly newspaper with all the houses for rent. You should have no trouble finding a place."

I flew to San Francisco for the first time in the spring of 1970, rented a car, bought a map—GPS was still in the future—and made my way through the city to the Golden Gate Bridge. What a stunning sight! (Architects also love bridges . . .) I stared at this spectacular bridge gracefully spanning the Golden Gate, a mile-wide strait connecting San Francisco Bay to the Pacific Ocean. The water far below was an incredible blue dotted with white sailboats. The buildings of the city off to my right were white and pink and everything shimmered. It seemed like a dream.

I left the bridge behind and followed the road as it wound steeply up the Waldo Grade and through a tunnel into Marin County. I found Blithedale Avenue but missed my turn and found myself on a narrow two-lane road in a redwood grove. Just ahead, the road split to go around a very large redwood tree. I had never seen anything so majestic! I pulled over, walked up to this tallest of living things and put my hand on the fibrous bark. "I'm home," I thought.

Mill Valley was too expensive, however, so I eventually found a small house to rent farther north, in San Rafael. A bonus? The house was walking distance to another Frank Lloyd Wright masterpiece: the majestic Marin County Civic Center.

The HOK San Francisco office was in the new Golden Gateway Center, a mix of apartments, offices and retail on the north edge of the Financial District. Dan Gale talked the landlord into renting HOK an unused double-height retail space on Davis Court. There

FIGURE 6.1 Author in new HOK San Francisco office, 1970.
Source: Photo courtesy of Patrick MacLeamy.

was a balcony at the back of the space, and HOK tucked three glass-fronted offices underneath it for the three office leaders. Dan, as marketing principal, occupied one office. Bill Valentine, the new design principal, had just moved into another. The third office would soon be filled by Bob Stauder, a top project manager under Kassabaum in St. Louis.

When I arrived, crews had just finished painting everything white and were painting supergraphics on one wall and a large red HOK logo on the other. The office also contained the Stanford Library project team, which consisted of six architects hired locally and led by Rolf Meunter, an HOK project manager who had transferred from St. Louis earlier. From this small beginning, we were determined to grow and become a large, successful office like St. Louis.

Working in Alaska

Bill immediately engaged me in our Alaska work, a diverse mix of projects. In addition to the ongoing Kodiak Island High School design, there was now a contract to create an adult corrections center near Anchorage—and many more. At the end of every week we prepared a package of the latest designs for shipment to St. Louis. And once a month, Obata flew to San Francisco to review our work. He eventually leased an apartment a short walk from our office.

A few weeks after moving to San Francisco I traveled with Bill Valentine to Alaska for the first time to meet with CCWC Architects, our partners in Anchorage. Since Alaska was the last frontier in North America, I was very excited to go there. Nonstop flights from San Francisco to Anchorage were in the future, so Bill and I took an afternoon flight to Seattle, then transferred to a 9:00 p.m. Western Airlines flight to Anchorage. All the passengers were on board and it was time to go, but the plane remained at the gate. Outside my window, a taxi drove across the tarmac to the plane. One of the flight attendants rushed down the jetway stairs to the taxi, took a leather satchel from the driver, then ran up the stairs to the plane. Then the crew closed the door and we pushed back, on our way to Alaska.

I had looked it up, and Anchorage lies at a latitude of 61° north, as far north as Oslo, Norway. It is also far west of Seattle, in the same time zone as Honolulu, so it took a three-and-a-half hour flight to get there. We arrived at 10:30 p.m. Anchorage time, and the moment we arrived at our gate, the crew repeated the unusual process I had observed in Seattle, but in reverse: a flight attendant rushed down the jetway stairs and handed the leather satchel to a waiting taxi, which then barreled off toward the airport gates. I asked her, "What's in the satchel that's so important?" "The latest videotape of *The CBS Evening News with Walter Cronkite*, just recorded in Seattle," she said. "It's on the way to the Anchorage CBS station for rebroadcast at 11:00 p.m." Alaska was so remote from the rest of the country that live television broadcasts were years in the future.

Anchorage was the largest city in Alaska but still felt like the frontier. Snow-capped mountains surrounded the town, and Cook Inlet, an arm of the ocean, provided access by ship. Small houses lined gravel streets, but downtown was booming with several midrise office buildings and hotels. Although it was close to 10:00 p.m. when I arrived at the

Captain Cook Hotel, the sun was still shining. People were out on the streets and playing softball in a park near the hotel. Someone told me later that on the longest day of summer, Alaskans always play a softball game there, beginning at midnight—and without lights.

Ed Crittenden, Lou Cassetta, Harold Wirum, and Ken Cannon, the partners at CCWC Architects, all came to Alaska from the Lower 48 for the opportunity and adventure. Their practice was traditional, with each partner responsible for marketing and delivering his own projects. CCWC was the largest firm in Alaska, with a staff of 15 working in a converted house near downtown. Senior partner Ed Crittenden seemed to know everyone in the state.

As we began to help CCWC with the project workload, Crittenden taught us about specialized design considerations for the Alaska climate, or Arctic Design. We learned how to design buildings over permafrost, ground permanently frozen even in summertime. He also taught us to design for too much sunlight in summer, followed by months of long winter nights. Ed was a natural teacher and loved to point out buildings with Arctic Design features as we traveled Alaska together. I learned how important it was to design specifically for a local area. In this case, weather was the focus. In other regions we had to consider different natural factors, like hurricane or earthquake risk.

Not long after we began working together, CCWC added a wondrous new, state-of-the-art technology to facilitate communications: a fax machine! The commercially available fax machines of the 1970s were slow, and it seemed to take forever to fax a standard 8-1/2 × 11 sheet of paper, but it was faster than sending it by plane. At the San Francisco office, we cut large drawings into 8-1/2 × 11 sheets, labeled them in order, and sent them through to the Alaska office for reassembly. This is another example of stretching the use of the tools of the time.

Some of our work was in remote villages where most residents were native peoples. I was assigned to work with CCWC partner Lou Cassetta on a new addition for the Indian Health Service hospital in the remote town of Bethel. This small town of predominantly Yupik peoples lies 400 miles west of Anchorage where the Kuskokwim River enters the Bering Sea. The entire area overlays permafrost and is treeless. No roads connect it with the rest of Alaska, so access was by air.

In the winter of 1970, Lou and I flew to Bethel for meetings with our clients. Bethel Airport consisted of a simple terminal and a runway built atop a layer of compacted wood chips. Lou explained the wood chips were insulation to keep the permafrost frozen, as melting would cause the ground to move and break up the runway. Since winter temperatures can reach −40 °F, CCWC lent me a parka with a big, fur-trimmed hood that projected out well beyond my face. Lou explained the fur is essential, because it holds a layer of warm air near the face. Inhaling extremely cold air can cause frostbite in the lungs. What had I gotten myself into? It was the first of many times I had to adapt to an exotic location in order to pursue HOK's interests.

Bethel had the look and feel of a frontier town in an old movie. Most buildings were made of wood and sat on pilings to lift them above the permafrost. Our hotel, the Kuskokwim Inn, was an eight-room barracks building, which is still there. The town had one taxi, and it only operated locally. Roads ended at the edge of town and there was nowhere else to drive. The owner kept the taxi running 24 hours a day in winter to keep the engine from freezing up in the extreme cold.

I was eager to experience life in remote Alaska, so Lou took me to Bethel's only restaurant for dinner. I looked over the menu and ordered fish. "Sorry, we're out of fish." "How about chicken?" "No chicken." The only meal available, until the supply ship arrived after the spring breakup of the sea ice, was hamburgers with French fries. After we ate, Lou suggested we stop at the town bar for a drink. We couldn't get in. The place was completely full, and a long line of people stood outside in the bitter cold, waiting to enter. Once someone inside ran out of money, the bartender threw them out and allowed the next person in line to come indoors.

We gave up on the bar and instead went to the movie theater. This big, wooden building—raised on pilings like all buildings in Bethel—was full of Eskimo kids, all sitting up on the seat backs with their boots on the seat cushions for some reason. The movie started, a grade B Hollywood movie about a biker gang running around in the Mojave Desert. About 20 minutes into the film, I realized my feet were numb. The floor had little insulation, and with the Artic air circulating below the floor, my feet were beginning to freeze. We soon joined the kids up on the seat backs.

We began work on the new hospital wing the next morning. The hospital was administered by the Indian Health Service, but Lou told me it was important to get input from the village elders first. I expected two or three people, but our hosts brought us into a room with about 20 people, both men and women. They spoke Yupik among themselves and one volunteered to translate. Their main desire was that the hospital have a two-story wing. We said, yes, that was possible, perhaps services would be downstairs and patient rooms upstairs. They were delighted, and the next—and most urgent—question was, "Will it have an elevator? We want an elevator because we want to join the modern world, and there is no elevator in our town." When the new hospital wing was finished Bethel had its first elevator.

The next time I traveled to Bethel was in the summer. The sea ice had broken up and a ship had arrived bringing provisions. Families bought a year's worth of supplies at one time and put them in their home storage rooms where the cold acted as a natural refrigerator.

Many other HOK people worked with CCWC on Alaska projects and traveled extensively in Alaska. My friend Terry Richert managed the Anchorage Federal Office Building project and spent much time in Alaska. A friend who worked for British Petroleum (BP), one of the companies extracting oil from the North Slope, invited him to go fishing. They flew a chartered pontoon plane to a large lake north of Anchorage, landed on the water and taxied to shore. After securing the plane to a tree, they walked a short distance to a pristine, gravel-bedded stream teeming with fish. Terry's friend had brought a gun, "In case we run into a grizzly." After putting on hip waders, Terry and his BP friend began fishing in a deep pool at a bend in the stream.

As Terry told us later, "We had just started fishing when a huge grizzly appeared out of the brush on the far bank. It stood up, wrapped one paw around the trunk of a tree, and snarled directly at us. That grizzly was about 25 feet away and had to be eight feet tall—but it seemed like ten feet to us!" I asked, "Where was the gun?" Terry grinned sheepishly,

"The damn gun was on the bank of the stream, too far away to do us any good." I asked, "What did you do?" "What do you think we did?" said Terry. "We got out of that stream as fast as our waders would go, and once we were on dry ground, put more distance between that grizzly and ourselves. As soon as we were out of the stream, the grizzly took over our fishing spot and began pulling out salmon . . . we had been fishing in his spot!"

San Francisco Projects

Fortunately, Alaska work kept our San Francisco office busy, and then, after a few years, we won our first project in the city of San Francisco itself. Dan Gale had become friends with the engineers at International Engineering Company (IECO), a large firm of experienced railroad engineers. They invited HOK to be part of their team to pursue a new project for the San Francisco Municipal Railway (MUNI), the transit agency for San Francisco. MUNI had recently replaced its fleet of aging trolley cars with modern light rail vehicles (LRVs) and needed to replace the old trolley-car repair shops with an up-to-date LRV repair facility. It doesn't sound glamorous, but remember, there's no such thing as a bad project. MUNI selected the IECO team and I was thrilled when Bill Valentine asked me to be the lead HOK designer for the project.

The triangular MUNI site was next to Balboa Park in San Francisco's Outer Mission District. MUNI had an ambitious program for maintenance, repair, and overnight storage for the LRV fleet. As our team leader, IECO's first task was to plan the site to accommodate the ambitious MUNI program. My job was to design the buildings IECO needed after MUNI approved the site layout.

I attended our first client meeting, where IECO presented a design for the site, with separate buildings for maintenance, repair, and painting. Tracks seemed to be going everywhere, with lots of loops and switches, leaving no room for overnight LRV storage. Jerry Cauthen, the MUNI engineer for the project, was not happy. He rejected the IECO design and demanded the team come up with a new layout for his review the next week. After Cauthen left, the IECO engineers did not seem to know how to proceed, so I got my big chance. I suggested locating all maintenance and repair functions in one building, with parallel MUNI tracks leading in one end and out the other. Each track served a different function—cleaning, repair, body work, painting, and wheel truing. The site design I came up with was simple and efficient. I didn't know it then, but looking for elegantly simple solutions was going to be one of my contributions to HOK. It's just how I'm made. IECO accepted my concept and we worked together as a team to refine the new layout.

I didn't know it then, but looking for elegantly simple solutions was going to be one of my contributions to HOK.

We presented the new design to Jerry Cauthen the following week. He was enthusiastic, saying "This design solves our overnight storage problem, and that's good. And having all maintenance operations in one building simplifies our operation since all staff will be in one place. How did you come up with the layout?" To their credit, our IECO colleagues said it was an HOK design. There is a famous Harry Truman quote that comes to mind: "It's amazing what you can accomplish if you do not care who gets the credit." I was just thrilled to be able to put my design and organization skills to work solving problems. I smiled toward the end of the project, when Cauthen said, "The next time we put a project out for design, we're going to ask the architect to be in charge, with the engineers as consultants!"

After the success of the MUNI project, the San Francisco office began to win more local work. Our reputation strengthened as a San Francisco firm. Work in Alaska continued for several years, but now Bay Area work drove our growth.

While still in St. Louis, Dan Gale had participated in the first HOK justice project, a new federal prison in Marion, Illinois to replace Alcatraz, the famous prison in San Francisco Bay. Dan was able to leverage this experience to win new justice work for us, first in Alaska, then in California and other Western states. I had just finished the MUNI project, when Dan asked me to accompany him on a marketing trip to Boulder, Colorado, the town I had dreamed of moving to years before. Boulder is a university town with a large liberal population, but is also the seat of Boulder County, a largely conservative area of ranches and rugged mountains. The sheriff of Boulder County wanted a new, larger jail, but a vocal community group in town wanted a smaller jail and was actively working against the project.

The Boulder County Commissioners hired HOK to conduct a criminal justice study and recommend the final size of the new jail—in other words, to get the heat off themselves. We put together a team, including a legal scholar, the retired head of the Federal Bureau of Prisons, and a statistical consultant from accounting firm Touche Ross (before it merged with Deloitte).

I liked the challenge of working with elected officials and the public, kept orderly track of meetings and managed to stay calm when things got heated. I became friends with the sheriff and one of the judges. Dan saw how I was handling things and soon left for another project, leaving me in charge. I spent many weeks in Boulder, but after living in the San Francisco area, it had lost its appeal as a potential home.

We found a middle path that satisfied both sides, a great learning experience for me. First, we helped Boulder County adjust its booking practices so the new jail could be smaller. Then we found a site for a new jail and convinced the sheriff and supervisors it was the appropriate location. I spent many nights putting the final report together, and Dan asked me to make the final presentation in Boulder. In front of a packed room, I reported that the solution for the county's needs was a series of diversion programs and a smaller jail. Mentally ill people would be taken to a hospital, and those with drug issues would enter a detox program instead of going straight into jail. After supportive public testimony, the Boulder County Commissioners approved our report and recommendations.

My friends, the sheriff, and the judge, took me for a celebratory drink after the meeting. One drink led to another and soon I was concerned about missing my flight back to San Francisco. The sheriff said to relax and called a patrol car. He and I got in the back seat and, with lights flashing and the highway patrol moving cars out of our way, we zoomed straight to the airport in time for my flight.

Building on our successful experience in Boulder, HOK San Francisco began to win more justice work. The State of Arizona hired us for a statewide study of its prison system. I learned the importance of George Hellmuth's admonition to be sincerely interested in the client during that study. I recommend this to all architects. Over the course of the study, we established a trusting relationship with the client. After the consulting work was finished, it was natural for the clients to prefer us—the team they trusted—to design the needed buildings. As a result, HOK received more commissions for projects, and I was always on the project team as the dependable advisor to the client.

Chapter 6: To Design a World-Class Firm

1. Give your people the opportunity to have many jobs at your firm, so they can build a career, and you will deepen your company's reservoir of experience and knowledge.
2. Design buildings just for their special setting, taking advantage of the best of the natural surroundings to inspire your scheme.
3. Design specifically for a local area's weather and other natural factors like hurricane and earthquake risk.
4. Seek design solutions that are elegantly simple.
5. Adopt the Harry Truman philosophy: "It's amazing what you can accomplish if you do not care who gets the credit."
6. Find a middle path that satisfies both sides in politically contentious situations.
7. Show sincere interest in your clients and you will become their trusted advisor, leading to more work.

CHAPTER 7

Managing Versus Leading

The flood of project work coming into HOK was a nice problem to have, but it was also a challenge for the San Francisco office, and for me personally. I no longer had time to design, and instead shifted my attention to helping the project team deliver the work on schedule. I am not a "that's-not-my-job" kind of guy. Plus, I had really bought into HOK's culture of both self-responsibility and helping each other to succeed, so I was happy to get involved in project management. I was personally well-organized and found it rewarding to organize project work.

Becoming a Project Manager

One afternoon Bill Valentine asked me to a meeting in his office with Bob Stauder. Bill said, "We've been watching you help your projects stay on schedule and believe you have a natural management ability. Your career is at a fork in the road, and you need to choose between design and management. If you choose management, you have a bright career ahead, but you will no longer be able to lead project design teams—and you will report to Bob Stauder, not to me." I thought it over for a few days, then agreed. Over the next several years I managed all kinds of projects in San Francisco and learned more about management—and a great deal about leadership.

The Toilet Seat Lesson

I learned an early lesson with my first project manager assignment, a new courthouse in Oakland, across the bay from San Francisco. The chief judge was our main client contact, and our team met in her chambers weekly to review design progress. On one occasion, the project designer and I met with her to review our design for the judge's chambers in the new courthouse. Chambers typically have a private half-bath, and she marched us into hers to take a look. The toilet seat was an institutional black with an open front designed for men.

"I *don't* want that," the judge said, pointing. "I want a full toilet seat—and I want it white, not black." I wrote it down, and after we returned to the office the project secretary typed up the meeting notes and filed them away.

> **H**ow could we lose something so important to the client in the mountain of project information? There had to be a better way...

A year later the courthouse was under construction. I toured the courthouse as it neared completion and discovered the chief judge's chamber had a black toilet seat with an open front. What went wrong? I had taken dutiful notes, but once filed away, we lost the information. I was embarrassed, and arranged for the installation of a new, white toilet seat with a closed front at HOK's expense. Although this was an inexpensive fix, it showed me there was a flaw in our system. How could we lose something so important to the client in the mountain of project information? There had to be a better way . . . if only we had a computer, we could make a list of all the important details in the project and track them so they wouldn't get lost. The toilet seat lesson led me first to computers, and years later to Building Information Modeling (BIM). More on that later. For now, let's just say that all architecture firms need to develop strong computerized systems for noting—and then tracking—the important details of their projects.

Managing Versus Leading

The other big lesson I learned as a project manager is that the title is deceiving. What did it mean to be a project manager? As a young architect, I thought, "That's the boss, the person who gives directions. If I become a manager, I'll get a nice office. People will come in, I'll tell them what to do, and they'll take care of it." One of the lessons I learned as a project manager was that managers who *manage* aren't doing it right. People don't follow managers. Instead they start watching the clock for quitting time.

The project manager role is less about *managing* and more about *leading*. People will follow a leader who shows confidence, enthusiasm, and clarity about the way forward. This is something Dwight Eisenhower demonstrated, first as a general, and then as president. He called leadership "the art of getting someone else to do something that you want done because he wants to do it, not because your position of power can compel him to do it."[1]

Here's another way of explaining it. There's a famous cartoon of Pharaoh building the pyramids. In the top panel, Pharaoh is standing over the workers on a stone while shouting and snapping a whip. That's managing. In the bottom panel, Pharaoh's got a rope over his shoulder, pulling like everyone else and he's out in front of the team. That's leading.

Whether it's a project manager, a managing principal or some other kind of manager, management is not what people need. People need leaders at all levels in the firm, to be out in front with the attitude that they won't ask anyone to do something they won't do

---

[1] Dwight Eisenhower, "What is Leadership?," Remarks to the Leaders of the United Defense Fund, April 29, 1954. Accessed August 6, 2019. https://www.dwightdeisenhower.com/190/Leadership-Organization.

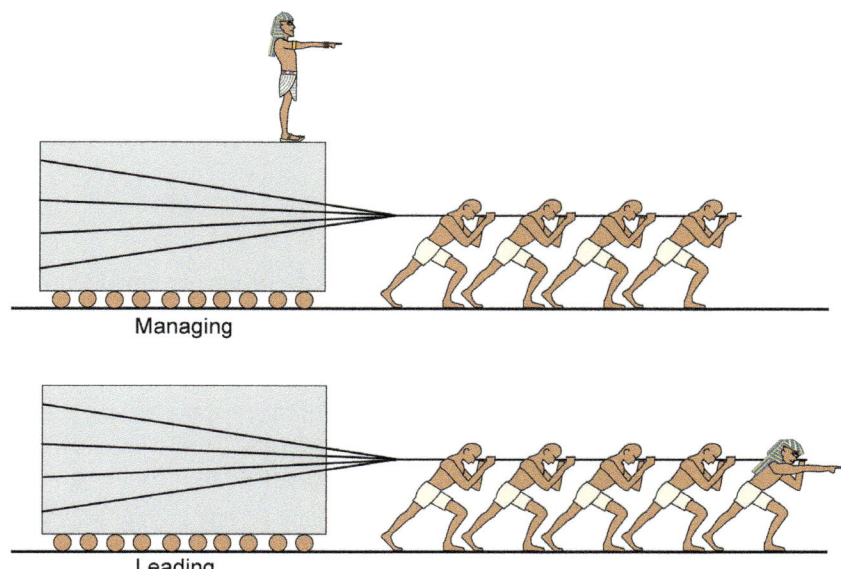

FIGURE 7.1 Managing versus leading.
Source: Cartoon by Patrick MacLeamy.

themselves. Whether they are building the pyramids or building a modern building, people will follow if they have a leader.

Managers direct: "Do this! Do that!"

Leaders encourage: "Let's solve this together!"

Manager is an overrated term. I learned that when leaders lead, people start taking the initiative on their own. They are unshackled from following orders and start putting their own ideas into practice. It's exciting to see the good ideas people come up with, and always a thrill to see someone exceed what they think they can do.

Why don't we call them *project leaders* instead of *project managers*? At HOK we tried this for a while, but not everyone understood. The term *project manager* has a distinct meaning in the practice of architecture, but the best project managers lead—they don't manage.

People love titles with the word *manager* included. *Director* is another favorite, director of design, or director of interiors. How about director of coffee making? I have learned to be skeptical of titles, and when people are in a big hurry to impress me with their lengthy title, they are probably not leadership material. I would sure like to impart this lesson to others: It doesn't matter what you're called; it matters what you do. Actions are more important than words.

Here's another way of putting it. The best leaders are selfless. Think of all the frontline officers who put themselves in the perilous position of going first as they lead their troops into battle. They are not asking their troops to do anything they would not do themselves.

They are right there with them. Leadership is about the mission, not the individual. Perhaps the best example of true leadership is parenting, where the welfare of the kids comes first. Parents lead but also sacrifice so their children can grow up to become responsible, successful adults. My own leadership skills were about to get a giant new test.

Case Study: Moscone Center

During the 1970s, the San Francisco Hotel Owners Association lobbied the city for a new convention center to replace the undersized, subterranean—and stupendously ugly—Brooks Hall beneath City Hall plaza. Everybody loves to visit San Francisco, and the city is a favorite trade show destination, so the outdated convention space was a lost opportunity. It should have been generating big business for hotels, restaurants, and the tourism industry, but it wasn't. Where could a spacious new convention center fit in this relatively small city?

San Francisco's Market Street begins on the east side of the city at the Ferry Building and extends west toward Twin Peaks. In the 1970s, Market Street separated two completely different San Francisco neighborhoods. The North of Market (NOM) neighborhood was vibrant, with the Financial District, the Union Square shopping area, the theater district, and many fine hotels and restaurants. South of Market was a wasteland of relics from the city's maritime past, including warehouses, light manufacturing, and rundown housing tenements.

The San Francisco Redevelopment Agency identified a convention center site in the beleaguered South of Market neighborhood, but not too far from the fine hotels and restaurants North of Market. Their strategy was for the new convention center to stimulate development, so that the South of Market neighborhood could become an equal partner to the bustling NOM area.

This being San Francisco, opposition soon formed to the project. One group wanted to use the site to replace housing that would be lost when the site was cleared. The city reached a compromise, agreeing to build more housing nearby. Another vocal group believed the new convention center would be too large and bulky for the neighborhood, and that the site should become a city park. This led the city to agree to a second compromise, to place the entire convention center underground and reserve the rooftop for public use. It would be a design and engineering challenge for some lucky firm.

HOK was recognized as a San Francisco firm by the time the City of San Francisco began to consider architects for the convention center. We put together our best team and brought Obata from St. Louis to lead design. Our structural consultant was the eminent T.Y. Lin, a native of China famous for his pioneering work with pre-stressed concrete. In addition to his consulting practice, Lin taught at the University of California at Berkeley. Remarkably, this eminent engineer used a computer for detailed structural computation but also carried a small abacus for quick calculations.

San Francisco Chief Administrative Officer Roger Boas took personal charge of the project. He was an intimidating figure, with a speaking style laced with swear words acquired during his World War II experience as a tank commander under General George S. Patton. He knew how to get things done, but through fear and intimidation. Acting on good advice, Boas first selected Turner Construction Company as the construction manager. He wanted design and construction to act as a team from the beginning of design through the end of construction, departing from the tradition of selecting the architect first. Boas and Turner reviewed proposals from a long list of architects, then interviewed just three firms: Charles Luckman from Los Angeles, our old rivals, SOM—and HOK.

Boas was inspired by Obata, but not convinced HOK had the experience to design such a challenging project. He asked to visit some of our past work to assess our ability, so we arranged for him to visit the National Air and Space Museum in Washington, DC and meet with Director Michael Collins. Boas was impressed with the museum and how well it handled the huge crowds; he was more impressed with remarks Michael Collins made about his great working relationship with Obata. It was not the first—or the last—time having the National Air and Space Museum on our resume helped us.

When Boas returned to San Francisco, he called us into his City Hall office and said, "Everybody I know says to select SOM because they have had an office in San Francisco for a long time and are the safe choice, but I have a different opinion. I want HOK. But if you let me down, I will personally see to it that you sons of bitches NEVER do another San Francisco project!" Our excitement at being selected was tempered by the challenges we faced, both with the project and with our cantankerous client.

In a city with an underground convention center that everyone despised, we were being asked to design an underground convention center that everyone would love. It was a tall order. We needed to overcome the suffocating feeling of being underground and avoid creating a heavy, oppressive space with too many columns. Yet we needed to design a structure strong enough to support the weight of a future park and other public uses on the rooftop. Obata, Bill Valentine, and T.Y. Lin met in a series of early design meetings. In a moment of pure, magical collaboration between Obata and Lin, they conceived a grand space without a single column. An array of paired, reinforced concrete arches would gracefully span a convention hall fully 300 feet across and 800 feet in length. Valentine's contribution was to find the way for natural light to penetrate from the Howard Street lobby directly into the convention hall, 40 feet below ground.

We knew our concept was elegant, but getting Roger Boas to understand it was almost impossible. In all my years of experience with clients, Boas stood out as someone completely unable to comprehend floor plans, models, or perspective drawings. He eventually based his approval on the strength of his relationship with Gyo Obata, supplemented by asking everyone else at City Hall what they thought of the design. It was one more reminder that strong relationships matter.

I served as the project manager for the convention center and made up for a lack of experience with hard work. That, by the way, is entirely doable and a great lesson for younger professionals: If you're green, get busy. The old expression "drinking from the end of a fire hose" describes what it was like. The HOK team was required to partner with the Turner team, and after a few weeks, we became friends and colleagues. Turner attended our design meetings and provided feedback about cost and constructability. The project was technically challenging, and under constant attack by the same San Francisco groups that had opposed it from the beginning. The HOK-Turner team worked together to solve every issue.

FIGURE 7.2 Moscone Convention Center, San Francisco, California.
Source: Photo by Peter Aaron. Photo courtesy of HOK.

While working on the Moscone Center project, I learned some valuable lessons. You must recognize and resolve small problems quickly. I'm talking about things like imperfect technical details, threats to staying on budget and on schedule, or relationship issues between team members. I kept a list of unresolved problems to go over during weekly reviews with my team. It doesn't work to avoid conflict or bury your head in the sand. If you neglect little problems they become big problems. And if you neglect big problems they can spiral out of control and become disasters.

I also learned something important that has served me well from working with the irascible Roger Boas: have the courage to tell the truth, even if it is not what someone wants to hear. If I disagreed with something Boas said, I told him, and gained his respect. By the end of the project, he relied on me for straight talk, whether about the convention center or San Francisco politics. Even though Boas was our client, the design required approval from Mayor George Moscone and the San Francisco Board of Supervisors, chaired by Dianne Feinstein, long before she became a U.S. senator. It was a grueling process, but after two years of design and several rounds of approval, Turner Construction broke ground in July of 1978.

Two months later, Mayor George Moscone was assassinated in his office by a disgruntled former member of the Board of Supervisors. Dianne Feinstein became interim mayor and our project was renamed Moscone Convention Center to honor the deceased mayor. Opening day came, in 1981, and 20,000 people visited the new space that day. The building was full of people, but I remember a feeling of emptiness. Moscone Center was ours during design and construction, but now it belonged to San Francisco.

Moscone Center has expanded three times since the initial construction, and has hosted many memorable events, including the 1984 Democratic National Convention. The annual Macworld Expo is held at Moscone Center. And Steve Jobs unveiled the iPhone there, in what is now a legendary presentation.

Moscone Center served as the catalyst for San Francisco's South of Market area revival, just as the Redevelopment Agency predicted. Later, HOK Sport designed Pac Bell Park for the San Francisco Giants baseball team, adding to the growth of what is now called "SOMA," an area worthy of a trendy nickname. Today, it's a dynamic neighborhood of housing, dot-com companies, baseball, and an always-busy convention center.

HOK as Matchmaker

I have often said, "HOK provided pretty much everything for me." It is certainly true that HOK gave me a great career, lifelong friends, and plenty of fascinating travel. But HOK was also to provide a crucial missing ingredient in my life: my wife.

By early 1974, I had become very busy with work and needed help. While I was away from the office visiting my family in the Midwest, Bill Valentine hired talented architect Jeanne MacArthur as my right-hand woman. She started at HOK on her birthday, April 10th. I returned from vacation a week later and met her for the first time. As soon as I saw her, I knew she would become my wife—but had the good sense not to say so just then. Her reaction was a bit different. She initially thought I was a building products salesman! My not-so-suave line to try to get to know Jeanne better was, "Maybe we could have a beer sometime and talk about criminal justice work."

Jeanne and I began working together on a justice study for the Northwest Council of Governments in Washington State. We learned about each other by working together. On one business trip, we ate dinner together every evening and managed to discuss one forbidden, but critical, topic each night: religion, politics, children, and so on. We never had a real date. As we were returning to SeaTac Airport in a rental car, we continued talking about what we wanted in life—and decided to get married! Three months later we were married in Sutro Heights Park overlooking the Pacific Ocean with my HOK friend Terry Richert as best man and our HOK colleagues in attendance.

I have said that architects tend to run in families. In our case, it happened by marriage. Many other HOK colleagues have gotten married over the years and the firm has supported them. I understand why some companies prohibit "fraternization," but HOK has never had a rule like that. I think it's because architecture isn't just a job, it's a calling. If you're going to ask somebody to put their heart and soul into their work, it's possible they will also find their heart's desire or their soulmate at work. I would encourage any creative firm to keep this in mind when making its personnel rules, because married couples can be an asset rather than a detriment.

By the time we got married, Jeanne was no longer working under me. Her keen talent and endless work ethic caught the attention of the San Francisco principals, and she soon ran her own projects with aplomb. Jeanne eventually became the first woman architect to be promoted to vice president at HOK. Since we still worked at the same firm, Jeanne and I believed it would be more professional if we retained separate last names, so she remained Jeanne MacArthur. I was born and remained Patrick Leamy.

However, to acknowledge our marriage, we announced an informal family name: "MacLeamy," a blending of our two last names. I worried that my father would be offended by the change, but, after our wedding, he told us the story of his grandfather who emigrated from Ireland with the last name "McLeamy"! My great-grandfather had dropped the prefix to sound less Irish, since Irish immigrants were regarded as a low class of people at that time. My father said, "It looks like you have come full circle with the name MacLeamy!"

After just a few months of living in the fog of San Francisco, we moved to an Eichler home in Marin County, where the sun shines nearly every day. Joseph Eichler was a Bay Area developer famous for home developments perfectly suited to the California climate. As architects, we knew all about him. Our house was post-and-beam construction, with an open floor plan and large floor-to-ceiling glass windows opening to a private courtyard. We loved that house and spent the first 10 years of married life there.

We continued to have separate last names, and the names Leamy, MacArthur, and MacLeamy were a puzzle to our mailman. One day I was in the yard when he came to deliver our mail. As I stood waiting, he sorted our mail, saying "Here's one for Pat Leamy, one for Jeanne MacArthur, and another for the MacLeamy family . . . is this a commune?"

After three years of marriage, Jeanne and I were expecting a son. "What are we going to call him?" she asked me. We had grown to love our combined last name and filed papers to legally change our last names to MacLeamy. However, our son was born before we could schedule a court date. When the nurse asked us what name to place on his birth certificate, we explained our dilemma about his last name. We were surprised and delighted to learn we could give our son any last name we wished, so he became Patrick MacLeamy, the first person in our family with the new last name.

One month later, a judge heard our petition in Superior Court in that beautiful Frank Lloyd Wright-designed Marin County Civic Center. The judge granted our petition—after quizzing us to be sure we were not running away from old debts—and the MacLeamy name was legal at last.

Jeanne took six months off to be a full-time mom, and eventually decided to stay home with baby Patrick. She said, "I looked at his little face and couldn't bear to leave him." HOK kept her on the personnel list for three years in the hope that she would return to work. Instead, Jeanne founded her own firm at our home to be available for Patrick and his sister, Elisabeth. They are grown and gone, but Jeanne's office is still going strong.

Chapter 7: To Design a World-Class Firm

1. Develop a strong, computerized system for capturing and tracking details of each project.
2. Lead, don't manage, your people. Think of it like leading them into battle rather than cracking the whip from behind.
3. Be skeptical of titles. It doesn't matter what you're called; it matters what you do. Actions are more important than words.
4. Make up for any lack of experience with hard work. In other words, if you're green, get busy.
5. Recognize and resolve small problems quickly. Neglect little problems and they become big problems. Neglect big problems and they can become disasters.
6. Have the courage to tell the truth, even if it is not what someone wants to hear. Straight talk will earn you respect.
7. Consider that married couples can be an asset rather than a detriment at your firm.

CHAPTER 8

Transitions: Succession Planning

George Hellmuth was set to turn 65 in 1972. It had happened fast. Under the terms agreed to by the founders, he was required to sell his HOK stock back to the company. He was not ready to retire—many architects work late into their lives—and believed his marketing skills would continue to win more significant work for HOK, a belief the future would confirm. He approached Obata and Kassabaum with a proposal to extend his mandatory stock sale five years, to age 70. They resisted at first. Both were about 15 years younger than Hellmuth. and looked forward to running the firm by themselves after he stepped down. After much discussion—some of it heated—they finally agreed to the extension if it would apply to themselves as well.

Naming Successors

Hellmuth was grateful for the extra five years. It's funny how the age you consider "old" when you're young, looks quite different when you reach it. Plus, people age at different rates and being "young" is largely a product of attitude. Hellmuth still had a lot to offer.

Nevertheless, Hellmuth recognized that it was time to identify and groom a next-generation HOK marketing leader. He believed the firm would be well served if his partners also publicly identified their successors. Since HOK was set up as a corporation, not a partnership, this made good business sense. All along, the founders had planned for HOK to outlast them. Now it was time to prove they meant it. It's a good lesson for all architects, designers, and other creatives: You must face your own mortality if you want the company you built to live on. After much more discussion, all three agreed to name one next-generation leader each and include them in leadership meetings. It was a prescient decision that became critically important in the future.

> **A**ll along, the founders had planned for HOK to outlast them . . . You must face your own mortality if you want the company you built to live on.

67

King Graf: Marketing

Hellmuth selected King Graf to become the next marketing leader. King had been with HOK almost from the beginning and achieved many marketing coups. He was tireless, a natural leader and dedicated to HOK. He was born in St. Louis in 1930 to a family of artisans from the Alsace-Lorraine region on the border between Germany and France. King's father Horace was a graphic designer and his mother Ellen was an accomplished professional pianist and writer. Uncle Fred Graf was an architect, yet another instance of architecture running in families.

King grew up in suburban St. Louis and had gifts for art and music. He was also a born athlete who became a track star in high school. It seemed natural for King to enroll at Washington University, right in St. Louis. He studied architecture under none other than faculty member George Kassabaum. When King recollected his career decision, he would always say, "Architecture is the only art job with a paycheck." He met his future wife, Pat Demick, in Webster Groves, Missouri, and they both knew right away that they would marry.

After earning his Bachelor of Architecture degree in 1953, King entered the U.S. Navy, where he toured the Pacific as an ensign aboard an Andromeda-class attack cargo ship, the USS *Diphda*. He was good at his job and his leadership ability came to the attention of the navy brass. King was set to complete his tour of duty in 1956 when the navy offered him an attractive position as an admiral's aide in Europe if he would re-enlist.

While considering this offer during shore leave in San Diego, King telephoned Kassabaum, his Washington University mentor and professor, for advice. Kassabaum, who by then was a partner in a new firm called HOK, was brief but effective: "If you're going to be an architect, King, maybe you'd better begin."[1] Six weeks later King was back in St. Louis working for HOK.

He was a good-looking man with a big smile that quickly made him everyone's friend. He gave the impression of being a tall and lanky cowboy out of uniform; if you put a Stetson and some boots on him, he'd have looked the part. He was fun to be around and well-liked. King listened to each person with his full attention and made them feel special. Sound familiar? He definitely fit into HOK culture.

Obata noticed King's natural ability to make friends. In 1959, when Hellmuth had accidentally scheduled two presentations to prospective clients on the same night, Obata recommended King Graf handle one, and sent him off to meet with a selection committee in Paducah, Kentucky. King didn't win that project, but Hellmuth recognized his potential as a superb marketer and invited him to join his team. At first King called on prospective clients with Hellmuth, then began going on his own. He learned many marketing lessons from Hellmuth, but the most important was "If you want the job, you have to be sincerely interested in the client."

King's innate ability to gain the trust and confidence of everyone he met became especially important in his relationship with the founders. Hellmuth, Obata, and Kassabaum were partners, but with very different personalities and ways of working. King was

---
[1] Walter McQuade and Paul Grotz, *Architecture in the Real World: The Work of HOK* (New York: H.N. Abrams, 1985), p. 22.

FIGURE 8.1 King Graf and mentor George Hellmuth.
Source: Photo courtesy of HOK.

trusted by each founder and eventually became instrumental in helping all of them sort out priorities and make decisions together, serving as the catalyst to hold the leadership together. Bill Valentine called him "the Peacemaker." I met King during my first week at HOK. He was the principal in charge of my first project, the Pittsburgh Great High Schools. He played a key role in landing the project for HOK, and, in addition to leading the project team, maintained a good relationship with our Pittsburgh clients.

King played racquetball at the YMCA along with a group of others in the St. Louis office. I took up the sport shortly after joining HOK, and soon had a match with King. He had me running ragged in short order by his sheer mastery of the game. Then he did something I will always remember: he eased up so I wouldn't feel so bad. Others in the office told me the same thing, but King would never admit to slacking off. He was so sensitive to other people's feelings that he wanted them to feel competitive, not dominated —a great lesson, whether in sports or business.

One of his more unusual talents was to throw pushpins at the tack wall in the conference rooms, which we used to pin up drawings for meetings. By spinning the pins as he threw, King was able to make them hit the wall point-first and stick. No one else could master this feat, but King made it look easy. He was always a gentleman and never swore or raised his voice. People followed him because of his interest in them and his willingness to try new things. He cheerfully moved his family to Dallas, in 1974, to lead the new office, and it flourished under his leadership. In 1984, King returned to St. Louis to become HOK's firm-wide marketing leader.

Bill Valentine: Design

FIGURE 8.2 Bill Valentine in shirt and tie for a change.
Source: Photo courtesy of HOK.

Obata selected Bill Valentine as HOK's future design leader. Bill was a hard-working, energetic designer with an infectious enthusiasm for projects, clients, and the design team. He always put clients first, seeking design solutions that were faithful to their needs.

Bill was born in Winston-Salem, North Carolina, in 1937, and grew up in Whiteville, a small farm town surrounded by tobacco fields. Whiteville farmers lived on credit between harvests. Each year, after they sold the tobacco crop, they paid off the grocer, the feed store and other creditors. The once-yearly pay cycle affected nearly everyone in town because for most of the year no one had money. Bill's family was affected by this cycle too, which he always recalled as "on the edge of poor." He was determined to improve his circumstances and applied himself during high school and college. Bill was able to enroll in the architectural program at North Carolina State University in Raleigh, and what he lacked in educational background he made up for with endless hours of study and work. If you're green, get busy! Still, he found time to marry his high school sweetheart, Jane, in 1959.

During Bill's senior year, Henry Kamphoefner, dean of the NC State Architecture School, asked Bill what he planned to do after graduation. "I haven't thought about it much, but I guess I need to find a job working for an architect," Bill said. Dean Kamphoefner had bigger plans for Bill and replied, "Bill, you have talent and you're a hard worker. I think I can get you into the Harvard Graduate School of Design." While awaiting acceptance to Harvard, Bill worked for an architecture firm in Durham, followed by a six-month tour of duty in the army. He was accepted to Harvard, discharged from the army, and he and Jane had their first child, Karen, just two weeks before graduate school began. "Oh my, what a confusing time!" he says of that year.

Bill loves to tell the story of how he came to HOK. Architects from around the country frequently visited Harvard to recruit design students. Most talked about how great their firms were, but didn't seem interested in the students. Bill and his colleagues were put off by this behavior and tended to ignore these recruiting visits. One day, a tall, friendly man came to the graduate studio. He didn't talk about himself or his firm. Instead he went to each graduate student's desk and asked, "What are you working on?" He really listened to what they were saying and seemed genuinely interested in their work and in them. After talking with all the students, he left. Bill and other students were so impressed by the man that they followed him out to the lobby to find out who he was, and from what firm. He was King Graf, from a new firm called HOK. After graduation, in 1962, Bill made the decision to join HOK. King Graf had followed George Hellmuth's best marketing advice when meeting with Bill and the other students: Listen more than you talk.

I got to know Bill during the Great High Schools project and gladly followed him to San Francisco. We became great friends and liked to swap stories from our childhoods. His farm-town roots were very different from my industrial town upbringing, yet each of our childhood experiences had led us to a shared desire to better ourselves.

If HOK believed in mutual respect, Bill Valentine was its leading practitioner. To Bill, the clerk who made the coffee was as deserving of respect as the best designer in the firm. He has a huge heart, a great regard for others, and tends to overlook people's faults. I might say, "Bill, that person is disrupting the entire project team." He would answer, "Patrick, sometimes good people do bad things." Bill believed if he set a good example, it would induce loyalty and good behavior in others. We had many discussions and some disagreements about this, but have remained fast friends.

Jerry Sincoff: Production

Kassabaum selected Jerry Sincoff to become the firm's next-generation production and operations leader. Jerry had been his lead assistant for several years, after becoming one of HOK's top project managers. Jerry was hardworking and loyal. His focus was on clients and projects, not on himself. Come to think of it, selflessness was a shared trait among many early HOK leaders and would serve any firm well. Jerry thought deeply about strategy and process and was eager to apply his thinking to the entire firm.

I met Jerry Sincoff shortly after joining HOK. At that time, he was the project manager for the new Ralston-Purina headquarters building in St. Louis. He was soft-spoken and thoughtful, with a slight build. His default facial expression was a smile. Jerry was born in St. Louis in 1933 and grew up near Washington University. He recalls always wanting to be an architect. Like the founders and King Graf, Jerry attended Washington University and graduated with a Bachelor of Architecture degree.

"I wanted to work at HOK. All us young architects did," he said. "I got out of the Army in 1958 or 1959 in the middle of a terrible recession, and got an interview with George Kassabaum, who said he didn't have any work and didn't hire me. I got a job with another St. Louis firm, worked for two years, and passed my architectural license exam. Then I went back to HOK, in 1961, only this time I interviewed with Obata and tricked him into thinking I was a designer!"

FIGURE 8.3 Jerry Sincoff.
Source: Photo courtesy of HOK.

Obata hired Jerry because the big Southern Illinois University project was underway. Two people led the project: George Hagee, Obata's top assistant for design, at the time, and Chester Roemer, top project manager under Kassabaum. They assigned Jerry to work on the administration and science buildings. The contract required most of the work to be done in Illinois, so HOK leased space in the Spivey Building, the only high-rise building in East St. Louis, a struggling city directly across the Mississippi from St. Louis. Jerry and other team members were not happy to be relocated away from the main HOK office, and—in protest—walked across the historic Eads bridge to the East St. Louis office on the first day.

The first floor of the Spivey Building was occupied by a federal agency called Aid to Families with Dependent Children. As Jerry recalls, "The week after our office opened, we heard gunshots from the first floor. Two women in line at the welfare office were chatting and learned that their children had the same father—so one of them shot the other." That event induced the project team to relocate to nearby Belleville, which remained an HOK branch office for many years. The state broke ground on the university in 1963 and held the first classes on the new campus in 1965.

By the time Jerry returned to St. Louis, HOK had hired Bill Valentine, who was developing a reputation as a strong designer. Jerry decided to seek his HOK future as a production architect and approached George Kassabaum, who said, "Great, why don't you work for me?" In a short time, Jerry proved his value as a hardworking and loyal member of the production department. He went with his true talent and never looked back.

Obata had just completed design of a new office building for Alcoa in Century City, Los Angeles. Alcoa insisted that HOK partner with a local architect who understood Los Angeles codes and requirements, so Hellmuth selected Charles Luckman Architects. HOK needed to place a loyal HOK employee in the Luckman office and Kassabaum selected Jerry. He was thrilled by the challenge of working with another architect in a different city and moved to Los Angeles in 1965.

"The first day I was there, two of Luckman's senior project managers invited me to lunch on Sunset Boulevard," Jerry recalled later. "The first thing they did was order a martini, so I had one, too. We went back to the office after lunch and I was a little weary, so I put my head down on my board for a minute . . . and then someone was tapping my shoulder. I picked my head up and they introduced me to Charles Luckman."

After HOK finished the Alcoa project, Jerry returned to St. Louis, where he grew to become Kassabaum's top assistant.

Adding HOK New York

Hellmuth still wanted a New York office. In 1973, he engineered a merger with Kahn & Jacobs, a well-established New York firm with a good reputation for Manhattan office buildings. Bob Jacobs agreed to stay on and help the two firms form an integrated office. Hellmuth sent Jerry Gilmore, one of his trusted marketing lieutenants, to New York to help the new office look for work. Obata sent Chi Chen Jen, the designer who had had the breakthrough idea for the Air and Space Museum, to provide day-to-day design leadership.

The transition was difficult from the first day. The merger coincided with a slowdown in Manhattan construction, and the new office soon needed more work. But the larger challenge was cultural. The Kahn & Jacobs people were slow to embrace being part of HOK, and some were openly hostile. They were brash New Yorkers, used to operating in the Big Apple, and couldn't be bothered with HOK's soft-spoken Midwestern style. Nor did they respect HOK's designs. The stress became too much for Gilmore, who fell seriously ill and eventually moved back to St. Louis.

That's when Hellmuth sent a substitute who almost couldn't refuse: his own son, George William Hellmuth. Founder George Hellmuth and his wife had followed family tradition, giving their son his father's name, but a different middle name. The younger George, who I will call George W., earned degrees in engineering and business. But his real gift was for marketing, just like his dad. George W. was a chip off the old block, who liked to meet people and win work for HOK.

It's unclear whether having one of the founders' namesakes in the New York office helped or hurt in the culture clash. What is clear is that the cultural problems there caused so much friction that HOK finally took action, moving the office from Park Avenue to Rockefeller Center, and removing the Kahn & Jacobs name from the front door. The old space had been Kahn & Jacobs' office and their turf. We needed a fresh location that represented HOK, and other firms might discover the same. HOK also asked some of the most divisive Kahn & Jacobs designers to leave. Sometimes that's an unfortunate necessity. Things improved from that time forward.

George Hellmuth Triumphs

Hellmuth continued to work with Bob Jacobs to market to New York clients. In the fall of 1974, a letter arrived on Jacobs' desk addressed to Kahn & Jacobs/Hellmuth, Obata & Kassabaum, asking if the firm would be interested in designing a new university in Riyadh, the capital of Saudi Arabia. Jacobs alerted Hellmuth, who swung into action. He flew to Riyadh without an appointment—talk about going to potential clients—and made daily calls to the office of the rector of the University of Riyadh.

After many unsuccessful attempts, Hellmuth finally arranged a meeting with the rector and vice rector. He drank many cups of tea with them while discussing the problems and challenges of major university construction. Once again, Hellmuth was engaged in active listening. He learned their biggest concern was their lack of experience in constructing an entire university from scratch. He advised them to hire an architect with a great deal of experience—like HOK.

The university project received many expressions of interest from architects, engineers, and contractors around the world. After examining the credentials of each, the selection committee narrowed the list of candidates to 18 companies, including HOK, and asked for more detailed information. In March 1975, the university notified Hellmuth that HOK was one of three firms on the final list for consideration. The others were from Austria and Japan. The client required each finalist to select consultants from a prequalified list of architects and engineers, and then make a final proposal to the university as a team.

As Hellmuth reviewed the list of prequalified firms from around the world, he realized that a team that shared a common language would be of great advantage. He selected four English-speaking firms and quickly invited them to form a consortium to be called HOK+4. It was another example of seizing the moment, a wily move and Hellmuth at his shrewdest. If you ever find yourself in this unique situation, never forget the power of actually being able to talk to your teammates. While Hellmuth's new team was discussing its final proposal in English, other groups were struggling to communicate through interpreters and translators.

HOK delivered its proposal documents to the university in the spring of 1975, bound in folders of Moroccan leather dyed the royal green of the Saudi monarchy and packed in a suitcase of the same leather. The custom leather packaging cost $4000, a bargain if we landed the massive project. Sometimes glitz matters. After nine months and a total of four trips to Riyadh by Hellmuth, the university selected HOK+4 to design the new $3.5 billion King Saud University on a 2,400-acre site on the outskirts of Riyadh. It was a dream job.

Hellmuth's greatest marketing coup of all had occurred when he was 68 years old. He had the vision to buy Kahn & Jacobs in New York, and the tenacity to vigorously follow up on the Saudi invitation that landed on Bob Jacobs' desk. Hellmuth's last great gift was to lift HOK to prominence on the international stage. The goal of designing a world-class architecture firm was one step closer.

George Hellmuth turned 70 in 1977, and HOK's revised bylaws required him to sell his stock back to HOK. He was no longer an owner—but still not ready to retire. After much more discussion, Obata and Kassabaum agreed to keep Hellmuth busy marketing for HOK, but not directly. Instead they created a new subsidiary company, HOK International, and installed Hellmuth as president. It was a solution that satisfied everyone, giving Hellmuth a role, but giving Obata and Kassabaum more control. I recommend that all architects look for creative options like this in times of succession. Hellmuth had always preached the wisdom of keeping talented people. Now the other founders had found a way to keep *him*.

Hellmuth's loyal secretary, Dorothy Forrest, followed him to HOK International, where she worked with him, as always. One Monday morning she did not show up, and Hellmuth grew increasingly concerned. This was totally unlike her. Hellmuth thought of her as family and would not leave it to someone else to go look for her. HOK takes care of its people. He drove to Dorothy's home and rang the bell. When she did not answer, he called the police to enter the house. Dorothy Forrest had died of a heart attack over the weekend. The end of an era was approaching.

George Kassabaum Dies

In August of 1982, George Kassabaum died unexpectedly of a stroke. He was only 61. His passing sent shock waves through the firm. In addition to the loss we all felt, we wondered how HOK would carry on without him. He was the founder who made things work, who fixed problems when they arose, and whose steady presence reassured both clients and employees. George Kassabaum's funeral was in the Graham Chapel at Washington University, where he had been a student, faculty member, and advisor.

Kassabaum had practiced what he preached his entire professional life, engaging fully in the profession and in society, rather than withdrawing, as so many architects do. At the time of his passing, he was a member of the Washington University board of trustees. After serving as AIA president, he had gone on to be chancellor of the AIA Council of Fellows. In 1968, he was named Man of the Year by the Missouri Council of Architects. But that wasn't all. In addition, Kassabaum had served as a trustee of the St. Louis Symphony, and supported the revitalization of St. Louis' historic Laclede's Landing district. After his death, the city dedicated a park in his memory and the Missouri Botanical Garden named a dwarf conifer garden after him.

FIGURE 8.4 Founder George Kassabaum, 1920–1982.
Source: Photo courtesy of HOK.

This renaissance man had been a lifelong student of the *Meditations* by Marcus Aurelius, the Roman emperor and philosopher. He became interested in the *Meditations* when he learned President Truman kept a copy by his bedside. At the time of his death, Kassabaum was writing an interpretive book on the *Meditations*. In 1984, with the support of family, friends, and HOK, selections from his manuscript were published as *Conversations with Myself, an Interpretation*. It was one more reminder that HOK's founders didn't just care about buildings. They cared about ideas.

Chapter 8: To Design a World-Class Firm

1. Name successors publicly long before you retire. Include them in important meetings and decisions so they are prepared to take over.
2. Be selfless. Set aside your ego and put clients and projects first.
3. Give leaders of acquired firms a chance to embrace your company culture, but if they don't, replace them and don't look back. Culture is that important.
4. Keep current leaders involved while at the same time increasing the participation and authority of their likely successors.

SECTION TWO

THE OBATA ERA, 1982–1993

CHAPTER 9

A Designer Leads the Firm

Gyo Obata was 59 years old at the time of Kassabaum's death and the last active HOK founder. George Hellmuth had not been part of HOK leadership for five years, although he remained president of HOK International, the subsidiary company created for him. HOK had grown to 700 people with five major offices and needed good leadership to hold the firm together and chart a course for the future.

The stock-ownership restrictions originally adopted by the founders contained a final provision allowing the last remaining founder to purchase enough HOK stock to retain control of the firm. Kassabaum's death triggered this provision, and Obata bought enough of Kassabaum's stock to own 52% of HOK, giving him a free hand to shape the future of the firm.

How would Obata—a designer—handle HOK's business? How would he market for new work? Thanks to Hellmuth's advice years earlier, second-generation leaders King Graf and Jerry Sincoff had been participating in leadership discussions and had been groomed for more responsibility. Bill Valentine, the other second-generation leader, was still based in San Francisco and did not participate regularly.

Within a few weeks, Obata announced formation of the office of the chairman (OOC). Obata himself became HOK's chairman and design leader. He promoted King Graf to vice chairman for marketing and Jerry Sincoff to vice chairman for management and production. In one stroke, Obata restored the three-person leadership structure that had served HOK so well since the founding.

Building Buildings Again

Formation of the OOC coincided with a turnaround in the U.S. economy. President Reagan assumed office in January 1981. A national mood of optimism under Reagan seemed to replace national malaise under President Carter. For whatever reason, clients around the country and the world regained confidence in the future and—lucky for us—began to build buildings again.

HOK was well-positioned to take advantage of the growth. The firm's leaders weren't the only ones who specialized. HOK now employed designers who specialized in different building types, such as aviation, justice, healthcare, higher education and more. And unlike smaller firms in which everyone needed to be a generalist, able to do everything and anything, HOK was much larger and able to support this kind of specialization. This evolved into a huge advantage. HOK also had a growing geographic reach, with offices in major cities from the Atlantic to the Pacific. That helped us take the pulse of different regions and know when new buildings were in the works. Fortunately, clients in cities across the country were beginning to emphasize hiring the best, most experienced talent for their projects, even if those firms were based somewhere else.

Rise of Project Specialists

As HOK evolved, offices began to organize differently in response to the diverse mix of project types. Instead of design and production departments, offices began to form specialized project teams for airports, university work, justice projects, and more. These teams started to design and deliver successive buildings of the same project type over many years.

Aviation is a good example. Whereas some aviation team members asked for reassignment after one or two projects, others developed a deep interest in airport design and asked to work on the next aviation project. Some young architects thought committing to aviation work was limiting, a narrowing of career choices, but this turned out not to be the case. They began to understand that within aviation, avenues were open to them for careers as specialized designers, project managers, project architects, and marketers.

Keeping people on a particular building type also benefitted HOK—and clients. To continue with the aviation example, an architect's continuing experience on multiple projects led to a growing understanding of aviation business and operational issues. With so much exposure, they came to understand airports from the client's perspective. There was one logistical challenge: the assignment process was messy and depended on timing. Sometimes HOK was ready to begin another airport project, but, if not, the firm had to assign aviation specialists to other types of buildings.

The New Marketing

Bear with me while I spin the aviation example out one more degree: Once HOK gained deep experience designing airports, the charismatic marketing George Hellmuth pioneered became less necessary to win the next project. We were no longer dependent on one charming guy and his protégés. Instead, HOK developed specialized marketing that trumpeted our profound understanding of aviation—or healthcare or education or some other specialty building type. We shifted from a charm offensive to a knowledge offensive.

Clients in the past had been content to speak with Hellmuth, but now they began to ask for interviews with the team that would be assigned to their project. Thus, as HOK's marketing became more focused by building type, it also broadened from one individual to a team effort. Clients demanded that HOK people with the most-specialized building type experience meet with them to sell their knowledge and ideas directly. Being in demand reinforced project specialization as a career choice. Everyone wants to be sought after for their ability and experience. King Graf called this the "New Marketing," where teams of specialized, experienced HOK people sold themselves to clients in interviews and meetings.

Obata was the best of the new marketers. He had met clients from the first days of the firm, but by now had earned a reputation as a fine designer of airports and much more. Obata was in demand to personally participate in the most important interview opportunities in different offices around the firm. Yes, he was a thoughtful designer, but even as he grew successful, he continued to really listen to clients and was better able to win them over in an interview setting than anyone else. If George Hellmuth launched HOK's success with pioneering marketing, Gyo Obata extended and strengthened it with the New Marketing.

Marketing for a specialty like aviation work often led to an unbroken chain of successive contracts, with each new project building on the experience of the last. The good reputation Obata earned as a designer of Lambert Airport in St. Louis led directly to being offered the Dallas-Fort Worth airport commission. Dallas-Fort Worth, in turn, led to other airport opportunities, including the King Khalid airport in Riyadh, Saudi Arabia.

Another example of an unbroken chain of work was in higher education. George Hellmuth landed the job for HOK to design a new campus for Southern Illinois University (SIU), in Edwardsville, Illinois. The SIU commission led to an unbroken chain of other university work at the University of Wisconsin, State University of New York, Stanford University, and eventually King Saud University in Saudi Arabia. It happened by accident at first, but soon HOK began to consciously try to parlay one project into another opportunity, something I recommend to all service firms.

The HOK Matrix

Building type specialization was a natural extension of the founders' individual specialization in marketing, design, and production, and was to become the main driver of future HOK growth. Projects designed and delivered by specialists were more responsive to client needs and the technical and operational requirements of their project types. Specialization helped establish a virtuous cycle:

- Specialized architects created better projects.
- Better projects burnished the HOK reputation in the project type.
- A growing HOK reputation led to more project opportunities.

Specialized practices took on the names of the markets they served—aviation, justice, and healthcare—and became collectively known as HOK's "market practices." Over time, other market practices emerged. For example, the higher education practice designed many different types of academic buildings, including laboratories. Over time, an even more specialized market practice—laboratories—grew from this work. That specialty then evolved further into designing laboratories just for the healthcare and pharmaceutical industries.

Everyone in HOK was aware of the growing success of market practices and every HOK office wanted to develop some of their own. Obata and his fellow firm leaders recognized that the increasing HOK reputation in these specialized building types was a major advantage and began to actively encourage all HOK offices to participate.

During meetings to discuss market practices, Obata or Jerry Sincoff usually began at the flip chart, where they drew a grid diagram to illustrate the growth of HOK's market practices. Offices were listed across the top and market practices down the left side. The resulting grid was filled in, with an "X" showing which offices hosted, say, an aviation or healthcare or justice practice. St. Louis, as the oldest and largest office, had all the boxes filled. San Francisco had a few boxes filled in—and some offices had none. This became known as the HOK Matrix, and for a while, the firm's leaders encouraged every office to develop all the specialty practices. Nobody wanted to be the office with blanks on the HOK Matrix.

However, the idea that every HOK office should become expert in everything was to prove inefficient, expensive—and divisive. I would not recommend it to any new firm still flexible enough to determine its own structure. HOK would eventually find a more logical way to organize the market practices, but not until some years in the future.

Growing Pains

People in the St. Louis office understood the expectations of the founders for internal harmony and collaboration, with everyone helping HOK to succeed. And they got the suggest-don't-tell style of communication. This HOK company culture was embedded in the office, needing little reinforcement. However, as the firm grew and added offices, no one thought about how to spread that same culture to new locations around the world. They just figured HOK culture would somehow naturally grow.

The San Francisco office was an early success. Bill Valentine and I were different people with different personalities, but we shared HOK culture and made sure it was adopted by local San Francisco employees. Bill often described this process as "vaccinating" people with HOK culture. By contrast, in other locations, like Washington, DC, a mix of HOK veterans and local people led the office. Offices like that often struggled to establish HOK culture, because the non-HOK people had their own way of working and were strongly resistant to change. Sometimes, it was only after HOK replaced key leaders with HOK people, as we had done in New York, that an office would begin to reflect HOK culture. We didn't know it then, but a cultural crisis was brewing.

As HOK grew into a firm of many offices, with many new people who had little or no exposure to the founders, or to HOK St. Louis, the collaborative nature of HOK culture began to erode. To make matters worse, as the market practices developed, multiple offices housed specialized teams that did the same thing, and those offices began to compete with each other for work. They went after the same clients in overlapping geographic regions. Sometimes offices won work on the strength of HOK's international reputation, but then lacked the local talent or experience to design and deliver first-rate work in that project type. Instead of sharing the work with experienced people in other HOK locations, an office would keep the entire fee for itself, designing and delivering an inferior project. That, in turn, damaged the reputation of the entire firm. It was a counterproductive mess on the inside that made us look bad on the outside.

The collaborative HOK culture was not the only thing that was changing. Firm-wide operations, which were relatively easy to manage when HOK was just one office, began to show strain as HOK added more locations. Some new offices were led by good architects who were terrible managers. This resulted in poor financial performance on projects and poor financial results for their office. Sometimes the problem was devastatingly simple: new offices would drag their feet in billing and collecting their fees from clients. No firm can succeed when its people are working for free. These issues simmered for several years but were masked by growth. When growth inevitably began to slow, financial troubles—especially anemic cash flow—became too big to ignore. It's a cautionary tale for other growing firms.

Some new offices were led by good architects who were terrible managers.

Signs of Trouble

HOK had always maintained enough cash to meet expenses, and under Kassabaum's leadership, Central Accounting in St. Louis had always managed firm-wide cash flow. Payroll was the biggest expense and the highest priority, and HOK always paid employees on time. The firm paid engineering consultants and vendors when cash was available. Crucially, Central Accounting maintained a line of credit with Boatmen's Bank in St. Louis that could be tapped when clients were slow to pay, then replenished when payments were received.

However, project accounting and client billing operated in a decentralized way, with the accountants managed by the leadership in each office instead of by Central Accounting. Over the years of expansion, each HOK office evolved different processes for project accounting and client billing—some better and some worse than others. While the firm was expanding, cash flow was not a problem. Growing fees led to larger billings, and if a client or two were slow to pay, expansion generated enough cash to pay the bills.

But by late 1982, uneven office leadership allowed more clients to fall behind on payments, resulting in cash flow problems. HOK continued to meet biweekly payroll expenses, but was forced to delay other payments, first to vendors, then to the engineering consultants who served project teams. Finally, the situation grew so bad that HOK had no choice but to begin using the Boatmen's Bank Line of Credit to pay bills. It was like using a credit card to pay your mortgage—unwise and unsustainable. Over the months, the firm's leaders dipped deeper and deeper into HOK's line of credit, causing a serious cash flow crunch.

Obata sought the advice of trusted St. Louis business friends, who told him HOK had grown too large for the original three-person leadership structure. Kassabaum's role had, in fact, been a dual one with him running both production and firm-wide operations. HOK had succeeded with only three firm-wide leaders due to Kassabaum's superb personal organization and talent for selecting good helpers to support both responsibilities. Acting on his friends' advice, in 1983, Obata promoted Bob Stauder to the OOC as Vice Chairman for Operations. Bob had been one of George Kassabaum's project managers in St. Louis before becoming managing principal of HOK San Francisco and had a reputation as a no-nonsense leader who knew how to get things done.

In 1983, I was just finishing the Moscone Center project in San Francisco and spending time marketing for the office. Bob Stauder and Bill Valentine called me in to Bob's office and explained Bob would immediately transfer back to St. Louis to begin his new role. They asked me to take his place as managing principal for San Francisco. I was 40 years old and had been at HOK 15 years. The new role was an exciting challenge, a stretch that would require more learning on the job.

Bob flew to St. Louis the next day and tackled the cash-flow problem. HOK had always made it a goal to pay all invoices within 30 days, but with money tight, that wasn't happening. Payroll always went out on time, but engineering consultants might have to wait 60 days to be paid, and suppliers 90 days. When Bob asked, "Where is the money from this office? Did they do their billings?" Central Accounting couldn't say for certain. Their answer was often, "We don't know . . . that office doesn't tell us."

Stauder concluded HOK needed to reassert Central Accounting control over the offices and began by imposing a freeze on raises, new hiring, and new office leases. All offices had to get approval before spending money for travel, promotional events, and even office Christmas parties.

Stauder also worked with Central Accounting to develop a list of unpaid invoices, with emphasis on clients who owed us the most or were the slowest to pay. Then he and our CFO called each HOK office and assigned collection responsibility and a deadline to the managing principal and the project manager for each client on the list. As a result, the flow of money into Central Accounting increased, gradually allowing HOK to reimburse the line of credit and resume paying bills on time.

Bringing in the Pros

Bob Stauder's firm-wide operations role went beyond solving the cash flow problem. He began to review all central departments—accounting, human resources, and legal services—and learned they had not kept pace with growth. General Counsel Paul Watson ably led the legal department but needed help to keep up with the growing workload.

Accounting and human resources lacked professional leadership. After consulting with the firm's three other leaders, Stauder began to search for a CFO and a director of human resources. Sometimes architects are so focused on design roles that they neglect other important departments. It was time to bring in the pros.

Stauder hired John Mahon as the first HOK director of human resources (HR), in 1985. John was a St. Louis native, a graduate of St. Louis University, and a human resources professional. Mahon began a series of initiatives to bring the outmoded employee benefit program up to date. Later, he established an annual evaluation process for all employees and initiated two recruiting programs, one for students about to graduate and the other for design professionals with work experience. By this point, HOK had been around for more than 20 years, so it's hard to believe that these programs were not already in place. HOK had been so focused on growing a diverse design practice, that it had neglected these areas.

I first met John in St. Louis a short time after he joined HOK. He was handsome, articulate, and possessed of good Irish humor. Like everyone, I found John an empathetic listener. He used to say "HOK is all about people. Treating people well is the first step. But if we want to keep the best people, we need to listen to their needs and do our best to help them succeed." As you can tell, John understood our company culture from the very start, a must for an HR leader responsible for bringing in the right talent. He earned the trust of everyone at HOK and soon became an advisor to HOK's top leaders—Obata, Jerry, King, and Bob.

In 1986, they hired Bob Pratzel as chief financial officer (CFO) with responsibility for accounting, cash management, and financial analysis. He was already familiar with HOK from his 10-year career at Deloitte, where he was responsible for the HOK annual audit. Bob was born in St. Louis and raised in nearby University City. He earned an MBA from Northwestern University. His first task was to improve the level of accounting at HOK, and he replaced two senior accountants with Tim Tynan as controller and Jan DeWeer as financial analyst. Bob Pratzel worked closely with Bob Stauder to regain control of HOK's finances, improve cash flow, and maintain a good working relationship with Boatmen's Bank.

Bob was short, lean, and friendly. He was always neatly turned out in a dark suit, white shirt, and tie, and said he wanted to look like a banker. He liked being at HOK and said, "It's exciting to be around creative people instead of bean counters." Bob was approachable, at his best when answering questions about finance or accounting and always patient with explanations. He loved to laugh, so he loved hearing a good joke. Bob took very good care of himself, was discerning about what he ate, and exercised regularly. This high level of self-discipline was evident in his financial work at HOK, as well.

Both Bob Pratzel and John Mahon brought a new professionalism to HOK operations, and people were grateful to Bob Stauder for hiring them and stanching the bleeding. However, Stauder himself, who remained in St. Louis as operations director for several more years, began to garner some resentment. It may have seemed necessary for him to be rigid and controlling when HOK was in trouble, but in better times his style seemed overbearing to some. He got the job done, but at what cost? Compared to what we would face later, this early cash shortage was just a kerfuffle—but it was also a warning.

Chapter 9: To Design a World-Class Firm

1. Consider organizing your architects by design specialty—aviation, healthcare, hospitality—rather than by job function—design, management, production.
2. Encourage your people to focus on a specific building type so they begin to understand it from the client's perspective.
3. Shift marketing from a charm offensive to a knowledge offensive as your people develop deep specialties in certain building types.
4. Set a goal to create an "unbroken chain," where you parlay one specialty project into another and then another.
5. Prohibit branch offices from competing with each other for work. This is counterproductive and makes your firm look disorganized.
6. Be aware that growth can mask sloppy operations, poor cash flow, and financial troubles.
7. Don't neglect support services. Bring in professionals to lead accounting, human resources, legal services, and technology.

CHAPTER 10

Run Toward Trouble

The San Francisco office had grown to more than 100 people with a diverse workload. The office was now located in a larger space at One Lombard Street on the north side of the financial district, at the foot of Telegraph Hill. We had just completed the Moscone Convention Center, a large team was putting the finishing touches on the King Khalid airport in Riyadh, Saudi Arabia, and Bill Valentine was busy designing a new headquarters for Levi Strauss & Co. just down the street from us. The office was busy and profitable.

Becoming Managing Principal

I stepped into the role of managing principal for HOK San Francisco in 1984. I was excited about my new role and determined to do the best job possible. Bill and I were now partners in leading the office. We talked every day. He was the principal designer and my primary responsibility was to create a supportive environment for design to flourish. Of course, design can't flourish if there's nothing to design. I met weekly with the marketing staff to review leads and proposals. Bill and I usually participated with the project team during client interviews.

Recruiting young architects to work at HOK San Francisco was easy, because we had interesting projects, thanks to the new marketing, and they wanted the experience of working on them. However, much like me when I was just out of school, many of these young architects expected to move on to another firm when a commission concluded, following the nomadic pattern of work in the architecture profession. They were not necessarily thinking of a career at HOK, so I would share my own story with them, to try to make them understand. The personal touch often worked, and I recommend it. We were determined to follow Hellmuth's strategy of hiring and keeping good employees for long careers, not losing their talent at the end of a single project.

Meanwhile, I organized weekly meetings with project leaders to assess work for the week and address any problems with a design, client, or employee. I also found myself responsible for San Francisco's version of some of those long-neglected departments that had gotten HOK into tight spots, like accounting and H.R. As managing principal, I was even in charge of office support services. Maybe the most critical part of that: designers need fresh coffee at all hours of the day and night!

Run Toward Trouble

As with project management, I discovered my new job was 10% management and 90% leadership. I finally had a nice office of my own, just as I had imagined, but found that leadership happened elsewhere. I learned how important it was to get out of that little room and listen to what clients or HOK people had to say about our projects. I found that the lesson I had learned as a project manager was even more true when running an office. The most challenging part of problem solving is to identify complications early, before they grow into real trouble.

When I met with clients, I asked, "Are you happy with our progress? Our team?" And more importantly: "Any issues that need to be addressed?" In other words, I didn't just ask them if things were going well. I asked if anything was going badly. I had learned that clients would let me know if they were unhappy with some aspect of our work, but it was better if I asked first. The best client relationships were based on mutual trust, on being part of the same team, and trust grew from clear, honest communication. It helped if I gave them an opening for their honesty—good or bad.

I coined a term for this, and it became my mantra: "Run toward trouble." In other words, don't avoid conflict, seek it out. Instead of ignoring problems, hunt them down and resolve them. By running toward trouble, instead of away from it, you end up clearing up controversies earlier. As I had learned when I managed the Moscone Center project, early intervention keeps little problems from becoming big problems and big problems from becoming disasters. This was just as true when managing an entire office. If there is one piece of wisdom I am proud to share with readers, it is this one.

> *. . . early intervention keeps little problems from becoming big problems and big problems from becoming disasters.*

I repeated this advice so often that I frequently heard other HOK people saying it to each other: "Run toward trouble!" Usually everything on our projects was going smoothly, but not always. Often HOK project team members were reluctant to speak openly about problems, but a little encouragement and lots of listening generally worked. Sometimes I resorted to asking team members questions to help get to the root of an issue. This is a technique anyone can try. I was a bit of a pit bull when I sensed a problem, because I continued to believe that catching mistakes early was critical to our success.

Projects were complicated then and they have become even more complicated now. No set of architecture plans is going to be perfect—but some mistakes are bigger than others. One time, we even made a blunder that wasn't discovered until after the grand opening of one of our buildings. We had designed a new courthouse in San Bernardino County, California. The county sheriff wanted a bus ramp leading from the street to the basement, so he could securely transport prisoners from the jail to the courthouse for trial. Because of the shape of the property, the ramp made a sharp right-hand turn as it descended. The design team neglected to check the clearance requirements for buses and made the curved part of the ramp the same width as the straight section. It was a whopper of a mistake, but nobody caught it.

The contractor finished the building, the county accepted it, and the first time the sheriff's people tried to drive a bus down the ramp, it got stuck! The sheriff couldn't believe it—and didn't blame us at first. Instead, he asked his best bus driver to try driving down the ramp. His bus got stuck too. Now, the sheriff came back to HOK and said, "You stupid architects." The builder had to jackhammer out the walls on one side of the ramp to make it wider, and we had to eat the cost. I was embarrassed—and frustrated. If only we had "run toward trouble" and caught the mistake early, when it was still on paper, it would have been an easy fix. This and many other mistakes not caught until construction would later lead me to a professional epiphany, but not yet. I continued to think about this challenge, but soon I faced a very different kind of challenge.

Collecting Money

HOK San Francisco's billings and collections were in relatively good shape. Bob Stauder had seen to that when he was managing principal. However, one client in Malaysia had an overdue bill for $200,000. Stauder called me from St. Louis and asked me to travel to Kuala Lumpur to demand payment from a Malaysian development company. "If they don't pay, sit in their office until they do," Bob told me. "We need that money to make payroll."

That was my very first trip to Asia. I first flew to Hong Kong, a 14-hour flight on Pan Am Flight 1, their famous around-the-world service. Crossing the Pacific nonstop was at the limits of commercial air travel, and Pan Am had pioneered nonstop Pacific crossings with a specially modified fleet of Boeing 747s. Hong Kong was steamy hot and more crowded than any city I had ever experienced—so congested that the city had built elevated pedestrian walkways to prevent people from blocking street traffic.

After an overnight stay in Hong Kong, the flight to Singapore took another four hours. Then I boarded a smaller Air Malaysia plane for the 30-minute ride to Kuala Lumpur. Whew! I checked into my hotel, changed, and went straight to the developer's office. Malaysia was a former British colony and most people spoke English, so the meaning was crystal clear when the receptionist told me, "They're busy. Come back next week."

Instead, I returned the next morning, presented myself to the receptionist and announced, "I want to see your general manager about a past due bill, and I am going to stay here all day until he meets with me." A few hours later, one of his assistants came out to the reception room and I told him, "You have a past due bill with HOK for $200,000 and I have instructions to remain here until we are paid."

"We can't do anything today," he replied. "Come back tomorrow." The next day, the general manager himself came to the reception area to see me. He began by saying, "The bank is closed today. Come back tomorrow." I replied, "You signed a contract and owe us money—and I'm not leaving until you pay our bill." It was a test of wills, and my persistence finally wore him down. He called someone in his back office and a short time later they brought me a signed check for $200,000.

I took the check and caught the next plane to Singapore, then to Hong Kong and, finally, the long flight to San Francisco. I went straight to our office and sent the check by overnight courier to St. Louis. We made payroll that week, and I felt like a hero! The experience of collecting past due money was my introduction to the importance of cash flow, an experience that would shape my thinking when HOK faced a dire crisis later.

Working in the Middle East

The San Francisco office had won a commission to develop a master plan for expansion of the airport at Jeddah, the second-largest city in Saudi Arabia. I had an appointment to visit the Ministry of Air Transport there, followed by a visit to the HOK+4 project office in Riyadh. This was my first trip to the Middle East, and I was eager to see what it was like.

For this longer two-week trip, I even purchased a larger suitcase. It held a lot of clothing but couldn't be carried on the plane, as I preferred, and it was awkward to handle. I had always carried my bags on the plane with me, to avoid the hassle of checked baggage going to the wrong destination. When I traveled for HOK, I was in too much of a hurry for distractions like that. However, this trip seemed so far and so long that I gave in and bought the giant suitcase. I obtained my visa to enter Saudi Arabia in advance, thanks to a visa service that expedited paperwork with the Saudi Consulate in San Francisco—and it's a good thing I did.

Planes couldn't yet make it all the way to the Middle East nonstop, so I stopped in London overnight. It was October, and chilly when I took a long walk in Regent's Park to overcome the effects of jet lag.

The next afternoon I boarded a Saudia Airlines flight to Jeddah and landed at 10 P.M. Jeddah is the gateway to Mecca, the holiest site in Islam. Inside the Jeddah Airport, I found absolute pandemonium. It was the time of the Hajj, the annual pilgrimage to Mecca, and more than a million people were arriving from around the world. Some had saved money their whole lives to make the pilgrimage, including some without the proper documentation to enter Saudi Arabia. The entire arrivals area was filled with people jostling to go through immigration.

I stood there, clearly out of place in my suit, waiting for my turn at immigration. A customs official noticed me, took me to the front and sent me through. I picked up my large, awkward suitcase, went outside to look for a taxi, and almost wilted in the 109° heat. Across the street, a vast encampment of hajjis, those waiting to complete the five day pilgrimage, stretched as far as I could see, gathered around cooking fires or lying on bedrolls spread out in the sand. Pilgrims on their way to Mecca used to enter the port of Jeddah by boat, then travel the final 60 miles to Mecca by camel or on foot. Now they fly to Jeddah and take buses.

A long line of taxis stretched along the curb before me. Fortunately, the taxi dispatcher was multilingual, and after asking what hotel I wanted, called up a tiny Toyota cab and told the driver, who spoke no English, where to take me. I noticed that my driver was missing his right hand. It was only later that I learned what that meant.

I spent a week in Jeddah meeting with the Saudi air ministry to discuss an airport project for them, plus the new terminal at Jeddah. One day, we took a break for lunch and I walked to the souk, a marketplace of narrow streets covered with awnings and archways to block the sun. The souk was full of open stalls grouped by category—one area for spices, another for gold, and so on. People bartered for everything, with no fixed prices, which made buying a long, involved process.

The souk contained many small coffee houses, and I went into one and ordered Arabic coffee, a small cup of very strong brew with grounds at the bottom. I was sipping my coffee when two men rushed through the souk with long canes. It was time for noon prayers, and they struck the doorway of each shop with their canes to remind shop owners to close. As they neared the coffee shop, my host hustled me outside and pulled the door closed. I found myself on the street in the midst of men kneeling on prayer rugs. Women were praying in a group separate from the men. I stood against the wall quietly, trying not to interrupt. After prayers ended, I returned to my meeting and described what had happened. My hosts laughed and said the men with canes were religious police, tasked with enforcing Islamic laws, including closing of commercial establishments at times of prayer.

At the end of the week, I flew to Riyadh for meetings at the HOK + 4 project office for King Saud University, the one George Hellmuth had won for HOK. Like all foreign companies, our Riyadh office occupied a walled compound, allowing our workers to live a more relaxed lifestyle without the strictures of Saudi society. Inside the walls, a large house contained a spacious workspace for the project team and living quarters upstairs. Project manager Bob Hysell and his wife lived in a smaller house next door. Bob was Bill Valentine's classmate at Harvard Graduate School of Design, and also joined HOK after King Graf visited the school.

We held meetings in the large house, and I stayed overnight with Bob and his wife, enjoying their company. Over dinner, they talked about life in Riyadh and told me one story I will never forget.

Bob and Anne went to the Riyadh souk one weekend to buy groceries and supplies. As they were shopping, police carrying guns came into the souk and ordered everyone out and into nearby Deera Square. As they stood there under the hot sun with locals and a few other foreigners, a procession of officials came into the square, accompanied by police and two men who were obviously prisoners. An executioner carrying a long, curved scimitar was the last person in the procession. One of the officials read a long proclamation, presumably describing the offenses committed by the two prisoners. After the proclamation, the executioner cut off the hand of the first prisoner, then beheaded the second man. Bob and Anne could not leave—they were forced to see the punishment with the rest of the crowd. I asked, "Why did they make you watch?" Bob replied, "The Saudis use public punishment as a deterrent, a warning to others to obey the laws." Now I knew what had happened to my cab driver.

One day, as I myself walked down the sidewalk in Riyadh, I spotted a leather wallet lying on the sidewalk. My first instinct was to pick it up and turn it in to the authorities.

Instead, Saudi people were taking great pains to walk in a wide arc around the wallet, so they would not be anywhere near it. I asked Bob Hysell what was going on. "They are afraid if they touch the wallet, they will be accused of stealing it," he explained. "An eye for an eye" worked as a deterrent in Saudi Arabia, but at what cost? It was a culture of fear. I thought back to the criminal justice work I had done, designing courthouses, and even jails and prisons, where we had worked so hard to make the buildings humane. I was glad to be an American right then.

At the end of my stay, I boarded my Saudia Airlines flight to London. The aircraft was a McDonnell Douglas MD-11 with three engines, one under each wing and another in the tail. The temperature was 110°, and the plane had been sitting out on the tarmac for hours. As we took off, there was a huge *THUMP* from the rear engine and the entire plane shook. As I looked out the window, we began a gradual turn, and an excited member of the crew made an announcement in Arabic. Passengers who understood the language reacted with alarm, and I began to share their feelings. Just then, a big, drawling Texas voice said, "Ladies and gentlemen, this is the captain speaking. Waal, we got a lil' problem. One engine has overheated so we're gonna make a nice wide turn and bring 'er back in. We'll getcha on another plane ASAP."

It was a great comfort to hear that calm Texan twang! As we approached the runway, all the emergency vehicles were lined up and waiting, but we landed safely. I caught another flight to London and then home. The big bag I had purchased before traveling had been a nuisance all the way there and back. I gave it away and used just a carry-on for all future trips, no matter how long.

Chapter 10: To Design a World-Class Firm

1. Get out of your office and work directly with your people to show leadership.
2. Ask clients not just if you are doing well, but if you are doing less than well, to give them an opening to be honest.
3. Run toward trouble. Drill down to problems and resolve them early, because they will become bigger problems if you delay.
4. Ask lots of questions and really listen, to coax reluctant team members to be honest about problems with a project.
5. Don't give up if faced with a test of wills to collect money. You earned your fee; persist until you collect it!

CHAPTER 11

Growth: Project Specialists

In the years that Gyo Obata was in charge, HOK did not follow a grand plan or make major moves such as mergers, even though Obata still wanted to design a world-class architecture firm. Instead, Obata and the others were more incrementally opportunistic, finding expansion opportunities that arose from the growing HOK reputation in specialized project types. HOK added five new offices during this time, which came from a mix of opportunities, mostly involving clients and specialized projects. Other firms can also expand by honing teams that specialize in certain building types and becoming the go-to firm for those building types.

Lessons of Los Angeles

By the early 1980s, HOK San Francisco had established itself as a local firm able to compete effectively for Bay Area work. However, the office was not able to win work in Los Angeles—clients there were just as parochial as San Francisco clients had been when we first arrived. Bill Valentine and I made several trips to L.A. in 1982, to assess market conditions and speak to prospective clients. We became convinced we could win Los Angeles commissions, but only if HOK established an office there.

We flew to St. Louis to meet with the OOC and proposed opening a new L.A. office. Part of our argument was that George Kassabaum had originally wanted to expand into Los Angeles instead of San Francisco. Obata, King, Jerry, and Bob liked the idea of an L.A. office, but required that all expenses for it be paid by San Francisco. Bill and I were so confident in this expansion that we readily agreed to risk San Francisco's profit for a few months until the new office won some work and began to pay bills on its own.

Instead of sending people from San Francisco or another HOK office to lead the new endeavor in Los Angeles, we recruited local architects, believing they would understand the marketplace and have the best knowledge of local clients. This was a big mistake. Once again, our new employees had no understanding of HOK culture, or of what it meant to be a part of our company. The office got off to a rocky start and was not successful until we transferred HOK people to Los Angeles. Learn from our mistakes: when you open a new office, it's best to install a few key people from inside your firm, so they can spread your company culture to the new branch.

Sports Design Specialty

The story of HOK Kansas City began with Ron Labinski, who was born in Buffalo, grew up in Cleveland, and finished high school in Chicago. Labinski earned a Bachelor of Architecture degree at the University of Illinois and won a fellowship to tour Europe for six months after graduation. Then he joined the army and spent most of his tour of duty at Fort Riley, Kansas. The highlight of Labinski's military career was designing a crypt to memorialize the last remaining horse in the U.S. Cavalry.

After military service, Labinski moved to nearby Kansas City and joined local firm Kivett & Myers. He was assigned to work on Arrowhead Stadium, a new home for the Kansas City Chiefs and Royals. Labinski immersed himself in the work and became fascinated with the challenges of sports architecture. He found he liked everything about stadium design and began to dream of a specialized career.

Labinski was a natural marketer. As George Hellmuth would have done, he made a list of all Major League Baseball and National Football League teams and when their stadium leases would expire. Labinski discovered that many leases would expire in the 1980s, meaning new stadiums would be needed across the country. He also noted another group of buildings, still very much in their prime, that would create a second, even larger opportunity: "There was this huge bubble in the 1990s, when all the lease agreements at multipurpose stadiums were up," Labinski said. "I recognized through all the conversations I was having with owners that multipurpose stadiums were not the way they wanted to go in the future. They wanted out of those."[1]

In other words, Labinski scoped out possible projects before those projects even existed, a brilliant move that other architects would do well to emulate. Then, he began attending Baseball and Football League meetings at a time when no other architects specialized in sports architecture. He was the only architect there! Talk about becoming a trusted advisor to potential clients. He was the *only* advisor. Again, these are moves anyone could copy in some other field. Labinski met team owners and managers, learned about the business side of sports, and began to see how stadium design was fundamental to the business success of professional teams.

Labinski also understood that his future was not at Kivett & Myers because the firm had no room for a bright young architect to grow into the partnership. So, in 1973, Labinski and three friends formed the new firm of Devine, James, Labinski & Myers. Labinski continued to focus on sports, while his three partners developed their own practices. His firm was not much different from Hellmuth & Hellmuth or other traditional architecture partnerships, formed as a marriage of convenience instead of a carefully planned strategy for long-term success.

---

[1] Bill King, "Ron Labinski," *Sports Business Daily*, March 22, 2010. Accessed April 21, 2019. https://www.sportsbusinessdaily.com/Journal/Issues/2010/03/22/Champions-Of-Sports-Business/Ron-Labinski.aspx.

Labinski hired three young architects—Chris Carver, Dennis Wellner, and Joe Spear—to develop his growing sports practice. The four became close friends and began to compete for Major League sports work. The firm competed for the Hoosier Dome in Indianapolis but lost to Howard, Needles, Tammen & Bergendoff (HNTB), a large Kansas City engineering and architecture firm. But the Hoosier Dome clients were so impressed by Labinski's understanding of stadiums, that they asked HNTB to recruit him for their project.

When HNTB approached him, Labinski said he would join their firm if he could bring Carver, Wellner, and Spear along. All four joined HNTB in 1980 and continued to specialize in sports projects. However, HNTB was a firm of architectural engineers rather than designers, and Labinski and his sports colleagues never fit in. After three years, they began to look for another host firm.

In 1983, Labinski met Gerry Gilmore from HOK St. Louis, who was scouting Kansas City as a potential new office location. HOK represented an intriguing opportunity—a large firm led by architects instead of engineers, with a network of offices in cities across the United States. Best of all, HOK had an established reputation for good, innovative design. Labinski asked Gilmore to introduce him to HOK leadership. When Labinski met Gyo Obata, Jerry Sincoff, and King Graf in St. Louis, he offered to leave his partnership and open a new HOK Kansas City office with Carver, Wellner, and Spear—under certain conditions:

Seed financing. The first condition was that HOK would provide seed financing for the new office until it could become self-sustaining.

Sports only. The second condition was that Kansas City would have a singular focus on sports architecture, and not pursue any other type of work. Labinski believed this was the only way to assure success in the sports marketplace. Fortunately for him, it was a sentiment becoming more common at HOK, as offices were increasingly organizing their work around market practices.

Exclusive rights. The third condition was that Kansas City would have the exclusive right to pursue, design, and produce all sports work nationwide. This bold demand was the most difficult for the HOK leaders to accept, because it denied other HOK offices the opportunity to pursue sports work. Labinski explained that the condition was not based on greed, but on quality control and client service. Sports clients demanded high standards, requiring experienced sports architects to do the work. One unsatisfactory stadium designed by inexperienced HOK people would destroy HOK's reputation as a sports design firm.

Annual Bonus. The final condition was that a substantial portion of the Sport Group's annual profits would be returned to Kansas City as an annual bonus. This provision did not raise a red flag because it was similar to general HOK practice.

Gyo, Jerry, and King discussed each of Labinski's conditions after the meeting. All readily agreed to finance a Kansas City startup. They also agreed that dedicating one office exclusively to sports work was an interesting experiment that might inform the future development of HOK market practices. The OOC leaders were most concerned about Kansas City's exclusive right to all sports work nationwide—even in cities where HOK had an established office—but persuaded themselves that other HOK offices would eventually share the work in some way. Obata and his partners did not seriously question the annual bonus provision. After all, the Kansas City Sport office was just beginning. Profits and bonuses would be small at first. This final condition would emerge as a major quandary in later years, one I myself would have to tackle.

In December 1983, Labinski and his colleagues opened the new Kansas City office, which became known as HOK Sport. The first task for Labinski was to hang onto his existing clients and projects. He persuaded HNTB to allow the 14 current sports clients to decide for themselves whether to stay with HNTB or to follow Labinski. All but one chose to come to the new HOK Sport. If you are a sought-after specialist and maintain excellent client relations, giving clients a choice like this can seem risky, but can actually be a savvy move. HOK Sport was profitable from the very beginning and grew from the original 5 to 30 people.

In 1984, Miami Dolphins owner Joe Robbie hired HOK Sport to design the football stadium that would bear his name. Labinski sold Robbie on an idea that would forever alter the model for stadium and arena design. He proposed an air-conditioned mezzanine section that looked like the lobby of an upscale hotel, with bars and areas to sit and talk. This "club floor" would then provide access to fancy suites for upscale sports fans, each with a view of the field.

Corporations and wealthy individuals could buy or lease the suites for entertaining their customers and guests, and stadium revenue would increase. Joe Robbie loved the idea and leveraged the increased revenue model to finance the stadium. Every stadium built today has a club floor and individual suites and they continue to be moneymakers. Word to the wise: as designers, we can innovate to make our buildings not just beautiful and functional, but also profitable and we should look for opportunities to do so. This applies to any building that is open to a paying public, such as museums, restaurants, retail, and more.

Team Member in Tampa

Once, HOK opened a new office thanks to the persuasion of a talented team member. It wasn't necessarily the best business plan, but here's what happened. The story of HOK Tampa begins with Ed Bartz, who grew up in Belleville, Illinois near St. Louis. He, too, earned a Bachelor of Architecture Degree at Washington University and joined HOK St. Louis, where his outgoing manner came to Hellmuth's attention. Bartz became a member of the marketing team, with a focus on winning Illinois work. He helped Hellmuth win the Southern Illinois University (SIU) Edwardsville project and led the East St. Louis project office that was required by the commission. When HOK relocated its Illinois office to Belleville, in 1960, the founders placed Bartz in charge with a mandate to win more Illinois work.

Bartz maintained the Belleville office and marketed for new work in Illinois—or wherever Hellmuth asked him to travel. Some of that travel was to Florida, and Bartz, like so many Midwesterners, enjoyed Florida in the winter. He and his wife eventually bought a house in the Tampa area, and, in 1984, Bartz persuaded Obata and the other OOC leaders to let him open a new office in Tampa. HOK Tampa established itself and did some notable work, but did not grow into a leading HOK office. It's a good lesson that firms should choose their office expansion locations based on a market's true potential, not on a team member's desire for a sunny climate. Nevertheless, I visited HOK Tampa many times and learned about the Ed Bartz evening ritual: He walked to a nearby pond, smoked a cigar—and fed the alligators!

Retail Design Specialty

Over the decades, HOK had designed many buildings in other countries, but had not made the leap to opening an office outside the United States. That was about to change. Founder George Hellmuth wanted us to expand to multiple cities. Now we were about to expand to other countries. This story took some twists and turns, so hang on for the ride, because it was really another "unbroken chain" for HOK's design specialists, with one commission leading to another and then another.

Retailer Stanley Marcus, leader of the high-end Neiman-Marcus stores, planned to open a new store in the brand new Houston Galleria that was in the planning phase. Marcus was always personally involved in the selection of the architect and the design of his new stores, and interviewed a long list of architects, including HOK. He was favorably impressed by Obata and his HOK team, especially that patient, listening style of Obata's. Before Marcus made a final decision, he called the HOK office early on a Saturday as a test. Did HOK work on weekends? Someone answered the phone, and Marcus asked for Obata, who was working, as usual, and took the call. Marcus made up his mind to hire HOK on the spot.

After working with Obata and the team on design of the new Neiman Marcus store, Marcus became convinced that Obata should design the entire Houston Galleria, and arranged for Obata to meet Gerald Hines, the developer behind the Galleria project. What a great reminder that there are no bad projects and that every one is an audition for the next! Obata's proposed design solution for the Galleria was masterful: three levels of retail, topped by a barrel-vaulted skylight reminiscent of the famous *Galleria Vittorio Emanuele II* in Milan, Italy. Obata placed a year-round ice skating rink in the very center of the Galleria, with hotels, restaurants, and office buildings around the perimeter and a pedestrian walkway, called a "retail street" connecting everything together.

> *. . . there are no bad projects and . . . every one is an audition for the next!*

The Galleria became a hub of commerce filled with shoppers, businesspeople, and visitors that rivaled central Houston. It was a major success and set a new standard for urban design. Other retail developers began to visit the Galleria to study its success and apply the design principles to their own malls. Two of these developers invited HOK to design retail centers outside the United States, leading to the establishment of the first two HOK offices overseas.

FIGURE 11.1 Interior view of Houston Galleria including ice rink, Houston Texas.
Source: Photo by George Silk. Photo courtesy of HOK.

Opening in Hong Kong

HOK Hong Kong did not originate with local clients, or even clients from East Asia, but instead from Saudi Arabia. In the late 1970s, King Graf began making frequent visits to the Middle East to call on clients. As I had seen, doing business there was a challenge. "We quickly learned one thing, and that was patience," King recalled. "The first trip I took to Saudi Arabia, I was supposed to be in Riyadh for three nights and I was there for 29 days. I didn't have enough shirts!"[2]

---

[2] Fred Faust, "HOK Architects Outgrow St. Louis Roots," *St. Louis Post-Dispatch*, October 21, 1991. Accessed April 21, 2019. https://www.newspapers.com/newspage/141487402.

On one Riyadh trip, when King gave his name as he checked into a hotel, the front desk clerk grew flustered and said, "Oh, your highness, we didn't know you were coming!" King was tempted to see where this would go, but instead laughed and set the poor man straight. Once I asked King about his unusual name, and he chuckled and explained, "My parents were German-American, and they named me Horace after my father and Kingsland after my mother's family. With the name Horace Kingsland Graf, it was either HK or King, and King stuck."

But back to the unbroken chain of retail design. A group of Saudi investors approached King on yet another of his visits to Saudi Arabia. They were impressed by the Houston Galleria and learned it was designed by HOK. They asked King if HOK would design a retail development—not in Saudi Arabia, but half a world away in Jakarta, Indonesia. King began to think about how to design a project so far from home. St. Louis and Jakarta are 15 time zones apart, making real-time communication a challenge. Air travel between the two is arduous, and crosses the International Date Line, meaning travelers arrive in Jakarta an extra 24 hours later.

King concluded the project would require establishment of a project office. HOK leaders were interested in establishing a branch office in Asia, but not interested in Jakarta as a strategic long-term location. Would the clients accept Hong Kong as a project office location? Sometimes, if you politely push, you can get something you want, that is perfectly acceptable to the client. At that time, Hong Kong was still a British Colony where a large percentage of the population spoke English, a tangible benefit, as George Hellmuth had discovered. HOK could more easily recruit people to live and work in Hong Kong, a four hour flight almost due north of Jakarta. Plus, the two cities are in adjacent time zones, making them only one hour apart on the clock. King told me later that there was another reason for the Hong Kong location. "Hong Kong is on the doorstep to China," he said. "Someday they will open their borders to the outside world, and we'll be ready to work there."

HOK established a project office in the Wan Chai District of Hong Kong in 1984. The Jakarta project was named Plaza Indonesia and contained a large retail mall topped by a Grand Hyatt Hotel. We had learned from our mistakes, and a small St. Louis team was transferred to Hong Kong to lead the project team. HOK hired local employees from the large international pool of architects living in Hong Kong, and the project office became a blend of people and cultures.

HOK Hong Kong remained a project office for many years during the design and construction of Plaza Indonesia. Eventually, the office was able to win work in the region and establish itself as a permanent office.

Launching in London

After opening an office in British Crown Colony Hong Kong, HOK had the opportunity to open one in Great Britain itself. Interestingly, commissioners of the Church of England were responsible for investing church funds in real estate projects around the United Kingdom and decided to build a new retail center in Glasgow, Scotland. The commissioners toured retail centers around the world for ideas and, like other clients, were most impressed with the Houston Galleria. Our unbroken chain of retail design was about to get longer.

The commissioners asked HOK to design the St. Enoch Centre, with the conditions that HOK work with a British architect and do most of the work in the UK. They had given us just the excuse we needed. HOK established a project office in London and associated with Gollins Melvin Ward (GMW) architects, familiar partners from the HOK+4 team that had designed King Saud University. In 1987, HOK established its London office, with experienced retail architect Pierre Baillargeon from HOK Dallas in charge.

London was a grand opportunity for HOK to position itself in a great world city with many design opportunities. Just as Hong Kong was a gateway to China, HOK's leaders were also keenly aware that London was on the doorstep of continental Europe, with its potential for even more projects. This is a good strategy for expanding firms: Choose your new locations, not just on their own merits, but for the other markets they open to you. Just a year later, in 1988, Obata and team decided to make HOK London a permanent office. They transferred Tad Tucker from St. Louis as managing principal and Bill Stinger from San Francisco as marketing principal. But who would lead design in London?

Obata once again believed the St. Louis office was transferring too many talented designers to new offices and did not want to lose any more. Instead he recruited Larry Malcic, a member of the Washington University architecture faculty, as London's design principal. Once again, Washington University was like our personal talent agency. Obata and others at HOK knew Larry and were impressed by his design talent and articulate speaking skills. Larry was a St. Louis native who earned his Bachelor of Environmental Design and Master of Architecture degrees at the University of Pennsylvania before returning to St. Louis to join the faculty at Washington University.

When HOK invited Larry to join HOK London, in 1988, he thought it would be just a stopping point on his professional journey. Instead, he found HOK to be a far more interesting place on the inside, a big family with a huge diversity of talent. "If you have talent and ambition, there is a place for you at HOK," Larry said later. "People try things. Sometimes they work and sometimes not, but the culture to allow initiative is important."

Chapter 11: To Design a World-Class Firm

1. Expand by building teams that specialize in certain project types and become the go-to firm for those project types.
2. Place your own firm's people in a new branch, rather than hiring all local talent, in order to instill your company culture in the new office.
3. Look for opportunities to make your buildings not just beautiful and functional—but profitable. Your clients will love you. This applies to any building open to a paying public—stadiums, museums, restaurants, retail, and more.
4. Choose your expansion locations based on business opportunities instead of the climate.
5. Choose new office locations, not just on their own merits, but for the other markets they open to you.
6. Remember that there are no bad projects—and every one is an audition for the next.

CHAPTER 12

Selling Stock to Investors

In 1990, HOK's top brass began to consider how to generate enough cash to accomplish two big objectives. The first was to buy back Obata's HOK stock when he reached 70 years of age. In addition, the firm needed more cash to invest in growth, especially internationally. How could HOK generate the large sums necessary to meet both objectives? Unfortunately, this was one instance in which HOK's founders had not planned ahead. They had not set aside any cash for a buyback, something I urge other firms to do.

CFO Bob Pratzel explained that HOK had three options: generate cash from profits, from loans, or from investors. HOK could save some of its profits each year to fund the buyback, but it would take too long to accumulate enough cash. Borrowing money from a bank or other lender was faster, but expensive and came with restrictive covenants. Plus, HOK had just overcome a cash flow crunch and had no appetite for additional borrowing. The third way forward was to find an investor willing to invest cash in HOK in exchange for a share of ownership.

Kajima Invests

While attending a seminar at Harvard, Gyo Obata met Dr. Shoichi Kajima, chairman of Kajima Corporation, one of the oldest and largest contractors in Japan. Kajima told Obata his firm was interested in expanding outside of Japan, particularly in the United States. The Japanese economy was booming, and Japanese firms like Kajima were on a buying spree. Obata asked Dr. Kajima if his company would like to invest in HOK. Dr. Kajima was interested, and Obata brought the idea back to Sincoff, who thought it might be a way to pay for Obata's stock buyback and finance more HOK growth.

Sincoff represented HOK in more detailed discussions, and over the next several months Kajima and HOK reached an agreement. Kajima would buy 15% of HOK stock at a price well above the current book value. The Kajima investment meant the HOK stock price would rise, benefitting all shareholders. Obata's stock value would get a boost like everyone else's, and the Kajima infusion would give HOK enough cash to fund his stock buyout at the new price. The agreement also entitled Kajima to two seats on the HOK board of directors, the first time people from outside of HOK would weigh in on the firm's decisions. HOK leadership would provide semiannual briefings to Kajima leadership at their Tokyo headquarters.

Sincoff believed HOK needed to grow much more to be competitive in the future and wanted even more cash to support expansion. In addition to investing in HOK, Kajima agreed to loan the firm an amount equal to their stock purchase. The interest-bearing loan was to last 10 years and Kajima had the option of converting the loan into an additional 15% of HOK stock. Some would say this was a risky deal for HOK, but the firm's leaders felt there was more upside than downside.

Sincoff wanted to expand in Asia beyond Hong Kong and agreed to open a Tokyo office with a promise of support from Kajima. He also agreed HOK would introduce Kajima to clients in the United States. Finally, HOK agreed to host Kajima employees in selected HOK offices so they could learn how American firms conducted business.

The agreement with Kajima required approval by HOK shareholders. Obata owned 52% of the shares and could have approved the Kajima agreement by himself, but he wanted everyone to be together in this major decision. It was another instance of mutual respect at HOK and it's a good example for any firm in similar circumstances. Obata, Jerry, and King went to the HOK offices and discussed the agreement with Kajima and how it would help HOK succeed.

HOK held a special shareholders' meeting in St. Louis, in 1991, to consider the Kajima investment. Almost everyone voted in favor of the agreement with Kajima, including me. One or two people voted no, but the shareholder discussion was overwhelmingly positive. People were happy with the boost in the HOK stock value and excited about the prospect of new work in Japan.

Now HOK had a partner, for the first time ever. Kajima had been founded in the 1800s, then boomed as Japan rebuilt after World War II. By 1990, Kajima was the largest contractor in Japan and one of the largest in the world. The company was well-run and highly disciplined, with building and infrastructure construction divisions, supported by in-house architecture and engineering departments as large or larger than HOK.

Kajima turned out to be a good partner, respecting HOK design creativity and taking a relaxed view of HOK internal operations. Kajima's primary goal was to build a US construction practice, not operate a design firm. Kajima sent a few people to the United States to work in HOK offices, particularly St. Louis. We treated them like family, and they loved experiencing American culture. When I asked them for their impressions of the United States, they always shared their astonishment at the large size of the United States compared to Japan, where 90% of the people crowd onto the flattest 10% of the land, with the rest too mountainous for major cities. One Kajima visitor traveled to the western states and told me, "I drove to Montana and could not believe it—as far as I could see there were no people!" Several of them dreamed about remaining in the United States, but all eventually returned to Kajima and Japan.

Our good working relationship with Kajima was the result of due diligence—with a dose of good luck. Other firms looking for investors should never neglect their due diligence—and luck never hurts.

Expanding in Europe and Asia

Not long after the shareholder meeting to approve the agreement with Kajima, Obata and the other leaders began to consider investing some of the Kajima money toward expansion. HOK already had a toehold in London, and they liked the idea of expanding into mainland Europe. The Berlin Wall had fallen in 1989, opening Eastern Europe to the outside world.

HOK's leaders also liked the idea of expanding farther into Asia. HOK had an office in Hong Kong and had now committed to a new office in Tokyo. But Asia was developing so rapidly, that opening still more offices in the region could make good business sense.

After 20 years of opening new offices, Obata, Jerry, and King were aware that expansion is challenging and decided to appoint leaders to shepherd HOK growth in Europe and Asia. They selected Larry Self to lead European expansion. Larry was the managing principal of HOK Dallas and had successfully led the office since King Graf moved back to St. Louis. Larry decided to relocate from Dallas to London to tackle his new position.

The HOK leaders chose me to lead Asian expansion. I was the managing principal of HOK San Francisco, and by then had some experience in Asia and the Middle East. Jerry Sincoff called to give me the news, and I was excited to have a larger role. At the end of our conversation he gave me my first assignment. "I want you to go to Tokyo and meet the people at Kajima," said Jerry. "They are our new partners and we want to be good friends. They will help you start the new Tokyo office." Gyo Obata had asked Bill Valentine to go too. Kajima would help us open the new HOK Tokyo office and Bill would help Kajima with some design challenges.

Traveling to Tokyo

What followed was a grand cultural adventure. Bill Valentine and I traveled to Tokyo to visit Kajima's offices, meet their people, and assist them with a design competition for a new airport project in Kyoto, Japan's second-largest city. But the real purpose of the trip was for us to become more comfortable with the Kajima people and nurture the partnership. We flew out of San Francisco on a Monday at 1 p.m. and arrived at Narita Airport outside Tokyo on Tuesday evening, after crossing the International Date Line. I was very curious to see Japan. The trip from Narita into Tokyo is about 30 miles, and the Narita Express train was still under construction. Taxis were extremely expensive, so we took the bus.

Everything we saw out the window was different. We passed miles of rice paddies full of people in water up to their shins. Rice growers in California sow their rice fields by dropping seeds from an airplane. Here, the stalks were started from seed, and men and women were planting them in the paddies by hand, one stalk at a time. As we prepared to meet our new colleagues, I wondered if it was a metaphor for how American and Japanese people do business differently.

Tokyo is spread out, like Los Angeles, but much more densely developed, with 25 million people, twice as many as metro Los Angeles. As we approached the center of Tokyo the bus got stuck in a massive traffic jam. Bill and I were tired from the flight, and the bus ride seemed to take forever. We had agreed to keep each other awake so we could sleep at our hotel, and I had to poke Bill about every five minutes to keep him conscious! After a total of three hours, we reached our destination, the Akasaka Prince hotel, designed by famous Japanese architect Kenzō Tange. Kajima had built the hotel and arranged for us to stay there; they wanted to showcase one of their projects.

Our new partners sent a driver the next morning to take us to Kajima headquarters. One building contained Kajima Construction and the other Kajima Design, with a cafeteria, meeting rooms, and other common facilities connecting the two buildings.

We had severe jet lag but went to meet the Kajima leadership anyway. Kajima Chairman Dr. Shoichi Kajima, a direct descendent of the founder, was educated as an architect and earned a Master of Architecture degree at Harvard. He had personally approved the Kajima investment in HOK and showed great interest in our work. We were grateful that he spoke very good English, as did most of the top Kajima leadership.

Every man in the Kajima offices wore a suit and tie, and for this occasion Bill Valentine wore one, too. Kajima had enjoyed great success after World War II rebuilding and modernizing Japan, then expanding into the rest of Asia. Their next goal was to go global by expanding into the United States and Europe.

After the meeting with Dr. Kajima and a tour of headquarters, a group of our new colleagues took us to a traditional Japanese restaurant for dinner. Upon entering, all our new friends took off their street shoes, stepped up to a raised wooden floor, then donned a pair of slippers provided by the restaurant. Bill and I followed their lead. They explained this tradition was practical, not religious. The Japanese are serious about cleanliness and do not want dirt from the street carried into their homes, or especially into restaurants. The staff took us to a private dining alcove separated from other diners by sliding shoji screens. Dining was on cushions on the floor around a low table.

This dinner was our first introduction to Japanese culture. Our hosts only invited men to the meal—typical of Japan at that time—and the food was served by women wearing beautiful kimonos. They brought us about 10 small courses of food. At the end of each course, after the dishes were removed, everyone toasted each other with beer or saké, and said "Kanpai!," which translates literally to "dry cup!" and in spirit means "bottoms up!"

Each person had to take a turn pouring the drinks, and our companions explained that it was an important gesture of friendship. You did not turn down a drink! The younger men finished every drink, but older men could leave a bit in the bottom. As the alcohol relaxed everyone, the businesslike air of formality melted, and we were able to laugh, talk, and become friends. By the end of the evening, after becoming best buddies with everyone from Kajima, we went back to our hotel and crashed.

After a night's rest, we were more observant of the city when the driver picked us up for the trip back to the Kajima office the next day. Tokyo was modern, busy, and full of skyscrapers, looking much like New York, except that space had been made everywhere for street trees and flowering hedges. Everyone working downtown was well dressed.

On day two at Kajima headquarters, we met the design department leaders to discuss design of a new airport. Bill and I explained it was important for us to understand Japanese architecture before beginning any design, and they told us the best way to learn was a visit to the old imperial capital of Kyoto. They assigned a young English-speaking architect to take us there to learn about the best of traditional Japanese design. We took our first ride on a bullet train from Tokyo to Kyoto. The Tokyo train station was huge, with many different levels, crowds of people, and signage only in Japanese. Without our young architect guide we would never have found our train. Kajima was hoping we would reciprocate with guidance like this—and more—as the big construction firm tried to break into the U.S. marketplace.

Centuries-old Buddhist temples fill the Kyoto valley, along with Shinto shrines, traditional wooden houses, and Imperial palaces that date from the time when Kyoto was Japan's capital city. The temples are in the traditional pagoda style developed originally in China that arrived in Japan with Buddhism 1,500 years ago. It was beautiful and different. The Japanese landscape and the architecture placed in that landscape were truly unique and it's a good thing we took the time to understand. Anyone serious about working in another country should try to do the same.

Kajima maintained a guest house in Kyoto for guests and employees, and we stayed there, learning the Japanese method of taking a hot bath. We first sat on wooden stools under a hot shower and scrubbed ourselves with stiff bristle brushes. After we were thoroughly clean, we settled in a hot, neck-deep bath for a good soak.

In Kyoto, Bill and I gained a special appreciation of Japanese craftsmanship and attention to fine detail. Contemporary buildings no longer use wood materials as in the pagoda style, but the legacy of quality and attention to detail continues in today's Japan, where the best architecture is always well-crafted with exquisite detail.

We returned to Tokyo for several more days of meetings with our Kajima hosts. At the end of each day they took us to a different restaurant and delighted in trying to find something we would refuse to eat! Since Bill and I were residents of San Francisco, famed for its Asian cuisine, we had long since mastered eating with chopsticks. They had to find other ways to tease us. One night, they brought us to a special restaurant. We took off our shoes, went to a private dining room and sat on floor cushions around a low table, as usual. But the table was different. A small stream of water containing live minnows ran through the middle. The waitress gave each of us a small net, and the game was for each of us to catch a minnow, swallow it live, then follow it with a beer chaser. Yes, I did it. Remember, our bosses had sent us to Japan to bond with our new partners. How could I refuse? I can tell you that the minnow tickled all the way down to my stomach. Our hosts explained the tickle was part of the dining experience!

FIGURE 12.1 Bill Valentine and the author catching minnows at Tokyo restaurant.
Source: Photo courtesy of Patrick MacLeamy.

Our first trip to Tokyo was an unforgettable experience, and the beginning of a long relationship with our new friends at Kajima. We learned much about Japan and gained an appreciation of Japanese architecture, culture—and food. We also grew comfortable with our new Japanese partners and they with us. Bill and several other HOK designers made more trips to Tokyo to work with Kajima designers on the competition for the new airport at Kyoto, but our team did not win the job. Despite this, we made many new friends at Kajima and began to build a solid working relationship.

HOK Tokyo

The next time I traveled to Japan was to open a new HOK Tokyo office as part of our agreement with Kajima. Our timing was perfect. The building marketplace was red hot, and the U.S. Commerce Department had reached agreement with the Japanese government to open its economy to outsiders, including architects. It would have been impossible for us to take advantage of this political change without our partnership with Kajima. Luck is when preparation meets opportunity, and all firms should be prepared to take advantage of an opportunity.

HOK got off to a good start in Japan. We transferred Dennis Cope from St. Louis to manage the office and look for work. Dennis and his wife Beverly saw Japan as an exciting opportunity and moved into a small apartment near the new office. With help from Kajima, we hired our first Japanese architects to fill out the office. We needed an HOK designer in Tokyo and moved Ernest Cirangle from San Francisco. Ernest was a native of New Jersey who earned a Bachelor of Architecture degree from the University of Illinois, my alma mater, before joining HOK San Francisco. Ernest loved Japan and quickly adapted to the culture.

His first project was the new headquarters for Tokyo Telecom, a dramatic building full of offices and equipment on new land reclaimed from Tokyo Bay. The only place to grow in Tokyo is up or out, so the Japanese often create new land in Tokyo Bay. Ernest also designed the new airport at Sendai, where Obata's father had lived before emigrating to California. Years later, in 2011, Sendai Airport served a key role after a major earthquake and tsunami struck the area. The airport survived intact and became the destination for aid shipments to the stricken area.

I went to Tokyo many times to visit the office and for meetings with our partners at Kajima. Every project required association with a local Japanese firm, and we worked with many of the best firms in Japan. But the office remained small, unable to grow to the size of more successful HOK offices in the United States and other countries. It had been easy to get work there when the economy was booming, but when Japan's economy went into recession, Japanese clients had little incentive to go to the extra trouble of hiring an American firm—a cautionary tale.

Dennis Cope remained in Tokyo for 10 years. Ernest Cirangle worked in Tokyo for several years, then transferred to HOK Hong Kong to lead the master plan for the new Hong Kong airport. He reinvented himself again years later, moving to HOK Los Angeles to become the design principal, where he works today. He's a great example of George Hellmuth's belief that HOK would thrive by attracting and keeping good people.

Sustainable Design

In late 1991, Obata and the others invited the HOK board of directors to a one-day retreat at the Bogey Club, Obata's suburban St. Louis golf club. The purpose of the meeting was to plan how HOK would invest the Kajima money to expand HOK around the world. The timing was ideal. Europe and Asia were growing and needed new airports, hospitals, and university buildings—everything HOK now specialized in designing. China would soon welcome foreign investment. The world was opening to HOK, and we had the resources to respond.

I was fortunate to be one of about a dozen board members in attendance. During the day, the board considered all sorts of grandiose ideas for investing the Kajima money. Participants had lots of suggestions: buy other firms, expand market practices, begin a construction business, develop a new entertainment practice. The list went on. Our ideas were all about what would best serve HOK. We didn't focus on what would best serve the world—until that night.

The highlight of the event was a dinner talk by Dr. Peter Raven. Raven was the director of the Missouri Botanical Gardens, for which HOK had designed a new visitors' center.

Raven was internationally acclaimed for his research into the relationship between mankind and the natural environment. He spoke for 45 minutes, without notes or illustrations, and mesmerized everyone with his compelling story of our planet at risk. He began with the big picture of Earth, and how all its life forms exist in a thin layer of land and water on the surface. He described how, over millennia, plants and animals formed an interdependent relationship. Raven then described how humans were doing great harm to our world, destroying plant and animal species at a terrifying rate, and altering the intricate relationship between all living things.

His challenge to us as designers was to change the way we thought about buildings, to see them as part of the environment that all of us share. Could HOK design buildings to become sparing users of energy, like plants and animals are? Could HOK design buildings that could be more efficiently constructed, with little waste? Could HOK design buildings with materials that are safe for human occupancy? And safe for the environment when the building is someday recycled? Here was something we had not even thought about investing in—and that didn't even have a name yet.

Peter Raven's talk led HOK in a fundamentally new design direction, one that still resonates today. We all responded enthusiastically to Raven's challenge, but none more than Bill Valentine. He developed a deep Interest in designing energy-efficient buildings constructed of healthier materials and became the HOK champion for what became known as sustainable design. Now we were investing in something good for the planet. And you know what? As often happens, it was good for HOK too, and would soon be in great demand. Doing the right thing can also be profitable, and that's synchronicity at its best.

> **N**ow we were investing in something good for the planet . . . As often happens, it was good for HOK, too.

Chapter 12: To Design a World-Class Firm

1. Plan ahead for a source of funding to buy back large quantities of stock from your firm's founders.
2. Raise cash for a stock buyback in one of three ways: save cash from profits, borrow money from a bank, or get outsiders to invest in your company. Saving cash is the best, but it takes time—so start early.
3. Seek full shareholder participation in major decisions. It is not only necessary but also helps to build a consensus.
4. Understand the motivations of outsiders before asking them to invest in your company. The best will not interfere with your business but simply expect a good return on investment.
5. Understand local business and culture before working in another country. Really understand local business and culture before opening an office in another country.
6. Work to always be prepared so you can seize opportunities—some people call this "luck."
7. Embrace sustainable design to improve the planet, which can also improve your bottom line. Doing the right thing can be profitable.

CHAPTER 13

Transitions: Hiring Family

HOK felt like a big family but hiring real family members—relatives—can be a sensitive subject. It even has its own dirty word—nepotism—but it didn't cause any problems at HOK, because the firm enforced the same values of self-responsibility and mutual respect with family members as it did with everyone else. I urge all firms to apply the same standards to family as they do to other employees. A quick example: one summer I hired my teenaged daughter, Elisabeth, as a file clerk. On her first day, I told her, "Elisabeth, if you mess up, I personally will fire you!" And I would have. Fortunately, she didn't mess up.

Over the years, a handful of family members came to HOK. Founder George Hellmuth's son, George W., mentioned earlier, had a successful 30-year career at HOK. Gyo Obata's son, Gen Obata, worked as an architect at HOK San Francisco for several years, before moving on to pursue his real passions for art and music. But perhaps the most interesting family connection came when Obata hired somebody from one of the other founder's families. That was the real game-changer for HOK, but of course, there were also other important comings and goings during Gyo Obata's tenure as Chairman.

Bob Stauder Resigns

Bob Stauder continued as HOK operations director until just before the Kajima investment, but remained controversial because of his style of leadership. He was unhappy in St. Louis and missed his home in the Bay Area. Stauder proposed to his colleagues in the OOC that he return to San Francisco and bring the Central Accounting and legal departments along with him. Gyo, King, and Jerry were adamantly opposed to relocating these departments, and after a few months of disagreement, Bob Stauder resigned from HOK.

Clark Davis Helms St. Louis

By 1988, the St. Louis office needed new leadership after transferring so many talented people to other locations throughout the years. Obata's fears of a brain drain had come to pass. This is something all service firms need to watch out for. No executives were available to bring in from another HOK office either, so the OOC began a search for a senior leader and recruited Clark Davis as the new managing principal.

Clark was a St. Louis native, had earned a Bachelor of Architecture degree from the University of Michigan, and was an experienced leader. Clark was professional, ambitious, and thoughtful, and he soon had the St. Louis office running smoothly again.

Bill Hellmuth Joins HOK

Over the years, Gyo Obata had hired many new designers to join HOK, but in early 1990, he hired one with a familiar last name. Bill Hellmuth was founder George Hellmuth's nephew, and you would think Hellmuth would have been the one to recruit him. However, Bill was the son of Hellmuth's brother, Ted, who was estranged from the rest of the Hellmuth family. "I never really knew the Hellmuth side of the family. My father died when I was about 10 years old and we didn't spend any time with them," Bill explained later. "I always tell people I'm at HOK by accident. It's a wonderful accident, but it was an accident."

Bill grew up in Cleveland, instead of St. Louis where the rest of the Hellmuth clan lived. He went to the University of Virginia for undergrad and then earned a Master of Architecture degree from Princeton University. Early in his career, he worked at SOM in New York for 15 years. When he got restless, a friend in the business suggested that he talk to Gyo Obata at HOK in St. Louis. "I was intrigued, went to St. Louis and met Obata," Bill later said. "He was wonderful and charming." Obata hired Bill on the spot.

You would think this could have been awkward, but the St. Louis Hellmuth family embraced Bill and his family. "I got to know Papa George really well, and that was extremely special," Bill said. Once, his Uncle Hellmuth even filled in for him at bring-your-dad-to-school day, because Bill was out of the country on HOK business and couldn't be there for his son. "It was really wonderful," Bill said. "It's not very often that you get to connect with people that have your same DNA . . . and find that you really like them." Speaking of DNA, isn't it fascinating that Bill Hellmuth became an architect, just like his uncle, even though he was raised separately? Talk about nature versus nurture!

I met Bill Hellmuth in St. Louis shortly after he joined HOK and liked him immediately. Bill was of medium height and build, with an enviable head of thick gray hair parted at the side and swept back from his broad forehead. Bill wore distinctive glasses with clear plastic frames that made him look like a designer—or perhaps a professor of design. He invariably wore white shirts with button-down collars and striped ties—quite a contrast to Bill Valentine in his jeans and black crewnecks.

Two years later, in 1992, Obata asked Bill to take a trip to Washington, DC. "We're going to have to let the design director in that office go, so we want you to fill in for the time being," Obata said. "But don't worry, I would never ask you to move there." Next thing he

Chapter 13 Transitions: Hiring Family

FIGURE 13.1 Gyo Obata and Bill Hellmuth in the HOK St. Louis office.
Source: Photo courtesy of HOK.

knew, Bill received a call from a friend congratulating him on becoming the new design director of HOK Washington. "I hadn't even had time to tell my wife, Nancy, that I was going to Washington," he recalled later. "Everyone knew except for me that it was going to be my next step."

Bill was sorry to leave the Hellmuth family behind in St. Louis but ended up working with another Hellmuth in Washington. Founder George Hellmuth's son, George W., had transferred from New York to DC not long before, and served as the marketing principal there. The two worked well together. "I quickly learned that, at HOK . . . you could pretty much chart your course," Bill said later. "We realized it was up to our imaginations as to what we could do." If you lead, rather than manage, your people, you can create a company where the employees use their imaginations to chart an exciting course.

". . . at HOK . . . you could pretty much chart your course . . . We realized it was up to our imaginations as to what we could do."

One of Bill's most significant DC projects was design of the Udvar-Hazy Center, an enormous addition to the National Air and Space Museum located next to Dulles Airport in the Virginia suburbs. Bill created two vast, curving hangars with substantial, yet graceful, trusses capable of supporting the Smithsonian's largest air and space artifacts. The aviation wing features an artificial sky; the space section has a dramatically darker ceiling. The museum is beautiful—and meaningful to HOK. On a professional level, the Udvar-Hazy Center was a continuation of the work HOK began with the original Air and Space Museum. On a personal level, it houses the *Enola Gay*, the airplane used to drop the atomic bomb on Japan—launched from a bomb rack drawn up by a young Air Force draftsman named George Kassabaum.

FIGURE 13.2 National Air and Space Museum, Steven F. Udvar-Hazy Center, Chantilly, Virginia.
Source: Photo courtesy of HOK.

Gyo Obata Consults

Bill Hellmuth was one of Obata's last design hires. In accordance with the stock restrictions created many years before, Obata sold his HOK stock back to the firm in 1993, when he reached 70 years of age. He was the last of the founders. During that time, HOK had grown from 700 to 900 people and from five major offices to nine, including two international offices. However, like George Hellmuth before him, Obata was not ready to retire. He wanted to continue doing what he loved—designing buildings for clients—while giving up the burden of firm-wide leadership. This is a common situation in architecture; we love what we do, so it makes sense for firms to leverage the talents of older workers while also moving forward with younger leaders.

Jerry Sincoff and King Graf arranged a one-year consulting agreement with Obata, allowing him to continue working as a designer. At the end of one year, Obata was still not ready to retire, so HOK extended his consulting contract for another year. After the second year, Obata continued to enjoy his work, so HOK extended his contract for a third year.

FIGURE 13.3 Gyo Obata, c. 1993.
Source: Photo by Suzy Gorman. Photo courtesy of HOK.

This annual ritual continued for the entire term of Jerry Sincoff's leadership—and beyond. Obata continued to work as a consultant to HOK, for at least 26 years—on top of his original 37 years as one of the founders. As of this writing, he is in his late nineties, and only just now slowing down.

Chapter 13: To Design a World-Class Firm

1. Apply the same standards to family as to other employees and you can successfully hire family members without any problems.
2. Do not deplete the talent pool in one office by transferring too many people to other offices.
3. Create a company culture in which employees can imagine their own course of action and accomplish exciting things.
4. Consider allowing talented people to continue to contribute after retirement with a consulting arrangement.

SECTION THREE

THE SINCOFF ERA, 1993–2002

CHAPTER 14

Get Bigger or Get Better?

In 1993, Bill Valentine joined Jerry Sincoff and King Graf as the three-person HOK leadership group. All three shared much in common: each had joined HOK soon after graduation, had grown up under the tutelage of one of the founders, and had been designated a second-generation HOK leader. All were about 60 years of age, had been at HOK more than 30 years, and were close friends.

Kassabaum protégé Jerry Sincoff would lead HOK as CEO. Hellmuth's understudy, King Graf, continued as vice chairman for marketing. Gyo Obata's successor, Bill Valentine, became HOK vice chairman for design. One big change: Bill did not move to St. Louis, instead deciding to remain in San Francisco to be close to clients there. Bill was the first HOK leader not to live in St. Louis, the beginning of a long-term trend to spread HOK leadership across the firm. Nor did he dominate design across the firm as Gyo Obata had. Instead Bill Valentine established high standards for design quality with his own work, especially sustainable design, and encouraged design leaders in every office to do great work of their own.

HOK was again led by a three-person group, but it was no longer to be called the Office of the Chairman (OOC). Jerry renamed the leadership group the HOK Executive Committee (ExCom), the name the firm still uses today.

The Sincoff Strategy

Jerry Sincoff was the first HOK leader to succeed the founders. He was a strategic thinker and developed three big strategies to transform HOK from a large firm with a good reputation to an international firm with a stellar reputation.

Growth Above All

Jerry's first strategy was growth above all. HOK was already a large firm, with 14 offices and more than 900 people. Jerry believed HOK needed to grow even more—especially internationally—to compete for the largest and most significant projects worldwide.

Executives at IBM had almost passed HOK over for a new laboratory project in Los Gatos, California because they thought the firm was too small to deliver the work. That incident had made a big psychological impression on Jerry. Other large clients like developer Gerald Hines built many projects in different locations each year. How could HOK deliver work for marquee clients like these? We would need to grow and spread to more diverse locations. And we would need to present a more substantial appearance, no longer playing the midwestern upstart. Sometimes to nab big clients, you have to be—and look—big yourself.

Jerry believed HOK could grow in two ways. First, he wanted to reorganize market practices—HOK's project specialists in different building types—across the firm instead of by office. Second, he dreamed of growing by acquiring other design firms. And thanks to the Kajima investment, the money was there to fund his vision.

Focus on Clients

Jerry's second strategy was to focus on clients, not just on winning more work. From the beginning, HOK's success had been based on winning the next job, so much so that it became part of the firm's DNA. George Hellmuth was a marketing legend, with stories of his exploits told and retold. Obata also focused on winning new work. When asked what was most important about architectural practice, he would smile and say, "There are three important things—get the job, get the job, get the job!" He would then add, "Our practice depends on jobs. No jobs—no practice." Jerry celebrated winning new projects like everyone at HOK, but every job has a client. "All of us loved to work on buildings, but it was necessary to realize the buildings were not ours," Jerry recalled later. "They belong to our clients and we work for them—just as all professionals work for their clients." In other words, quality was just as important as quantity of work and doing a superior job would yield even more projects.

Jerry's key insight was that certain large clients were in a constant state of expansion and change, with a need for ongoing design and construction services. Large developers maintained a portfolio of projects, with many active at the same time. Large corporate clients required continuous interior design as they shifted entire departments from one building to another or from one campus to another. Airport clients were always growing, with ongoing needs for more gates, larger gates, improved security, or new retail space. Hospitals were consolidating, creating ongoing needs for new patient wings, surgical suites, or diagnostic facilities.

Jerry believed repeat business was the way to build a world-class architecture firm. Remember the HOK Matrix, where all local offices were encouraged to develop specialties in buildings types such as education, aviation, laboratories, and more? Many large clients with continuous needs for design services needed the precise types of design expertise in the HOK Matrix. Jerry's goal was for HOK to build a working relationship with these clients and help them with successive projects over many years. It's not that Jerry wanted HOK to lose its focus on winning the next job. Rather, his goal was to instill in us an equal focus on serving clients, so they would become repeat clients—another way of winning more work. Do a top notch job and they are likely to hire you again.

Firm-Wide Market Practices

Jerry was a voracious reader and studied the business practices of other professions for insights about how to improve HOK. He learned how other professionals were becoming specialized. Lawyers were shifting from general practice to corporate law, patent law, or litigation. Doctors were evolving from general practice to cardiology, dermatology, and orthopedics. Accountants were shifting to specialties like tax, audit, or estate planning. By contrast, most architects were still generalists. However, HOK had evolved from a general practice toward specialization in different building types. Jerry saw that as a huge advantage that we could exploit further if we organized our specialties firm-wide, instead of office by office.

Jerry analyzed HOK's revenues and discovered our specialized market practices in aviation, health care, justice, and sports were responsible for most recent growth. However, HOK was organized around local offices, not market practices. Until now, HOK leadership had encouraged every office to fill in the squares in the HOK Matrix and develop specialty practices that answered only to their own office leadership. The problem is that this structure actively discouraged collaboration between specialists from different offices. In fact, since everybody was trying to specialize in everything, offices would sometimes compete for the same work.

The firm's most organized market practice was HOK Sport in Kansas City, an office devoted exclusively to sports architecture, but not limited by geography. HOK Sport was our firm-wide sports architecture practice—period. The sport group was winning work across the country and building a stellar reputation. Sport specialization evolved to include baseball, football, basketball, and hockey. Then, over time, even greater specialization evolved within each sport. For example, in baseball, major league stadiums, minor league stadiums, and spring training facilities all had different needs.

Jerry was very impressed with the HOK Sport model and wondered if it was possible to transform other HOK offices into firm-wide aviation or healthcare specialists. When I asked Jerry about this, years later, he said, "If we had it to do over again, organizing HOK offices as specialists would have been effective. But the offices were too diversified and too well established as regional practices by the time we thought about changing." Here again, you can learn from our mistake and consider organizing your own firm around project specialists instead of around geographic offices.

Since our office-centric structure was already entrenched, Jerry began to think about creating organizational parity between local offices and market practices. He wanted to raise market practices up so that the two would be equal with each other. Ultimately, he wanted each market practice to be a firm-wide resource rather than having separate specialists in every office. He called this "fixing the matrix." Jerry knew this would require HOK to organize specialist groups more formally and identify leaders for each one.

In summary, Jerry Sincoff's goals for HOK were:

- Growth above all
- Focus on clients
- Firm-wide market practices

Jerry summarized his strategy in a paper called "The Futurity of HOK," emphasizing market-focused specialty groups as an organizing framework for the future and a way of nurturing ongoing relationships with clients. The paper addressed the question of how best to couple the specialty expertise of groups within HOK with the strong network of HOK regional offices. It was absolutely crucial that Jerry garner agreement and support from regional office leaders in order to achieve his vision.

Sharing the Strategy

Jerry carefully plotted how to sell his three goals to HOK leaders. Instead of a half-day or full-day meeting, he scheduled a three-day workshop in St. Louis to put his plan into action, inviting HOK leaders from around the world. Those invited included design, marketing, and management leaders from every HOK office and emerging leaders in the justice, aviation, healthcare, laboratory, and sports practices.

Instead of meeting in the St. Louis office, Jerry invited everyone to the newly restored hotel at historic St. Louis Union Station. There, The Rouse Company, a specialty retail developer, had commissioned HOK to convert the beautiful Richardsonian-style train station into a hotel and restaurants, and to transform the large train shed into a Tivoli-like recreation center. Jerry wanted HOK leaders to have a place after every day's meeting for more conversation over drinks and dinner. This would give them extra time to digest and discuss details of the unfolding strategy. Union Station had the advantage of being on nobody's home turf and provided the perfect environment. Plus, it reminded everyone what inspiring work HOK could do. Sometimes you must set the stage and provide the perfect backdrop if you want to announce a major initiative.

Bill Valentine and I flew to St. Louis with our market-practice leaders and met everyone from the other offices, ready for three days of hard work. Jerry opened the workshop by describing the growth of market practices and the potential for more success if we organized those practices across the firm. He highlighted examples of the justice practices in St. Louis, San Francisco, and Washington, DC, which operated as three separate groups, with no overall strategy for winning or doing work together. Other market practices were the same. Aviation was scattered in three offices, and each group operated separately. Jerry's message was simple, elegant, and compelling: Market practices would be more successful if we organized them as firm-wide practices, sharing leads for new work and sharing the best talent between offices.

Jerry's strategy placed clients first—where they belong—giving them the benefit of the best HOK team for every project, regardless of geography. But his plan required major changes. The current HOK structure was office-centric. Leaders in each office were responsible for all the people in their office, from hiring to project assignments, annual evaluations to levels of compensation. Jerry's strategy would require sharing those responsibilities with newly appointed market leaders, a big change to the central role of office principals.

After laying out his strategy, Jerry didn't give orders or issue mandates. His approach was to let everyone in the room work it out, trusting that we were all good people who would put HOK first. But his faith in the assembled HOK leaders to sort things out would be challenged. Our assignment for the next three days was to choose who should lead each market practice, then work out the details of how to share leadership decisions between offices and firm-wide market practices. Discussions continued all day, into dinner . . . and after.

As we grappled with how to organize firm-wide market practices, we gave some attention to what they should be called. How about focus groups? No, that sounds like modern psychology, we realized! Well then, how about centers of excellence, someone proposed. Ron Labinski from HOK Sport was in attendance and looked thoughtful. He said, "Well, if we called them centers of excellence and there was a problem with one of the buildings, we might get sued. The client's attorney would have a field day with the term centers of excellence. He would read out loud from Webster's dictionary during the trial and describe excellence as free of flaws—meaning we would be in big trouble." Ron sat back, rubbed his chin thoughtfully and said, "Well, I guess we could call them *centers of pretty good!*" Everyone laughed and the mood of the meeting brightened considerably. Ron had told us in a humorous way that getting the right name was not as important as getting the right relationship between specialized teams and regional offices.

Nearly everyone at the meeting understood the need for specialization and supported the concept of firm-wide market practices. Ideally, the overlap between regional offices and specialty teams would smooth out workflow among offices. Better yet, when an office experienced a slowdown in local work, many of its people would still be working in their specialty for a project in another locale. It all made sense on paper, but for the regional office leaders, it was difficult to give up control—and potentially revenue.

When it came time to decide which office should host each firm-wide market practice, every office volunteered to be the host. No one wanted to be left out, and there were plenty of comments like, "We should have the aviation group in our office. Even though we don't do airport work now, we have three airports in our city, and the office doing airport work only has one. Why is the aviation group located there?" The founders' goal of "collaboration inside" was being sorely tested.

The three-day workshop ended with full agreement about the *benefits* of reorganizing our specialized groups into firm-wide market practices, but with some sharp disagreements about the *details* of the plan. Who would lead each firm-wide market practice? Which office would host each one? How were project teams to be organized for each project?

Jerry had launched us in a brilliant direction. Emphasizing design specialties was the key for our future but required leadership for success. Jerry and his ExCom partners, King Graf and Bill Valentine, believed enforcing compliance with the updated matrix strategy was heavy-handed and would fail. Instead they had faith that office leaders would eventually see the merits of the firm-wide market practice strategy and adopt it on their own.

This belief in the good in people and hesitance to enforce compliance was well-intended but led to some chaotic years. Project specialists and regional offices sometimes worked well together and sometimes didn't. One office might hire someone to lead healthcare work even if there was no healthcare project at the time. When a healthcare project emerged, the office leaders would tell the healthcare market leaders, "We already have a healthcare expert in our office and don't need you," and keep the work for their own office.

I learned that when you are making a big organizational shift, explaining the concept is only the beginning. You need a structure of support and concrete consequences for nonadopters, otherwise real change won't happen. In this case, office leaders paid lip service to the firm-wide market-practices concept, but resisted real change, preferring to keep things as they were.

Firm-Wide Retreats

Jerry Sincoff saw that making market practices firm-wide and equal to the offices was only partly successful. Getting offices to voluntarily cooperate with each other and share specialized experts was always going to be difficult. He concluded that office and market leaders needed more time together to work out the details of their relationships. Many office and market leaders didn't even know each other, and Jerry wanted a forum where they could spend time together and build bonds of friendship. We weren't even friends, let alone the big, extended family the founders had wanted. Jerry believed fixing this was the first step to firm-wide collaboration.

Jerry and the ExCom organized the first-ever HOK leadership retreat in October 1994 and invited 90 leaders from every office and market practice to the Lake of the Ozarks, a recreation area near St. Louis. After welcoming everyone, Jerry described how important it was to our future to make market practices firm-wide. He acknowledged that we had not fully embraced the goal of sharing specialists and projects, and said his goal for the retreat was for all of us to become friends. His vision was that if we knew and liked each other, we would work together to fully implement the firm-wide market-practice strategy.

Jerry brought along a facilitator who organized team-building exercises for the first day. I vividly remember the first exercise at an outdoor tennis court. The facilitator lined us up, blindfolded us, then placed a rope in our hands and asked us to form a perfect square without letting go of the rope. The purpose of the exercise was to learn cooperation, but the result was chaos. People were yelling and hollering at each other, with no one leading. I heard someone yell, "I'm trying to make a corner!" Someone else said, "Let's count off equal numbers of people for each side of the square!" Several other people shouted out ideas, but they were lost in the general confusion.

Some people laughed at these exercises outright; others were completely turned off. I told Bill Valentine, who was next to me, "This is stupid. We're not getting anywhere." Bill was laughing hysterically. When he stopped laughing, he said, "HOK people are good people and will eventually work this out." His hope that people would catch on to what was expected of them remained just a hope. The exercise demonstrated, once again, that the culture of collaboration fostered by the founders had been diluted by growth. We were 40 years into HOK's history, and many people at the retreat did not know the founders or HOK culture. I concluded that it takes more than team-building exercises to build a team.

The next day we tried again, developing rules of engagement to support firm-wide market practices such as, "Treat each other with respect," or "I recognize the need to support market practices across the firm." After the retreat, a team refined the list and published it as the *HOK OneFirm User Guide*. The document was useless. It takes more than a user guide to guide a team.

. . . it takes more than team-building exercises to build a team . . . It takes more than a user guide to guide a team.

The most revealing part of the retreat occurred in the big meeting room when everyone spoke candidly about implementing the new firm-wide market-practices strategy. One office leader said, "If I send my best airport guy to another office, I'm worried that he won't ever come back. I won't be able to market airport work while he's gone—and the other office will poach him from me." He and other office leaders were describing a basic conflict between the goal of firm-wide market practices and individual offices.

Jerry was still hopeful. On the last day of the retreat, he asked everyone to endorse the new rules of engagement established during the meetings. Then Jerry went around the room and asked each of us, one after the other, to support the new firm-wide market-practices strategy. Every leader said yes, but many added qualifiers. "I'm in favor—but have reservations" . . . "I think it is a good idea but am not sure how it will work in my office." I overheard an office leader tell one of his colleagues, "I bet that SOB over there has his fingers crossed behind his back!" For all their good intentions, office leaders could not find their way to putting HOK first and their office second. The Ozark Retreat did help HOK leaders get acquainted, but HOK's office-centric structure held back full implementation of the new firm-wide market-practices strategy. In fact, some offices continued as if the retreat had never happened.

The ExCom decided HOK needed still another retreat, and, in 1996, hosted HOK leaders at a conference center near Dallas. This time there were no goofy exercises. Instead, HOK leaders developed a teamwork statement over the course of several days. During our concluding session, Jerry asked each HOK leader to sign an enlarged version of the statement in the presence of the other leaders. This effort was optimistic, but little changed after the retreat. Office leaders had learned that even if they didn't cooperate, there were no consequences.

The firm held two more leadership retreats, at Las Colinas, near Dallas, in 1997 and in Cancun, Mexico, in 2001. The level of cooperation between offices and market practices improved, but not enough. The goal of full cooperation across offices to make market practices firm-wide was still in the future. Perhaps the biggest benefit of the retreats was getting HOK leaders together so they knew each other.

Offices Push Back

Remember how the founders and early employees showed mutual respect? And how HOK leaders would suggest a course of action rather than commanding employees to do something, even though it really was a politely worded order? This respectful, non-authoritarian way of communicating continued to work well in St. Louis, and in San Francisco, which had been founded by transplants from St. Louis. But it did not work well in many offices, especially newer ones.

As the firm grew, and the next trio of executives emerged, they still utilized this same method of suggesting rather than telling how to proceed. However, since the HOK culture of collaboration had been diluted by growth, it didn't work. Some leaders understood and took the firm-wide market-practices suggestion seriously, doing their best to cooperate with other offices and building specialists. Other leaders had never been to St. Louis and didn't understand that what might seem like suggestions were really orders. They began to ignore ExCom "suggestions" and make their own decisions. If you are going to adopt a subtle communication style meant to demonstrate mutual respect, you had better find a way to explain it to new hires as you grow your firm.

Worse yet, some offices began pursuing work without checking to see if other HOK offices were pursuing the same client or project. I once received a call from a client saying, "I met with your office last week, and today another HOK office asked for a meeting." In one embarrassing example, representatives from an HOK office called on a client. When they stepped into his office and exchanged business cards, he said, "The name HOK rings a bell . . . oh yes, your colleagues from the Dallas office were here yesterday." Never let your branch offices compete with each other in pursuit of work. It's counterproductive—not to mention embarrassing.

Many of the offices—Kansas City, London, New York, Dallas, Los Angeles, and others—began to drift, feeling they were independent. Some leaders began to put their offices first and HOK second, operating quasi-independently. Disputes over clients, projects, and territories began to spring up, particularly between St. Louis and New York. Who gets the work in Ohio? Pennsylvania? Rivalry between offices meant we weren't putting our best foot forward. We certainly weren't "collaborating inside in order to compete outside," as the founders had envisioned, nor were we helping each other to succeed.

While some offices were practically ignoring their HOK connection, others were doing the reverse, leveraging their HOK reputation to seek work for which they had no experience. For example, one office won a healthcare project on the strength of the HOK brand, but no one in the office had healthcare experience. The office leaders planned to fake their way through it rather than leveraging firm-wide market practices. The ExCom did intervene in that instance, requiring the office to partner with healthcare experts in another office. Without intervention, the project would have been a disaster and damaged the HOK healthcare reputation. As your own firm's reputation for different building types grows, make sure all branches tap into the experts responsible for that reputation, so they don't damage it irreparably.

Chapter 14: To Design a World-Class Firm

1. Never forget that doing quality work is the best marketing. Quality of work is more important than quantity of work.
2. Seek out large clients with ongoing needs. Do a top notch job and you will earn repeat business.
3. Understand that sometimes to win big clients, you must be—and look—big yourself.
4. Consider organizing your architects by design specialty—aviation, healthcare, hospitality—rather than by geographic office location.
5. Create concrete consequences for nonadopters, when you are making a big organizational shift; otherwise real change won't happen.
6. Remember that it takes more than team-building exercises to build a true team and more than a user guide to guide that team.
7. Protect your hard-earned reputation in a building type. Insist firm-wide experts be included in each new project regardless of which branch won the contract.

CHAPTER 15

A Firm-Wide Role

When Jerry Sincoff became CEO, I continued as managing principal for the San Francisco office. By now, that meant a lot more than just managing projects in the Bay Area. We were occupied with a great deal of aviation work in Saudi Arabia, plus projects in Asia—especially in Hong Kong; Tokyo; and Jakarta, Indonesia. The Los Angeles Office remained a branch of San Francisco, so I was responsible for our projects there, too. Bill Valentine and I regularly traveled to all these places, plus to St. Louis. Bill went back to the mother ship for regular ExCom meetings with Jerry and King. I flew there twice a year for board meetings. Soon, I would be heading to St. Louis just as often as Bill. More on that shortly.

Innovating in Silicon Valley

Amid all the exotic international projects, there was something just as exciting going on closer to home. When the nation's tech companies started designing products that would change the world, many of them chose HOK to design the buildings where they invented those products. America's tech hub was shaping up from Stanford University all the way down to San Jose. It wasn't called Silicon Valley yet. We still called it the "South Bay" and HOK San Francisco had been active in this area since the 1970s.

That's when the Xerox corporation commissioned HOK to design a new research facility on a hillside next to Stanford University. Gyo Obata, with help from Bill Valentine, designed the Xerox Palo Alto Research Center (PARC) as a series of cascading steps down the hillside with a succession of landscaped terraces. I wish we could take the credit, but it was at PARC that scientists created the personal computer, the Internet—and more. The groundbreaking innovations at PARC are what spurred the creation of legions of new companies and cemented Silicon Valley as a force in American and international business. Lucky for us, we were involved from the start. If you can get in on the ground floor of a new center of industry, do it—whether it's high tech in Silicon Valley or biotech in Boston.

HOK went on to design Silicon Valley buildings for Adobe, Sun Microsystems, Symantec, Octel, Hewlett Packard, Advanced Micro Devices, Nortel—and more. These were exactly the kinds of big, important clients Jerry Sincoff wanted to have. Plus, one tech company contract tended to lead to another, the "unbroken chain" Obata had envisioned. But no project was more significant than when we got the opportunity to design an entire campus for Apple. It almost didn't happen.

On a Thursday in the early 1990s, Bill Valentine received a call from Bob McIntire, the gruff head of facilities for Apple. "We just bought a piece of land in Cupertino for our new headquarters, and we want you give us some master planning ideas," Bob said. "But please understand—we are only talking to HOK about a master plan. We will interview other architects for the design work." Bill agreed to put together some master planning concepts to show him the following Tuesday. Bill procrastinated and didn't work on the master plan over the weekend, as he normally would have—maybe because he was unhappy with McIntire's "master plan only" message. Instead, he started brainstorming on Monday, just one day before the meeting.

Instead of drawing something up, Bill elected to create a scale model of the site. He had developed a clever technique where he used an aerial photo as a base. I called it a "Valentine Special." This innovation really helped clients visualize his ideas. Building from the aerial photo, Bill could make a model fast, using lightweight foam to represent the buildings, colored paper for roadways, and lots of magic markers to denote other details. Bill arranged his foam Apple Headquarters like a college campus, with six buildings of four stories each grouped around an elongated oval of green space. This park-like common area would be accessible to all Apple employees.

Bill brought the model to McIntire's office wrapped in plastic, and, as he unwrapped it, the 3-foot-square model was so light it floated down and alighted on McIntire's desk. As the colorful model landed, McIntire said, "Give me that!" and walked out of his office without another word, leaving Bill to wonder what had just happened. About a half hour passed before McIntire returned. He placed the model back on his desk. "Forget all that crap about interviewing other architects," he said. Then he pointed to the site model. "We want that, and we want it right now!" And that's how HOK got the job—the whole job.

Apple would occupy that headquarters for decades. It represented the culmination of Bill Valentine's design thinking. Apple had expected an arrangement of buildings and parking, but instead got a headquarters with a heart. Clustering buildings around a central common was vintage Valentine. He believed green space was both soothing and inspiring. And, indeed, Steve Jobs and Apple developed the iPhone, the iPad and many other iconic products on that campus—and announced them to the world in our Moscone Center.

FIGURE 15.1 Apple Headquarters, Cupertino, California.
Source: Photo by John Sutton. Photo courtesy of HOK.

Doubling Your Reach

Whether working at home or abroad, I was grateful to be busy, because it meant HOK and the San Francisco office were a financial success. My own duties had grown, and I needed a savvy executive assistant to manage my schedule, my travel, and help with my responsibilities. I had various assistants over the years, but no one who really "got" me and could function as my right arm—or left, since I'm left-handed.

I asked the San Francisco HR director to conduct a search for the right candidate. In early 1995, I interviewed Susie Becker, a young Bay Area woman with good experience, first in banking and more recently working for the San Francisco office of developer Gerald Hines. Susie was bright, enthusiastic, and professional. She wanted a career, not a job, and was interested in HOK and our work. She was to become a wonderful addition—incredibly diligent and steadfastly loyal.

On her first day, Susie discovered several boxes of old files under her desk and asked if she could move them somewhere else. I said, "Let's see what they are. Maybe we don't need them." Susie went through the boxes and discovered the files were very old. After looking them over I told her she could throw them out. She said later, "When you told me I could throw out those files, I knew I was going to like this job!" It may sound simplistic, but Susie is a forward-looking woman of action and those files represented the dusty past.

I discovered Susie was eager to learn about everything I did at HOK. The more she learned the more helpful she became. Susie read my mind—and sometimes saved me from myself. She became so good at anticipating my needs that she doubled my reach. Susie continued as my miracle-worker assistant for the next 22 years—and remains at HOK to this day. I often wonder why I wasted all those years without a truly effective assistant. I can't do it over, but you can, so I urge you to take the time to find the right executive assistant from the start, one who will double your reach.

Overseas Adventures

Since I was now in charge of our Asia efforts, I had to travel there, and it's a long way to go, so I usually visited several HOK offices each time. For one memorable trip, I first flew to Tokyo, then to our new office in Shanghai, then finally to Hong Kong, landing at the old Kai Taki Airport across the harbor from Hong Kong Island. I avoided Hong Kong taxis. They were small and sure to end up on the losing end of a car accident. Instead, I asked Susie to book a hotel car belonging to the Grand Hyatt, which was my preferred hotel near our Hong Kong office.

Crashing in Hong Kong

It was hotter than blazes, and as I got in the car, the driver offered me a Perrier, and the man who opened the door handed me a copy of the Asian *Wall Street Journal*. To be honest, I was jet lagged and it was all a bit fancier than I was used to, so I got distracted and forgot to put my seatbelt on. I was sitting there reading and enjoying the water, while the driver made his way through the harbor tunnel to the Hong Kong side. We emerged from the tunnel onto a very congested elevated roadway and were probably going 35–40 miles per hour. My driver either fell asleep or had a momentary lapse and plowed into the back of a flatbed truck that was stopped in traffic. I looked up just in time to see the back of the flatbed crash through my side of the front windshield.

Everything seemed to be in slow motion as I watched the glass shatter inward. The checker plate steel on the back of the flatbed truck was headed right for my face. At the last second, the front of our car struck the rear axle of the truck and we stopped abruptly. Or, our car did. Since I wasn't wearing my seatbelt, I flew like a shot into the seat in front of me, ending up in a crumpled heap on the floor—and under the extended flat bed of the truck.

An ambulance came and took the driver and me to a Chinese hospital. I sat on a gurney in a hallway for quite a while, waiting. Turns out, they were looking for a doctor who could speak English. Finally, a doctor came and said, "Hello, my name is Dr. Toh." To me, it sounded like Dr. "Toe." I replied, "I think I need Dr. Ankle!" I guess I was in enough shock that it didn't hurt too much and I could crack a joke. He smiled and sent me for X-rays. The images showed I had broken the fibula and ankle of my right leg.

The doctor was honest and said he was not an orthopedic surgeon and couldn't fix my leg. Instead he put me in a temporary cast to keep my ankle stable until I could get home and see a good orthopedist in the United States.

Then he sent me to get fitted for crutches. The small Chinese man in charge took one look at this big American and started shaking his head. The standard Chinese crutches were too short for me. While muttering to himself, he got out a hand saw, cut two new, longer pieces of wood, and attached them to the crutches as extenders to accommodate my height.

By then, the Grand Hyatt had learned what had happened and sent me yet another hotel car—their biggest, longest limo, driven by their best, most careful driver—for the short drive to the Grand Hyatt. I had just arrived at my hotel room when Frank Whitcomb, the managing principal of our Hong Kong office, arrived with Bill Valentine, who was there working on a Hong Kong project. I told them my story, then added that my leg had really begun to hurt. Bill asked, "Did the doctor give you anything for the pain?" He hadn't.

"I know just the thing," Whitcomb said. He opened the mini bar in my room, pulled out two little bottles of Johnnie Walker Red Label scotch, poured them into a glass with a couple of ice cubes, and said, "Sip this. I *guarantee* in 20 minutes it won't hurt!" I didn't believe him—and the scotch tasted awful—but he was right! I didn't feel drunk, but I didn't feel any pain either. In fact, I felt so good—and so hungry—that I suggested we go downstairs to dinner. I am a scotch drinker to this day.

The hotel paid for everything, including that dinner and a first class ticket back to the United States. A third hotel car took me back to the airport, and the Hong Kong health service met me with a wheelchair. As I prepared to use my crutches to enter the plane and find my seat, the health representative said, "You must give the crutches back to me! They are the property of Hong Kong health services!" I couldn't believe it, but I gave up my crutches and literally hopped on one foot to my seat. When my flight arrived at San Francisco airport, my wife Jeanne met me and took me straight to an orthopedic surgeon, who said he needed to operate on me immediately. I was in surgery a short time later and am forever grateful that it all worked out.

After I returned home, HOK hired a service called "WeDriveU," where a driver chauffeurs you around in your own car. As I have said, the firm takes care of its people. That same person also carried my bags and belongings, because, let me tell you, it is impossible to carry things while you're on crutches. About a week later, I was back on another airplane, this time to an HOK board meeting in St. Louis.

Arrested in Saudi Arabia

I seem to get into trouble in and around airports. On a trip to Jeddah, Saudi Arabia to meet with the Aviation Ministry about the airport master plan, I got arrested. I was there with Ron Thompson, a member of the HOK Aviation Group. Our meeting with Air Ministry officials took place in their offices at the Jeddah airport. After the meeting, they offered to give us a tour of the new hajj terminal, built for Muslim pilgrims on their way to visit the holy city of Mecca. We accepted, and our hosts gave us visitor badges for the five-mile drive to the hajj terminal.

Our Air Ministry guide was an expat from Scotland who spoke with such a burr he was difficult to understand. My colleague, Ron, was originally from Ireland, so as we drove, I learned a new category of jokes featuring the Scots and the Irish. But what was soon to happen was no joke. SOM designed the hajj terminal to look like a series of giant Bedouin tents, with a huge expanse of fiberglass fabric stretched across giant poles held fast by large steel cables. The edge of the tent was so high that jumbo jets could park with their noses inside to shade passengers entering or leaving the planes.

The annual pilgrimage was winding down, so only a few hajjis were present, along with a large contingent of soldiers to keep order. Ron Thompson, a true aviation enthusiast, wanted to see everything, and asked if we could view the terminal from the outside. Our guide was happy to show us, so we walked through a boarding gate with a door to the outside. As we exited, I noticed a young Saudi soldier with a submachine gun watching us closely. Our guide told him, "I just want to show them the outside, then we'll be back." The young Saudi seemed to nod, and out we went.

We geeked out on the external view of the building, as architects will do, and then returned through the same door. The soldier said something to us in Arabic, which we did not understand, so we continued walking. Mistake! Next, he shouted at us and this time we stopped. We didn't understand Arabic, but we understood shouting. With his submachine gun clutched in his hand, he signaled that he wanted to see our badges. Our Aviation Ministry guide had a green badge, while our visitor badges were red. The guard communicated with hand gestures that our host was free to leave, but Ron and I were not. We were dumbfounded. "What did we do wrong?"

The soldier saw our confusion and pointed his submachine gun at the door we had just gone through. Finally, we figured out that when we went through the door to the outside, we left Saudi Arabia for international territory. That was acceptable, but when we returned, we were entering Saudi Arabia from international territory—without the proper ID. Our guide did his best to talk the soldier out of detaining us, but it was no use. The more he tried, the more agitated the soldier got and the more he waved his gun around. Our host eventually decided to drive back to the Aviation Ministry and return with an Arabic-speaking official. We agreed and he left us with the soldier.

Ron and I sat in a couple of chairs under the watchful eye of our young captor, who seemed to be waiting for his superior to arrive. I was content to wait, but Ron was not. "This is ridiculous," he huffed. "I'm just going to get up and walk out of here." Ron stood up and took maybe one step before the young Saudi soldier pointed his submachine gun at the two of us and shouted something in Arabic. I didn't speak Arabic, but the message was loud and clear: "Sit down and shut up!" I yelled to Ron, "Sit down! Do you want to get shot?" The soldier was probably only 18 or 19 years old and he seemed nervous, which made me nervous. Ron sat down and stayed down.

We waited for the better part of an hour until finally our guide returned. He brought both a Saudi army official and a Saudi Air Ministry official, figuring that's what it was going to take to set us free. They spoke to the young soldier in Arabic, and I could tell from his gestures that he was explaining we had entered Saudi Arabia illegally, and he was under orders to detain anyone who did. With the right officials speaking the right language, it was all straightened out in a few minutes, but we were still shaken. It was a reminder that working in foreign lands brought HOK great opportunities, but also exotic challenges.

Joining the ExCom

I had been on the HOK board for some time, but the major decisions happened in the much-smaller Executive Committee. Jerry Sincoff, King Graf, and Bill Valentine had decided to add new members to the ExCom in anticipation of King's plan to retire at age 65. After some deliberation, they invited Larry Self and me to join the ExCom and called each of us with the news. I was delighted with opportunity to help shape the future of HOK. Larry, who was in London, was just as excited. Larry and I began to meet regularly with Jerry, King, and Bill. I chose to remain in San Francisco to be close to clients there and a bit closer to clients in Asia. Larry Self remained in London for a few years before relocating to St. Louis.

I had always wondered how it would feel to attend an ExCom meeting. The topics were heady, ranging from implementing Jerry Sincoff's three strategies to fixing problems in a broken office. HOK held most ExCom meetings in St. Louis, so Bill Valentine and I flew in from San Francisco and remained there for several days each time. Larry Self had to travel the longest distance, from London. The ExCom also had telephone meetings, but these were at irregular intervals.

More intense meetings occurred at the end of the fiscal year, when we met to discuss the size of the annual bonus pool as well as annual raises and promotions. CFO Bob Pratzel and HR director John Mahon often participated if we were going to discuss financial or personnel issues. Sometimes Paul Watson attended to advise on legal matters. Yes, original attorney Paul Watson was still with us, more proof that HOK was a place where people could build satisfying careers that lasted decades.

Voicing My Opinions

Jerry Sincoff continued to pursue growth above all, and welcomed fresh ideas for forming new HOK offices, market practices, or services. For example, people in the HOK Tampa office created a specialized design service for the entertainment industry called HOK Entertainment. They believed entertainment businesses like Disney World, as well as big hotels offering live entertainment, like those in Las Vegas, would be potential clients. Another group established a small construction firm, HOK Construction. And so on.

The creativity was beautiful, but the execution could be ugly. Lots of HOK people put ideas forward for new offices or new market practices, but just because they had ideas did not always mean they had the leadership ability to turn them into successful practices. This is an important point: Ideas are not enough. You must have the know-how to execute them. Failing offices and struggling market practices became a drag on the rest of the firm. Although some offices consistently maintained a good reputation and made money, others struggled to establish a good reputation and lost money.

For a while, firm-wide growth once again masked the weakness of individual offices and certain market practices. But underneath the growth, HOK was a patchwork of profitable and unprofitable sections. Cash flow became an issue again. Some offices billed and collected fees on time, but others did not. Unprofitable offices were the biggest problem. Even if they billed and collected fees, the revenue they brought in was not enough to pay their way. Collaboration between offices was still uneven, despite the retreats, with some offices working in concert and others not at all. The HOK culture of helping each other to succeed was eroding.

Jerry, Bill, Larry, and I discussed what to do about failing offices during ExCom meetings. They don't teach you this stuff in architecture school. I believed we needed to establish some simple financial metrics for offices to follow and insist on their compliance. I brought up the same issue at every meeting and became a thorn in everyone's side. Jerry and Bill were natural optimists and believed good HOK people would eventually figure things out without formal metrics. They worried that metrics were too rigid for creative people, and would cause them to either sidestep the rules or leave the firm. By contrast, I saw myself as a pragmatist and wanted to find a balance between creativity and responsibility. I still believe it can be done.

I believed we needed to establish some simple financial metrics for offices to follow and insist on their compliance.

I was a lone voice for a long time. Bill Valentine often said, "You can't *make* people do something; you have to help them want to do it." He had a great point—very similar to that famous Dwight Eisenhower quote—but how? It would be a few years before I would get the opportunity to find an answer to that question.

Chapter 15: To Design a World-Class Firm

1. Get in on the ground floor of a new center of industry.
2. Help clients really see your vision, by creating a simple 3-D model.
3. Take the time to find the right executive assistant, one who will double your reach.
4. Remember that new ideas are not enough. You must have the know-how and leadership ability to execute them successfully.
5. Beware that firm-wide growth can mask failing offices and specialties, just as it does sloppy operations and poor cash flow.

CHAPTER 16

Embracing Technology

When I joined HOK in 1967, architects drew all their designs by hand on paper or Mylar. Computers were still in the future, although a few large, room-sized computers were in use by the government and some academic institutions. The personal computer revolution did not begin until 1981 and PCs were first used for word processing, then for spreadsheets. In 1982, Autodesk was among the first companies to offer computer-aided design or "CAD" software.

Computer-Aided Design

Obata looked at CAD technology and said, "This is to help draft. We need something to help us design." HOK continued to be interested in innovation and hired a small programming staff to create custom software for the design process. The program HOK DRAW was ready for use by 1983 and enthusiastically adopted around the firm. Early PCs were not powerful enough to support HOK DRAW, which ran on UNIX servers, large computers located in a special air-conditioned room in each office. Computers were still a novelty, and the HOK San Francisco computer room had a large glass viewing window where we took clients during tours of our office.

HOK DRAW was so successful that HOK began to sell the program to other architects. HOK created a new version of DRAW for the emerging Windows operating system in 1993 called DrawVision. But HOK was a design firm, not a technology company. Autodesk and other companies began to offer newer versions of their software that matched or exceeded DrawVision's capabilities. Obata eventually decided to freeze further DrawVision development and sales, although the firm used both HOK DRAW and DrawVision for many more years. It was a good reminder that you should innovate early and often, but you also need to recognize when it's better to stick to your core competencies.

HOK adopted AutoCAD software in 1996, although some people continued to use DrawVision for a few more years. The transition from drawing by hand to creating buildings by computer took longer than the software transition.

Tech 2000

I had been interested in computer technology from the beginning, so I kept a close eye on all this. Like all firms, HOK was at the beginning of a technology transition. Younger employees were usually the first to use computers, whereas many older employees continued to draw by hand. Although every office used HOK DRAW and DrawVision, some offices also began to buy software from Autodesk or Bentley Systems. Some clients began to ask for drawings created using specific software, so the HOK office serving that client bought still more software. At the same time, HOK accountants, administrators, and marketers adopted Apple Macintosh computers for budgets, word processing, and producing proposals.

By the mid-1990s, technology at HOK was a mass of confusion, with three operating systems: a mix of Unix workstations, Windows PCs, and Macintosh computers. Technology use was office-centric, and no firm-wide strategy existed. It did not take a genius to see technology was getting better every day and would soon transform HOK's organization and how we would design and produce projects. The confusion of computers, operating systems, and software around the firm was a hindrance to progress that we needed to address. We also needed a firm-wide strategy for systems like email instead of leaving it to individual offices to set up different programs. As the newest member of the ExCom, I brought up the need for a firm-wide technology strategy. My colleagues "rewarded" me by giving me the responsibility to lead the effort. The task suited my organized, structured personality perfectly. If you're going to raise your hand and say that the firm needs to do something, be prepared to be asked to do it yourself!

I asked three HOK people to join me in forming a committee to study technology and make recommendations. Ken Young, the San Francisco IT leader, was an architect who had become deeply interested in technology. Ken Herold was trained in architecture and technology, and HOK had originally hired him to develop HOK DRAW. Hal Kantner was the leader of graphic design in Houston and brought his special knowledge of technology for work processes.

We met regularly in my San Francisco office to review the current level of technology at HOK. We began to explore a series of technology options, and brought in experts from outside the firm for advice. Susie, my new assistant, arranged each meeting and kept track of our deliberations and decisions. Over the next six months we created a five-year program to bring technology to HOK, partly to spread the large investment over several years, but mostly to give people time to adjust to a new way of working. The time period concluded in the year 2000, so of course we named our strategy Tech 2000, and I shared a summary with my ExCom colleagues:

Computers: Issue a computer to every employee—desktops for most people and laptops for road warriors. This sounds obvious in retrospect but was a big initiative—and expense—at the time.

Operating System: Reduce the number of operating systems from three to one. We recommended Microsoft Windows because most of the available CAD programs ran on Windows.

Network: Build a Local Area Network (LAN) in every office, enabling teams of people to share project files. Build a Wide Area Network (WAN) to connect all the HOK offices together. The WAN would, for the first time, enable people in different offices to work together on the same project. The WAN also enabled Central Accounting, legal, and HR employees to support people and projects in every office.

Email: Establish a firm-wide email system for all employees with a common address protocol: firstname.lastname@hok.com. Although it sounds quaint in retrospect, this was a huge step forward, giving everyone in HOK the ability to communicate with clients, consultants, and each other. All you needed to know was a fellow employee's name and you could email them.

Phone: Establish one firm-wide phone system, including voice mail. Several offices already had voice mail systems from different vendors, but they were incompatible with each other.

Website: Create an HOK website to showcase our best projects. The website would become our new front door where clients and others could learn about HOK.

Digital Images: Digitize the more than 10,000 project images in the HOK slide library and make them available online for everyone at HOK.

Intranet: Create an internal HOK website for employees, filled with information about HOK projects, offices, people, and more. Could technology bring us together at last?

My ExCom colleagues were intrigued but concerned about the cost of moving HOK to a unified technology strategy. When he heard that I wanted to issue every single employee a computer, Jerry Sincoff said, "Patrick, that's going to cost a lot of money." I said, "Yes it will, but technology will help people be more productive—and technology is cheaper than people." I also argued that buying the best, most up-to-date technology is not spending money, it is investing money—an argument I recommend to anyone pushing for a vital technology upgrade. Things like personal computers, email, and websites are now old news, but the same principles apply to whatever cutting edge technology your firm may be considering.

My fellow ExCom members also wondered how people would react to the hassle of a transition. Would some employees freak out when their Macintosh computer was replaced by a computer running Microsoft Windows? How would older employees react to the learning curve of a brand new desktop computer? I also argued that we needed to view Tech 2000 as more than a set of technology goals. It was a strategy to stitch HOK together with technology and common systems. On its own it was not enough to unify the firm, but it was a beginning. The ExCom agreed, approved Tech 2000, and asked me to oversee implementation.

My first task was to explain Tech 2000, beginning with the board of directors, then evangelizing it in every office. Almost everyone was enthusiastic, but some people were intimidated by the challenge of learning how to use a computer. Others were reluctant to give up their Macintosh computers and resisted until a new Windows computer arrived at their desk. One accounting employee was so distraught at losing her Macintosh that she resigned, but most employees made the transition with a minimum of grumbling.

Remember, my group had studied not just computer needs but other technologies. For example, HOK maintained a master slide library in St. Louis, housed in a locked room and guarded and preserved zealously by a slide librarian. When someone asked for a slide, she created a duplicate from the master slide collection and sent it by overnight courier. We proposed to digitize this master slide collection.

Spending the time and money to digitize historic hard-copy assets is worthwhile so they are easily accessible and so your firm's history is preserved forever. Nevertheless, it was a long, tedious project. The librarian sent batches of master slides to a St. Louis vendor, which scanned, color-corrected, and removed scratches and other imperfections from them. Next, the librarian loaded the new digital images into a powerful HOK server and placed them in project folders. The entire conversion project took several years, but after that anyone in HOK could gain access to perfect project images.

Bill Valentine did not want to use the new digital images. He liked computers but *loved* his Kodak Carousel slide projector. Bill did a comparison test by projecting a slide image onto a screen next to a digital image. The slide image looked much better. Digital projectors were in their infancy and the digital images looked washed out compared to the slides. Bill continued to use his Kodak Carousel projector. As a technology true-believer, I did not give up. I pointed out the annoying flaws with slide projectors: the bulb tended to burn out during presentations; slides were sometimes upside down; and if the locking ring wasn't locked, slides ended up on the floor. Bill continued to do it his way—and the yin and yang of our relationship continued as always.

Bill Valentine was in St. Louis one day when Gyo Obata called him over to his desk, saying, "Take a look at this! Someone showed me how to pick digital images and put them in PowerPoint—it's so easy!" When Obata gave up slides, there was no way Bill could keep using them, and he finally retired his slide projector. Fortunately, digital projectors had improved by that time.

Two of my colleagues who helped shape the Tech 2000 vision received promotions in 1996. Ken Young became CIO (chief information officer), in charge of technology and training. Ken Herold became chief knowledge officer (CKO), with responsibility for developing and populating the HOK website and Intranet. HOK launched the Intranet in 1998 and its website in January 2000. Today, the website has become a virtual HOK front door, and the intranet is packed with information to help employees do their jobs.

HOK launched firm-wide email shortly after it adopted Tech 2000, relying on email servers in each office. The email system was an immediate success and grew quickly. One casualty was the fax machine, that mythical technology that had blown our minds in the 1970s when we were trying to coordinate with our partners in Alaska. Like people everywhere, we found sending an email with an attachment infinitely easier than sending a fax. HOK moved its email system to a cloud-based system in 2002, the beginning of a trend to move more HOK data to the cloud. You can't rest on your laurels with technology. Since it is ever-changing you must constantly evolve too.

Tech 2000 was expensive and challenging—and transformational. HOK joined the digital era. But more important, Tech 2000 became a kind of digital glue, helping HOK pull diverse offices together with a firm-wide strategy. I had hoped it would help. The initiative exceeded my expectations.

Going Paperless

I have always been organized. For me it is second nature and part of everything in my life and work. But my HOK duties were a test of my organizational skills. As a project manager I had worked with a secretary to document project decisions on paper. That paper was then tucked away in a long, gleaming row of filing cabinets. That was the easy part. The challenge was remembering to access that information later when we needed it. I was bothered by my inability to track important client requests, always thinking back to instances like the female judge who had asked for a white toilet seat and got the black one with a split seat. There seemed to be no efficient way to faithfully record client priorities and then remember to incorporate them into the project.

After the firm approved Tech 2000, HOK issued me my first laptop computer, in late 1995. I learned how to create and save digital files with a few mouse clicks and soon organized my files in folders on the HOK network so I could share them with my team. The big surprise was how easy it was to find a digital file. All it took was a few mouse clicks through a well-organized folder system or a quick search term, compared to digging through mountains of paper.

Using that laptop, I began to experiment with using Microsoft Excel for meeting notes—and everything else I did. Excel accommodated everything I needed: text, graphics, charts, numbers, and images. Every Excel workbook contains different sheets, with tabs for access. It may sound geeky, but I started to categorize the tabs for one project in a single workbook, with meeting notes on one tab, budget on another and client decisions on another. I also learned to hyperlink information from one sheet to another. This way, no client request—for a special toilet seat or anything else—would ever be lost in a mass of paperwork again. Yes, technology is always changing, but I continue to believe this rich use of spreadsheets is very effective and something others should try.

New CIO Ken Young's desk was a few steps from mine, and we talked daily about progress with Tech 2000. Ken suggested, "The future of work should be paperless, and you should set an example for HOK." I accepted Ken's challenge and began to learn to work exclusively digitally. I already used digital files and Outlook for email and contacts. The annoying remaining challenge was my calendar. I maintained three paper calendars: one on my desk, another in my pocket, and a duplicate version at Susie's desk. They *never* matched. Susie and I began to use a shared Outlook calendar and discovered it was blissfully simple. Either of us could schedule meetings, and updates instantly appeared in my calendar, Susie's calendar and my smart phone. Today, we take this technology for granted, but I'm proud to say I was an early adopter. Anyone still using a paper calendar—especially multiple ones—is missing out.

I found going online and paperless was utterly freeing. There was no paper in my office, except a little tray of notepaper to doodle on. I began to encourage others at HOK to go paperless as well. Susie took up the challenge, and particularly enjoyed pitching out yet more paper files. If someone at HOK sent me something on paper, Susie, the gatekeeper, sent it back, saying, "Patrick doesn't accept paper. Please send an electronic file." If someone outside the company sent something on paper that was worth keeping, Susie scanned it into our files. If it sounds a bit militant, I don't apologize for that and think everyone should join my paperless army. When I finished my HOK career after 50 years, all my files fit on a single portable thumb drive. Is going paperless for everyone? I would argue it's for anyone who wants to be truly organized. Going paperless is liberating.

buildingSMART

I came out of architecture school brimming with ambition, like all graduates, and believed design was a special calling to shape the human environment in ennobling ways. Yes, I had grand ideas! As I worked at HOK, I learned architecture was more demanding than other arts. Buildings shouldn't just be pretty. Architects must design buildings to meet client needs, adhere to building codes, fit within a budget—and much more. I also learned design was only the beginning of a long process leading to a finished building. The architect must coordinate the work of engineers and other consultants, document the design with detailed drawings and specifications, and work with the contractor during construction to complete the building.

Around 1990 I began to think about this in a different way. Here was my epiphany: The architect is responsible for orchestrating a vast ocean of information from design through construction. Once again, I came back to my embarrassment over the judge and her white toilet seat—a lost drop in the ocean of information. Was there a better way to capture information without forgetting anything? Shared digital files were a start. Computers were good for calculation and information storage. Could they help manage information in an even better way, all the way from design through construction?

I was not the only one thinking about this possibility. In early 1994, Autodesk representative Ian Howell asked to meet with me in San Francisco to discuss a new initiative. Ian was part of an Autodesk team dedicated to solving the problem of information-sharing across the building industry. His team had developed a promising approach but needed a consortium of firms with real-world experience to test and verify the concept. Ian invited HOK to join the consortium, explaining that our size and geographic reach made us his first choice. I spoke to my ExCom colleagues about the commitment and possible benefits, and gained their support. A successful initiative would help HOK manage and coordinate information—and might even help the entire building industry. When you get the opportunity to help both your own firm and your entire industry, the obvious answer is "Yes!"

I selected Ken Herold as HOK's technical representative for this effort. He was on the team that developed HOK DRAW and helped develop our Tech 2000 strategy. Ken and I attended our first meeting at Autodesk headquarters near San Francisco and met the other members of the consortium. Tishman Construction of New York was the general contractor. Jaros, Baum & Bolles of New York took the engineering slot. Three manufacturers of building equipment were in the consortium: AT&T for building communications systems, Carrier for heating and air conditioning equipment, and Honeywell for building control equipment. Lawrence Berkeley National Laboratory also joined the consortium to contribute their research on energy use in buildings. Autodesk even invited other specialized software companies to join in.

Pursuing Interoperability

After introductions, Ian Howell described the highly fragmented nature of the building industry. Architects, engineers, and contractors each played an essential part in bringing a building from design through construction. And each type of firm used software designed for its own needs, such as CAD programs for architects and scheduling programs for contractors. Of course, architects, engineers, and contractors needed to share information to design and construct a building, but their software programs didn't talk to each other. It was like a modern-day Tower of Babel. We all spoke different "languages" and that resulted in costly errors, delays, and inefficiencies.

Ian proposed that it was possible for our different software systems to talk to each other. He suggested that our goal should be to integrate all project information, from every type of construction profession, so that it was seamless. The idea was to create a kind of universal translator that would help different software systems understand each other. Ian envisioned a time when we would lose as little information as possible in translation. Ian described this concept as interoperability, a term commonly used in the software industry, but new for me.

> [Our] software programs didn't talk to each other. It was like a modern-day Tower of Babel. We all spoke different "languages."

All 12 companies were enthusiastic about our goal and committed to working together. We divided the tasks into projects. Ken Herold and others did most of the technical work, testing, and revising information exchanges. I served on the management team with the other consortium members, meeting monthly to review progress and plan next steps. After one year, we met to assess the results. Our test was a success. We were able to exchange important information between architect, engineer, contractor, and manufacturers seamlessly, with little loss of information.

Here's a simplification of how it worked, using a door in a new building as an example. An architect could create an elevation showing what the door should look like. An engineer could create technical specifications for the fire rating of the door. A door manufacturer could write a catalog telling how much the door cost. All of these would be separate documents—created using different software—but thanks to interoperability, these professionals could all access and understand each other's contributions. And a contractor could come along and view all this information in one place.

Going Global

People from all 12 companies were proud of our accomplishment, but it was just the beginning. After a year of working together, we concluded that our concept would work, but only if a neutral organization led the effort and provided open access for all software providers, not just Autodesk. We also realized that people around the world would want to participate in further development and proposed a world-wide organization with national chapters dedicated to that purpose.

The original 12 consortium companies agreed to form a nonprofit US chapter to continue development and opened the organization to new members. We originally named the new group the Industrial Alliance for Interoperability (IAI). The first word, *Industrial,* was awkward, referring to the fact that it was a group for the building *industry*, and we soon changed it. I was honored when my colleagues elected me chairman of the first IAI chapter. I felt like I was following in George Kassabaum's footsteps, by getting involved to improve our profession.

Ian Howell, Ken Herold, and I took a series of trips to Europe and Asia to share our concept with people in other countries and recruit new chapters. Autodesk arranged the first trip to Europe, with meetings in London, Paris, Munich, Stockholm, and Rome. Turned out, it was mostly an easy sell. In each city, those in attendance enthusiastically received the concept and agreed to form chapters in their country to share development work.

Our last and longest meeting was in Rome. After a translator converted our presentation from English to Italian, one of our hosts said, "Excuse us for a few minutes. We would like to discuss your concept with each other in Italian." This had happened before, so we listened attentively as the Italians began their discussion. A few minutes turned into a long, heated discussion of an hour or more. I had promised Ian and Ken we would tour the Vatican Museum after the meeting, but by the time the shouting had died down and we caught a taxi, the museum had closed for the day.

FIGURE 16.1 buildingSMART logo. Source: Image courtesy of buildingSMART International.

Despite the impassioned Italians, by 1996 IAI chapters were in operation in a dozen countries of Europe and Asia, and we held our first international meeting in London. About a 100 people attended and began to organize our work. One positive outcome of the meeting was a name change. We changed the word *industrial* to *international* and became the International Alliance for Interoperability. In later years, our organization renamed itself again, becoming buildingSMART, with the international office remaining in London, where we held the first meeting. We also adopted a logo designed for us by Ken Herold's wife, Mary. The logo is of four interlocking squares representing design, procurement, construction, and building operations—the life cycle of buildings.

Transitioning to BIM

In the early days of buildingSMART, architects used CAD, which was limited to two dimensions and not much of an improvement over drawing by hand. Later, improved computers at last allowed architects to design buildings in three dimensions using an electronic building model called 3D CAD.

Electronic building models began with architects, but soon engineers, contractors, and building owners found it helpful to embed even more useful information into the building model: How much does that door cost? What is the insulation value of that wall?

All you had to do was click on the door or wall to find out. Adding more information to the building model gave rise to a new term: Building Information Model, or BIM. But how was the raw information in BIM going to be exchanged between thousands of different software products? The mission of buildingSMART evolved to focus on open standards to convey BIM information seamlessly among all participants during building design and construction, and later during building operation.

On a grander scale, BIM became a game changer for sustainable design. Modeling buildings in three dimensions is a necessary first step to designing green. Designers can now model buildings in three dimensions, then use software to adjust the design for optimal energy performance.

Today, buildingSMART is a vibrant international organization that supports open standards, not only for the building industry, but also for the infrastructure industry—roads, railroads, power companies, and more. A small professional staff coordinates the work of buildingSMART chapters in 22 different countries and 50 large corporate and institutional members to develop open digital standards. The organization has published standards widely adopted by software companies and has developed collaboration agreements with other standards organizations including the International Standardization Organization (ISO). One thousand people from more than 80 countries attended our last summit. I have served as chairman of buildingSMART International for 20 years and will continue as long as the group will have me. Why invest HOK's money and my time in this effort? There are two principles at play here that will benefit any firm that relies on technology: openness and standardization.

Chapter 16: To Design a World-Class Firm

1. Point out when the firm needs to do something—but be prepared to take charge of it yourself.
2. Buy the best, most up-to-date technology. It's not spending money; it is investing money.
3. Use technology and common systems to stitch your people together into a cohesive team.
4. Digitize historic hard copy assets so they are easily accessible, and you preserve your firm's history.
5. Evolve constantly in your use of technology, since it is ever-changing.
6. Go paperless to clear the clutter, clear your mind, and be truly organized and liberated.
7. Volunteer in your profession to improve the entire industry.
8. Support openness and standardization in your industry's technology.

CHAPTER 17

Growth: Buying Firms

Under CEO Jerry Sincoff, HOK's expansion accelerated. Remember, his first of three goals for HOK was growth above all, to transform HOK from a large firm with a good reputation to an international firm with a stellar reputation. Founder George Hellmuth had wanted to create a "depression-proof firm" by diversifying to multiple cities. Jerry wanted to extend the idea to multiple countries. If the economy was bad in one part of the world, maybe it would be strong elsewhere. Instead of opportunistic expansion as in the past, Jerry began to use money from the Kajima investment to proactively buy other firms. Jerry was in a hurry and wanted HOK to grow quickly. This was in direct contrast to HOK's early growth, which had mostly been incremental, typically taking advantage of a large new project in another city to establish a project office and later making the office permanent. Jerry believed more aggressive growth was the way to design a world-class architecture firm.

CRS, Houston

Sincoff's first purchase was CRS, a Houston-based firm with a long history and a good reputation. The firm was founded in 1946 by two Texas A&M professors, Bill Caudill and John Rowlett. Wally Scott, one of Caudill's students, joined them later, becoming Caudill, Rowlett & Scott (CRS). Another Caudill student, Willie Peña, developed a technique called "problem-seeking," a rigorous process for gathering complete information about the needs of the client and project before beginning design work. Problem-seeking was a great success, adding to the CRS reputation for innovation. When I heard about the technique, I loved it. After all, "problem-seeking" sounds a bit like "running toward trouble."

CRS was innovative in other ways. The founders wanted to expand and decided to take the firm public to generate funds for growth. In 1971, CRS was listed on the American Stock Exchange, a rarity for design firms. Any investor could buy and sell CRS stock, the opposite of HOK where stock ownership was limited to active employees. CRS bought industrial engineering firm J.E. Sirrine in 1983 and changed its name to CRSS. As a public company, CRSS began to expand into other areas of business unrelated to its roots as a design firm. One of these businesses, the development of peak load power generation stations, plants that only run when there's high demand for electricity, grew rapidly and began to dominate CRSS. In an ironic twist, the original design practice no longer fit into the business CRS had created. This is one risk of being a public company. So, in 1994, CRSS put the original CRS design business up for sale.

When Jerry Sincoff learned CRS was for sale, he moved quickly to arrange a visit to Houston to meet the design team and learn the terms of sale. He invited a group of HOK leaders to join in the assessment, including me. I had always admired CRS for their thoughtful, innovative approach to each new client or project, and thought adding the CRS abilities in thoughtful innovation to our diversified practice could be a master stroke.

The CRS design offices remained in what was called the "White House," the firm's original Houston headquarters, while the much larger CRSS offices occupied a large, conventional building nearby. Here I go, an architect describing buildings again! The White House was located at the edge of a wooded bayou below street level with parking on the roof deck and offices below with dark, shaded views of the bayou. CRS also had smaller offices in Washington, DC; Sacramento, California; and Greenville, South Carolina.

The HOK team met some talented people at CRS, including Tom Robson, the architect in charge of the office. Tom was friendly and happy to see us. He let us know CRS's designers were eager to become part of a design firm again, and to be "rescued" from a firm to which they no longer belonged. We met other talented people too. Critically, the CRS people appeared to fit in well with HOK culture.

I joined Jerry Sincoff to discuss terms of a sale with Bruce Wilkinson, the CFO of CRSS Capital. Wilkinson seemed eager to unload CRS and offered to sell at a fair price. He was willing to include a large project in Saudi Arabia as part of the deal. CRS was designing "Peace Shield," a large Ministry of Defense project, in what had become a familiar country to HOK. CFO Bob Pratzel had advised Jerry that cash flow from Peace Shield would help pay HOK's purchase price for CRS, so this was a huge plus. In fact, it's worth pointing out to others that if you can buy a firm engaged in a lucrative project and that project is included in the deal, the acquisition may well pay for itself, which is a beautiful thing.

Wilkinson also offered to sell us the White House. We had learned it sometimes flooded during heavy Houston rains, and asked if the building was a mandatory part of the CRS purchase. Wilkinson said it was not, but if HOK didn't want the building, we would need to relocate the CRS office as soon as he found a buyer for the property. Our negotiation with Wilkinson lasted less than an hour. He was an eager seller and Jerry agreed to his terms, especially Peace Shield. Wilkinson was happy and so were we. He could focus on power plant development and we could grow a combined design firm with CRS. When you find a firm to purchase that is such a perfect fit and with such a fair price, you should move fast. Don't dither.

We completed the sale just months later, in 1994, and Jerry Sincoff named Tom Robson Managing Principal of the new regional HOK office. A few months later, the office moved from the subterranean White House to Williams Tower at the Houston Galleria, the groundbreaking project Obata had designed. The effect on morale was instant and positive. Tom Robson later recalled, "The move from an underground building to a high floor in Williams Tower, with lots of natural light and great views, made everyone feel the office was off to a fresh start."

Tom tackled the substantial challenge of transforming the CRS headquarters office into a regional HOK office. He eliminated CRS central accounting and reduced other overhead departments. He refocused the office's marketing from national and global to regional clients. He closed the CRS Washington, DC and Sacramento offices, and eventually the Greenville office too. But Tom didn't just tear things down; he also built them up. He helped turn CRS Atlanta into HOK Atlanta—a two-for-one bonus for HOK.

Tom also worked with Jerry Sincoff to merge the CRS problem-seeking team with HOK programming, creating a new market practice to advise clients making key real estate and space decisions. Fortunately, the Peace Shield project was very profitable, and as Bob Pratzel had predicted, it helped HOK pay for CRS. Within a year, Tom and his team had transformed HOK Houston into a growing and profitable office. HOK had landed another great new office and a great new leader. Later, Tom would take on an essential firm-wide role at HOK, a good reminder that sometimes top people come to you from outside your original talent pool.

Eduardo Terrazas y Asociados, Mexico City

The word was out that good things could happen to firms that agreed to merge with HOK. In 1994, Eduardo Terrazas, the owner of a medium-sized design firm in Mexico City that bore his name, approached Jerry Sincoff. He was nearing retirement age and offered to sell his firm to HOK. After a short evaluation, we agreed upon a price and Terrazas agreed to continue working for a short transitional period until Sincoff could find a suitable replacement.

Jerry asked Roger Soto to relocate to Mexico City and lead the new office. Soto was a talented young designer in HOK New York who was Chilean by birth and was raised in Mexico City. Roger agreed and was soon working alongside Terrazas and his staff. Soto began to market for new work in Mexico, but noticed he kept losing key commissions to Haldeman Associates, another US firm with a Mexico City office. Haldeman was led by Riccardo Mascia, an American from Chicago who had studied under Frank Gehry and Ricardo Legorreta while earning his Master of Architecture degree at UCLA.

Soto decided Mascia was so effective that he recruited him to HOK in 1996, a good strategy: If you can't beat them—hire them. A short time later, we transferred Soto to HOK Houston, which was growing fast and needed a new Design Principal to work alongside Tom Robson. At the same time, Eduardo Terrazas retired, leaving HOK Mexico City leaderless. The ExCom searched for another HOK leader to transfer to Mexico City, but found none who spoke Spanish. Riccardo Mascia saw an opportunity and offered to lead the office. The ExCom agreed and Riccardo had the small office organized for success in record time. HOK had gained a productive new office and another promising talent.

Jerry Sincoff sent me to Mexico City to see how the office was getting along, and I met Riccardo for the first time. He spoke flawless Spanish and had earned the respect of our clients and people in the office. In the evening, I had dinner with Riccardo and his wife, Sofia, who was also an architect—and the daughter of an architect. Riccardo was tall, charismatic and clearly in charge. He inherited good features from his Italian-American ancestors, with dark eyes and wavy hair. One of his hobbies was running marathons, so he had the physique of a long-distance runner. Riccardo remained the managing principal in Mexico City for several years, but soon HOK would have him running marathons for us elsewhere.

HOK Chicago

HOK had expanded from St. Louis to both coasts and overseas before getting around to establishing an office in nearby Chicago. HOK St. Louis leaders, led by Clark Davis, opened a small branch office in Chicago, in 1995, financing the new office with St. Louis profits, the same pattern used earlier by San Francisco to establish HOK Los Angeles. Chicago was the only new HOK office opened during this era that was not a purchase of an existing firm.

HOK Chicago was established in the Inland Steel Building, the office tower designed by SOM and the same building where I had interviewed with SOM for a job years before. Chicago remained a branch of HOK St. Louis for several years before becoming an independent office, joining the HOK Matrix of offices and market practices.

Cecil Denny Highton, London

By 1990, HOK London had grown to a staff of almost 50 but was still viewed as an outsider by UK clients. The office also needed new leadership after Marketing Principal Bill Stinger transferred to HOK Washington, DC and Managing Principal Tad Tucker retired and returned to St. Louis.

Only Larry Malcic remained as design principal. Larry first recruited two local architects to fill leadership positions: Ralph Courtenay as managing principal and Paul Purvis as marketing principal.

The new leaders believed the best way for HOK London to become an accepted local firm was by acquiring a well-established London design firm. Note to others: Sometimes buying or merging with a local firm is a short cut to acceptance in a new city or country. After an extensive search, they identified Cecil Denny Highton (CDH) as a top prospect. CDH had a good reputation and experience in institutional and UK government work, most notably design of the Commonwealth Office. Ray Cecil had retired five years earlier and John Denny led the office. The third partner, Michael Highton, had established a CDH office in Warsaw, Poland and was living there.

HOK approached CDH proactively and learned the principals there were interested in joining forces. The two offices were of equal size and had complementary experience: HOK London with commercial architecture and CDH with government and institutional architecture. HOK agreed to acquire CDH, but people in both offices saw it as a merger of two equals. We learned three lessons all in one with this move: First, approach a firm before it is officially up for sale, and you may get a mutually beneficial "yes"; second, it's a bonus if you can acquire a firm with complementary strengths; and third, be flexible with words. If "merger" makes people feel better than "acquisition," there's no harm in calling it that, if the two firms share a compatible company culture.

The 1995 merger was a great success. CDH fit in well with HOK London from the beginning, unlike years before when we bought Kahn & Jacobs in New York and had to strip their name from the door. Most important, UK-based clients began to accept HOK London as a local firm. Happily, the merged office began to win new commissions in both the public and private sectors. Within a few years, HOK London grew to 150 people with exciting new work in London, the UK, and the Middle East. The CDH Warsaw office became HOK Warsaw for a few years but was not able to grow as expected, and HOK eventually sold it to the local leadership group.

Urbana Architects, Toronto

HOK Canada had its beginnings in a great client relationship. Jerry Sincoff had managed two projects for Mobil Oil in the 1980s and developed a strong rapport with his Mobil client representative. Jerry and his client stayed in touch over the years, and his client eventually joined Nortel, the large Canadian manufacturer of telecommunications equipment, which was about to embark on a major expansion program. The obvious lesson here: keep in touch with old clients as they change companies; you never know when they'll be able to hire you again.

Jerry called on his friend, now head of global real estate for Nortel. As Jerry told me later, "I suggested that since HOK did a great job for Mobil, he should give us Nortel work. He told me Nortel also had a good relationship with CRSS, so he would split the work between CRSS and HOK." Yes, he was referring to the same CRSS based in Houston. In fact, in a classic coincidence, it was soon after that conversation that HOK bought CRS, which meant HOK got *all* the Nortel work, after all. Many former CRS people worked on it with us. That makes me think of another variation on the old saying: If you can't beat them *buy* them!

The large volume of Nortel work prompted Jerry Sincoff to think about a permanent HOK presence in Canada. He was introduced to Urbana Architects, a small practice working in a renovated townhouse in downtown Toronto. The three Urbana partners were organized like the HOK founders. Terri Comeau, Gordon Stratford, and Lou Mancinelli were responsible for marketing, design, and production, respectively. It was just one sign of a great fit.

HOK began to collaborate with Urbana, and though it was a bit complicated due to Canadian law, we were eventually able to bring Terri, Gordon, Lou, and their firm into HOK. The office grew quickly on the strength of the Nortel work and was able to successfully win new contracts with other clients. HOK Canada established a branch office in Ottawa, in 2003, and other branch offices throughout Canada by 2008.

Lobb Partnership, London

Since the time Ron Labinski and his four colleagues had opened their first office in 1983, HOK Sport had earned a reputation for designing ingenious stadiums that clients—and the public—loved. In fact, HOK Sport had grown to become the dominant sports design firm in the United States. The group had worked for all of the major professional sports leagues, creating iconic designs such as Camden Yards, home of the Baltimore Orioles; Nationwide Arena where the Columbus Blue Jackets play hockey; MetLife Stadium, which is shared by the New York Giants and Jets; and United Center, headquarters of the Chicago Bulls.

Still, Ron Labinski was not satisfied. He believed HOK Sport could become even more successful and began to travel extensively, looking for opportunities to expand HOK Sport. During a trip to London, Labinski met Rod Sheard, leader of the Lobb Partnership, a sports architecture practice based in the UK and Australia. The two hit it off, and HOK and Lobb agreed to collaborate on the new Wembley Stadium project. The teams enjoyed working together and the two firms agreed to merge in 1998, 15 years after the founding of HOK Sport. The merger created the world's largest sports architecture practice, so big that the magazine *Architect's Journal* covered it. "The global set-up will employ more than 300 people in London, Kansas City and Sydney," the magazine wrote. "Ron Labinski, HOK Sport senior vice president, said the new firm would have a portfolio of 450 sports projects on six continents, including 50 league franchises and 25 European soccer and rugby clubs."[1]

It was a symbol of the separation between HOK Sport and the rest of HOK, a rift that would only grow.

I expected the Lobb London office would relocate to share office space with HOK London, but that was not the case. HOK Sport insisted its newly formed partnership was better able to serve clients from its own London office. If we had it to do over again, I would not allow this. London was the first and only city with two HOK offices. It was a symbol of the separation between HOK Sport and the rest of HOK, a rift that would only grow.

Expansion in Europe

Larry Self was convinced Europe was a promising place to expand the HOK network of offices. Larry watched as six countries formed the European Union in 1993, then more joined until most of Western Europe and many eastern European countries were members. Larry noted that the European Union was similar in size and economic output to the United States. By this time, HOK had a network of 14 offices across the United States. Why couldn't we have an equal number in Europe?

---

[1] *Architect's Journal*, "HOK and Lobb Team Up to Form Global Sports Power," November 12, 1998.

HOK already had an office in London and, for now, another in Warsaw from the CDH merger. Over the next several years, working from his base in London, Larry started small offices in Berlin, Moscow, and Prague. These were marketing offices, established to help HOK win work rather than full-service offices capable of doing the work. Remember, founder George Hellmuth originally did the same thing in Washington, DC, successfully setting up a marketing office that grew into a real office.

I visited HOK Berlin in the late 1990s. The Berlin Wall had fallen in 1989, and our office was in former East Berlin. I asked HOK Berlin office principal Michael Bennett how he made the decision to locate the office there instead of West Berlin. Michael explained rents were much lower in East Berlin, and the office was near the historic city center. Most buildings in the area were in poor condition, but our office was in a well-maintained building. When I asked Michael why, he laughed and said, "This building used to be the headquarters of the communist party of the German Democratic Republic—East Germany—and they always took good care of their own buildings."

From Berlin I traveled by train through East Germany, crossed into Poland and on to Warsaw. The HOK office there was near the center of the city, in an area of traditional buildings beautifully restored after World War II. Michael Highton, the former partner of CDH, led the office of about 30 people, mostly Polish citizens. Many spoke English and were busy with a large new retail project. They were earnest and interested in HOK, but I wondered if they were going to fit into the HOK office network or adopt HOK culture.

We were to learn a hard lesson in Europe. Yes, it was about the same population as the United States, with about the same level of economic activity, but it was infinitely more difficult to build successful offices there, let alone establish HOK culture. After all, each new office was in a different country with its own history, language, regulations—and culture.

HOK Dubai

We opened HOK Dubai in 2000 as a project office for the Dubai Marina, an HOK Canada project. You can see how fast HOK was growing when you consider that an HOK office in a second country was winning work in a third country! Daniel Hajjar, a Canadian of Lebanese descent, transferred to Dubai to coordinate the project. Many other HOK offices were active in the Middle East, but Dan and his small office were the only permanent HOK presence in the region. Dan and his team began to assist other HOK offices with marketing, coordination during design and construction administration. The Dubai office also began to win new work on its own or in partnership with other offices. Once again, a strategic project office had grown into a regional office. Dan grew HOK Dubai for us, then eventually transferred to London as managing principal, another team member who proved himself and kept earning new "jobs," all of them at HOK.

Chapter 17: To Design a World-Class Firm

1. Move fast when you find a firm for acquisition that is a perfect fit, with a fair price.
2. Remember the most important thing you acquire when you buy a service business is the talent pool.
3. Recruit talented individuals away from other firms if you keep losing work to them. In other words, "If you can't beat them—hire them."
4. Buying or merging with a local firm can be a short cut to acceptance in a new city or country.
5. Acquire firms with different specialties from your own for greater diversification.
6. Opening a new office in a large country is different from opening an office on a large continent with many countries.

CHAPTER 18

Enforcing Financial Metrics

Jerry Sincoff did his best to persuade HOK office leaders to adopt better business practices and spread HOK culture, hoping it would have a trickle-down effect on their staffs and specialties. He also called on them to share leads and work. But most office leaders continued to see people from other offices as threats to their prosperity, rather than as partners on a path to greater success.

I spoke to Jerry about intervention. "Jerry, HOK has grown and diversified," I said. "We offer more services now, including engineering, landscape architecture, and others. This is wonderful, but if we weren't growing, we wouldn't make any money. Don't we need to work on our business practices and HOK culture?" I will never forget what Jerry told me. "Some CEOs work on growth. Others work on fixing their business," he said. "I chose growth because I believe that is our top priority right now."

Charm School

This is where I got into trouble. I saw that everyone did not share HOK culture, and learned some leaders were scheming to succeed at the expense of other offices. I continued to express my frustration to Jerry and Bill. I did my best to convince them to be more demanding, telling them, "There will be no change without consequences for those who don't comply." My frustration was growing, and I was vocal about it. That resulted in my being sent to what I called "charm school."

HR Director John Mahon took me to dinner in St. Louis one night. We went to his favorite Italian restaurant and had a great meal. John was savvy and got me relaxed with some good Italian wine, then said, "Jerry and Bill think you're too outspoken and tough. We know what you're trying to do, but you need some executive coaching to learn to engage others more productively. You know, they think you could be the next CEO." Jerry and Bill were rightly cautious about HOK going from being too relaxed to too rigid. A design firm is a creative place, and people must be supported in that creativity for the firm to thrive. Too little structure leads to chaos, but too much will smother creativity.

"If that's what I have to do to get the job done, I'll do it," I said. John found a well-regarded executive coach in San Francisco, who first came to my office to observe me at work for a few days. The coach had me take some personality assessment tests, and according to the results, I was "strong-willed and decisive." A list of synonyms included the term "bull-headed." The instructions suggested I ask a good friend or family member if they saw me the same way the assessment did, so I went home with that on my mind. The first person I saw was my young daughter, Elisabeth. I asked, "Do you think I'm bull-headed?" She had a quick wit and answered, "Why, no, daddy, I think you're bald-headed!"

I met with my coach every few weeks, and the biggest thing I learned is to be more patient with people, including giving them room to voice their own thoughts. The other big thing I learned is that people need to understand *why* something is important, not just *what* to do. After a few months, he said, "I think you're going to be just fine. You tend to come on strong. If you take the time to explain things to people, you'll accomplish more." It was valuable advice.

I began trying to listen to people first, to understand their problem or point of view. Looking back, it occurs to me that I was learning to practice "careful listening," Obata-style. Once I had listened, instead of telling people what to do, I explained why a certain result was important and asked for their suggestions. I learned that involving everyone in problem solving created consensus. Strong leadership meant cultivating engagement, not being bull-headed. Bill Valentine had hinted at this when he said, "You can't make people do something; you have to help them want to do it."

It took me about a year to regain Jerry and Bill's trust. Fortunately, by then, everyone on the ExCom had come to share my concern about the uneven performance of HOK offices and continuing problems with cash flow. With the encouragement of other ExCom members, Jerry Sincoff appointed me chief operating officer (COO) in early 2000. I was the first firm-wide operations leader since Bob Stauder. Would I be able to get HOK's operations back on track without alienating people? My new responsibilities were daunting, but I was determined to use my newfound charm school training to help the firm at this critical turning point.

My first priority was to get HOK's finances in order. I began to call every office monthly. Some were profitable and others were not. Some billed and collected fees on time and others did not. Some had a steady backlog of work and others did not. When I asked offices what they were doing to get back on track, the answers were more about hopes than plans. I needed to establish some clear, understandable financial metrics for office performance, to help office leaders measure success. This was something the firm had never done before. We were architects—what did we know about financial metrics? I believed these metrics must be clear and simple for the best chances of adoption. Clarity and simplicity are guiding principles in most everything I do, and I cannot recommend them highly enough. I reached out to CFO Bob Pratzel and Controller Tim Tynan to better understand accounting and finance fundamentals and began inhaling business books at night to educate myself.

The 50 Percent Rule

From my experience as managing principal of the San Francisco office, I knew people were by far the firm's biggest expense. After all, architects are service providers, not widget makers. The HOK accounting system had some metrics to measure the cost of people who worked on individual projects. But no metric existed for *everyone* in an office—project people, marketers, accountants, HR, IT, admin, and so on. Tim Tynan and I began to dig through lots of complicated financial information. After a few sessions, we boiled the complexity down to a simple metric I called the "50 Percent Rule:"

For any office, total annual salaries should not exceed half of annual fees.

When Tim tested the 50 Percent Rule against the financials for each HOK office, the results were clear. Offices that met the 50 Percent Rule were profitable, and those exceeding the 50 Percent Rule were not. As I said, I'm a big believer in the beauty and utility of making things simple. Now I had a benchmark to review with each office, a straightforward way to help them understand how to get to a state of profitability.

I gave offices with too high a payroll a short period of time to comply with the 50 Percent Rule. They could achieve this in three ways: by winning more work, loaning staff to a busy HOK office, or reducing staff. Laying people off was the hardest choice to swallow, so the 50 Percent Rule became an incentive for offices to market more successfully or reassign staff to help another office with its workload. We created this rule to help HOK balance its books, but it ended up encouraging offices to collaborate more, as well. Who would have thought a pragmatic business move would help HOK make progress toward one of its long-held goals? It was a start, but we had a long way to go.

The 90-Day Rule

Now that we knew how much money each office needed to make, we had to bring in that money. Collecting money is essential for any business, including design firms. I had learned that as I carried out my little "sit-in" in the developer's lobby in Kuala Lumpur years before. I met with Bob and Tim to learn why clients didn't always pay on time. My method for understanding an issue was to ask as many questions as it took to get to the root of it. This became known as the "MacLeamy drilldown."

In this case, I learned that HOK, like most design firms, used an accrual accounting method, where fees are counted as earned when the design work is done—not when the client pays the fee. This left offices with little incentive to send out bills and collect their fees. The HOK accounting system didn't hold anyone responsible for bringing in the money! I proposed another simple rule to encourage billing and collecting. This became known as the "90-Day Rule":

Fees not billed and collected in 90 days will be "unearned."

Offices had a lot at stake when it came to fees. Year-end bonuses were based on fees and profits, making unearned fees a serious blow. Bob and Tim were happy with the 90-Day Rule, which reduced the monthly arm-wrestling discussions between Central Accounting and offices in which leaders did their best to convince Tim that a client payment was imminent—the old "check's in the mail" routine. After that, Tim even kept a sign on his desk highlighting the need to convert estimated fees, called accrual, into cash: "Accrual is an opinion. Cash is a fact".

During calls with the offices, I explained that fees were no longer considered earned until they were collected. It was blindingly obvious, yet something we had never, ever done. Office leaders inevitably asked me, "But what if fees are collected *after* 90 days?" (There was going to be a lot of that going around for the first few months.) I explained that those would be restored as earned fees. My goal as COO was to be firm, but fair. That's how I hoped to straddle the line between allowing chaos and nurturing creativity. With the 90-Day Rule, the incentive for offices changed from just earning fees to collecting them within 90 days. Collections began to improve. It was another simple rule for a complicated problem and another step in the right direction.

The 10-Month Rule

Every design firm depends on new work to replace work completed each month. George Hellmuth's depression-proof-firm strategy was based on keeping valued HOK employees busy by winning a steady stream of new projects to replace the ones each office finished. HOK had grown into a large firm with 20 offices—of different sizes with different leaders who had different styles. We needed another simple metric to indicate if the flow of new work, called backlog, was adequate to keep people busy. And the metric had to work for every HOK office, regardless of size.

Back again to Bob Pratzel and Tim Tynan for another drill-down session. The question this time: how much backlog was prudent? Of course, the more backlog the better, but how much backlog was enough to keep the design teams in each office working steadily? We sorted through a great deal of HOK history, looked at large and small offices, and discovered backlog adequate to keep people busy could be expressed by a third simple metric, the 10-Month Rule:

> **Every office needs 10 months of backlog to maintain current staff.**

Office leaders knew how much fee they earned each month. If their backlog of work still to be done was 10 times each month's earnings, they were in a steady state, neither shrinking nor growing. Offices with less than a 10-month backlog were shrinking, and those with more than a 10-month backlog were growing. Now every HOK office, large or small, had a formula for assessing their future needs and could plan accordingly. Growing offices were able to plan for expansion, and shrinking offices had an early warning to redouble their marketing efforts. The 10-Month Rule also served as another incentive to collaborate. Offices with less backlog had an incentive to partner with offices with more. Offices with more backlog had an incentive to tap the talent at offices with less. This was a baby step toward fulfilling both George Hellmuth's long-desired strategy to share work across HOK and Jerry Sincoff's hope for more collaboration among offices. But, as you will see, it was not enough.

Simplified Accounting

Each time I worked with Bob and Tim to dig into our financials and get information, I was bothered by the complexity of the HOK accounting system. The firm's fiscal year began and ended in the middle of the calendar year. I asked Bob, "Why not align it with the calendar year?" He said, "We get a lower price from our auditors with a mid-year setup." Most confusing of all, the HOK fiscal year was divided into 13 accounting periods of 4 weeks each instead of 12 calendar months. No one except the HOK accountants knew what period we were in or when it began or ended. I asked Bob why HOK used this system, and he said, "Our payroll is every two weeks, and two payrolls fit evenly within a four-week accounting period." I concluded that the HOK accounting system worked well for the accounting department—and was baffling to everyone else.

I went to my fellow ExCom leaders and proposed changing the HOK fiscal year to a calendar year with 12 monthly periods. Remember, I'm a big believer in the beauty of simplicity. They agreed, and this time it was the accountants who grumbled, but we made the changes. Now everyone knew when each monthly period began and ended, and everyone knew when the HOK fiscal year began and ended. Not only was it simpler, it was more motivating. Offices could now easily grasp their deadlines for getting fees earned, billed, and collected.

I wasn't done yet. Every month, Central Accounting printed and bound financial reports for each office, with details of fees, expenses, and profits. To make it even more complex, these numbers were further broken down by project. The reports were big, bulky, and hard to read, with long columns of numbers carried out to the penny. Even after everyone at HOK had a computer, Central Accounting printed financial reports on paper and distributed them to each office by overnight courier. The paper reports were difficult to use during my calls with the offices. I kept two or three months of reports on my desk and had to flip madly from one to the next to understand the trends. Were fees, profits, and collections going up or down? It was hard to say. We needed to simplify our financial reports.

I met with Bob and Tim yet again to overhaul financial reporting. They agreed future reports would be digital, sent electronically to each office. I insisted that reports contain numbers rounded to the nearest thousand dollars to make them easier to read. "But we need to keep accounts to the penny for our auditors," Tim argued. We finally agreed that auditors needed pennies, but HOK leaders only needed dollars. They would be delighted with *less* detail. From then on, the accounting department prepared its reports using Microsoft Excel, a flexible tool for showing trends in profit, backlog, and collections over months and years.

> **S**ometimes less is more. Having the right *information is more important than having* all of *the information.*

Another great lesson: Sometimes less is more. Having the *right* information is more important than having *all* of the information. These accounting changes may sound nit-picky, but, as you will see, they ended up helping us save HOK.

Expanding the Board

The HOK board had remained the same size, made up of 10 to 12 senior leaders, since HOK was one office in St. Louis. By the time I became COO, the firm had grown to 1,600 people spread over a global network of 20 offices. I believed the board structure had not kept pace with HOK growth and proposed it be much larger to include a leader from every major office and market practice.

My ExCom colleagues agreed, but the eventual solution prompted a change in the HOK company structure. The original parent company board, elected annually by the shareholders, was reduced in size to include just ExCom members. Then a new HOK company was created to oversee all HOK companies worldwide, and this company was led by a new, larger board of directors, including the ExCom, office and market-practice leaders, discipline leaders, and others.

The new board consisted of about 30 people and was a positive step toward building rapport and restoring HOK culture, but met only twice each year. I believed board meetings would be even more helpful in bringing us together if we held them more often. Everyone at HOK used a computer by this time, so I proposed that in addition to meeting in person twice a year, the board meet virtually every month to review the latest monthly financial reports. We originally organized the virtual meetings using a conference call and networked computer system.

Monthly board meetings were another early plus. Because the meetings were virtual, I added an attendance sheet to the Excel workbook, with a column for each month and a row for each board member. Attendees received a green square next to their names, and absences remained white. It was a bit like the original HOK Matrix where nobody wanted to see an empty square. Attendance improved—people didn't want a white square for "absent" next to their name. Later, we purchased a high-end videoconference system so people in every office could see and hear each other on one large screen and view financial and other information on another large screen. This was a great example of leveraging technology to build teamwork across HOK.

I made a final suggestion to rotate the in-person board meetings from office to office instead of always holding them in St. Louis. Regional offices began to host board meetings, giving board members the opportunity to meet people in their offices. Host offices used the opportunity to show off their latest work and introduce emerging leaders. Each host office invited the board for breakfast in their office to meet local staff and review local projects. Host office leaders also joined the board dinners, even if they weren't on the board. Rotating board meetings turned out to be another important step in the right direction for HOK. The pattern of virtual monthly board meetings and twice-yearly rotating, in-person meetings was set, and it continues to this day.

Chapter 18: To Design a World-Class Firm

1. Remember to explain to your team *why* something is important, not just *what* needs to be done.
2. Balance the design and business functions of your firm. Too much structure will smother creativity, but too little structure leads to chaos.
3. Make clarity and simplicity guiding principles in everything you do as an architect or businessperson.
4. Adopt financial metrics that are clear and simple so people will understand them, embrace them, and use them.
5. Limit total annual salaries at your firm to X percent of annual fees to assure profitability. At HOK, X equaled 50%.
6. Know that if you do not meet your firm's version of the 50 Percent Rule, you must earn more in fees or be required to reduce staff.
7. Consider "unearned" any fees that are not billed and collected within 90 days. Don't count fees as earned just because you have a contract and have done the work.
8. Have backlog—projects you have won but not yet completed—equal to X months of work to maintain your current staff. At HOK, X equaled 10 months.
9. Simplify your accounting system so nonaccountants can understand how the company is doing. Having the *right* information is more important than having all the information.
10. Include stakeholders from every part of your firm on your board of directors to increase collaboration and emphasize firm-wide goals—even if it requires restructuring your organization. Meet virtually every month between in-person meetings.
11. Establish an executive committee to keep your large board of directors organized and focused on the right things.
12. Rotate board meetings among your office, if applicable, so board members can get to know those offices and vice versa.

CHAPTER 19

Transitions: The Second Generation

Jerry Sincoff and King Graf filled a big psychological gap left by the founders, giving everyone in HOK the confidence to succeed by continuing the work the founders had begun. Looking back, it was so important that Hellmuth hand-picked King and Kassabaum chose Jerry, because it signaled to the rest of the firm that these new leaders deserved our confidence. They had performed admirably as the second generation, and we now knew that HOK would be able to carry on successfully with future leaders too.

King Graf Retires

King Graf retired from HOK in 1995 at age 65 after a 39-year career at HOK. He had learned marketing under George Hellmuth and spent his career winning new work for HOK. He was a pioneer marketer in the United States, Asia, and the Middle East, and was responsible for winning significant projects leading to the initial HOK expansion.

King loved HOK and was a friend and supporter of everyone at the firm. He was from a family of artists and returned to art in retirement, creating beautiful paintings and drawings, including paintings of some of his favorite HOK projects. The wild stories he loved to tell about HOK's early days continued to be passed down after he retired, but nobody ever mastered his technique for tossing pushpins.

George Hellmuth Dies

Founder George Hellmuth died in 1999, at age 92. He had retired as president of HOK International 13 years earlier. Bill Valentine and I flew back for his funeral, which was held in the very first HOK-designed building, St. Sylvester's Church in Eminence, Missouri. He was buried nearby, on a spot he had selected years before, at his beloved farm—The Sinks, the same farm where he had invited hundreds of HOK employees over the years. We

FIGURE 19.1 Founder George Francis Hellmuth, 1907–1999.
Source: Photo courtesy of HOK.

remembered George Hellmuth as the founder who designed HOK as a totally new type of architecture firm.

As part of Hellmuth's depression-proof-firm strategy, he had wanted to hire and retain talented people. HOK had grown from a staff of 27 at the founding to 1,900 at his death. He believed the firm would thrive under specialized leaders, including full-time marketers, and each HOK office was still run by a designer, a marketer, and a production architect. Finally, Hellmuth believed diversity of cities, services, and specialties could insulate a firm from economic downturns. HOK now had offices in 26 cities and employed at least eight types of design professionals, not just architects. Hellmuth's idea to diversify led directly to the formation of HOK market practices specializing in different building types, driving yet more growth. It was quite a legacy.

Paul Watson Steps Aside

Paul Watson had been HOK general counsel since 1963, to our knowledge the first-ever in-house attorney for a design firm. In 1994—almost three decades later—Paul finally decided to hire another lawyer to help him keep pace with HOK growth. Amazing. He chose Bob Staed, someone he knew well. As a boy Staed had caddied for avid golfer Paul, and earned his law degree from Paul's alma mater, St. Louis University. At HOK, Bob proved to be diligent, hardworking, and loyal.

In 2000, Paul Watson became HOK senior counsel. He had served the founders and successive HOK leaders for more than 30 years with skill and a deep commitment. His role as general counsel was taken over by Bob Staed. In his six years at HOK, Bob had earned the confidence of Jerry Sincoff and other leaders, and continued Paul's tradition of commitment to HOK and our culture.

Shortly after becoming general counsel, Bob decided he and Paul needed more help, and hired Dennis O'Leary as a part-time attorney. Next he hired Lisa Green, a native of Waukegan, Illinois who earned her law degree in 1988 at Washington University. Lisa was bright, industrious, and a dedicated addition to the legal staff. The four lawyers worked well together, with plenty of room for humor. Lisa often teased Paul that she was born the same year he became general counsel—and Paul never thought it was funny! It was exactly the sort of friendly, somewhat corny humor that had been part of HOK culture since the beginning.

Mahon and Pratzel Join the ExCom

HR Director John Mahon and CFO Bob Pratzel had been advisors to the ExCom since joining HOK in 1985 and 1986, respectively. As HOK grew, the need for advice from Bob and John grew also, until they attended most ExCom meetings. In 2001, they were elected to the parent company board by the shareholders and joined the ExCom, the first and only nondesign professionals to be members. It was a sign that HOK was growing up—architects acknowledging that things like professional accounting and recruiting mattered.

It was a sign that HOK was growing up—architects acknowledging that things like professional accounting and recruiting mattered.

FIGURE 19.2 John Mahon and Bob Pratzel at an HOK party, c. 2001.
Source: Photo courtesy of HOK.

Jerry Sincoff Retires

Jerry Sincoff stepped down as CEO in 2000, then spent a transitional year as chairman of HOK. Later, he consulted for the firm, helping build up corporate services, the newest HOK market practice dedicated to serving large corporations with ongoing space-planning needs. Jerry's top priority as CEO had been growth and, indeed, HOK grew from 900 people in 14 offices to 1,600 people in 20 offices during his tenure. His second objective had been a focus on clients, in hopes HOK would form long-term relationships that brought repeat business. This goal was well underway. As you have heard, his third ambition was making market practices firm-wide instead of siloed at each of the offices. He wanted market practices to be equal to HOK's offices, and for the two to enthusiastically collaborate. Here, he got half of what he wanted. Market practices did become the major driver of HOK growth during his tenure, but true teamwork among offices and market practices remained elusive. There was much more work to be done.

Chapter 19: To Design a World-Class Firm

1. Know when it is time to step aside and install someone else in the hot seat.
2. Invite nondesigners to join your inner management circle if you find you are often relying on them for your biggest, most important decisions.
3. Remember that professional accounting and recruiting matter.

CHAPTER 20

Confronting Crisis

It was HOK tradition that an outgoing leader took the lead in choosing his successor, just as the founders had chosen theirs. When Jerry Sincoff was planning to retire, he conferred with Bill Valentine and John Mahon about who ought to be the next CEO. This could have gone multiple ways. HOK had been envisioned by George Hellmuth, a marketer; led by Gyo Obata, a designer; then led by Jerry Sincoff, a production architect and manager. As one of the prospective candidates, of course I was not privy to their discussions. I have always assumed they were still worried that I was too bull-headed and didn't have the temperament to be CEO. However, I later learned that Jerry just "decided not to decide" about a CEO, instead hoping that, as president, Bill Valentine would continue the work Jerry himself had begun.

Yes, Jerry left the CEO position vacant. This did not seem terribly strange, at the time, given that, under the founders, nobody had used the title "CEO" and when Gyo Obata ran HOK, his title was chairman. At the annual meeting, in 2001, shareholders re-elected the ExCom with no changes. Bill Valentine remained HOK president, effectively making him the firm-wide leader, and I remained as COO.

Bill was a designer, first and always, and not totally comfortable in his new overall leadership role. He remained head of HOK for two years. Problems that had been festering for years made it quite a ride. In that short, 24-month period, three major crises emerged to threaten HOK's very existence. After 32 years of working side-by-side in San Francisco, Bill and I thought of ourselves as partners and best friends. It was natural for him to reach out to me for help with these looming challenges.

The Kajima Crisis

The first crisis involved Kajima. Since its investment in HOK 11 years earlier, Kajima had been satisfied with HOK operations and content to let us run the firm as we wished. That was about to change. Kajima executives called Bill Valentine, Bob Pratzel, and me to the firm's Manhattan office for a meeting. There, our Kajima colleagues complained that their investment in HOK stock was not growing because our profits were too small, and because we gave too much of that small profit to employees as bonuses. That left little for stock growth. Our Japanese colleagues were polite as always, but clearly unhappy. We had been taking them for granted and assuming the status quo would never change. Big mistake.

Kajima's proposed solution was painful. Since HOK stock was not growing, our investors wanted HOK to pay them an annual dividend, suggesting this was fair compensation for their investment. I interpreted their proposal as a demand to "pay up"—couched in polite words. As an investor, Kajima had serious leverage. They could sell their stock back to HOK at any time, and demand cash payment—and we didn't have the money. We promised to consider the Kajima proposal carefully and reply within a few weeks. They agreed. Acting calmer than we were and asking for more time were the only smart things we did in that meeting. Alarmed, Bill, Bob, and I left Kajima's offices and found a nearby restaurant to have a coffee and talk about what in the hell we were going to do.

The Bank of America Crisis

We had just sat down for our coffee—yes, it was the very same day—when Controller Tim Tynan called with the second disaster. Our bank had just phoned and demanded to speak to HOK's leadership. By now, HOK's longtime bank, St. Louis-based Boatmen's, had sold out to NationsBank, which had, in turn, merged with Bank of America. The personal connection was lost somewhere along the way, something we had failed to address. So, in the clatter and chaos of that busy New York restaurant, we dialed in to a conference call with Bank of America representatives who we didn't really know.

They told us we were in violation of covenants governing the HOK line of credit with the bank. What were we going to do to get back into compliance? What assurances could we offer? Our problem was the same: we didn't have the money. Our coffee grew cold as we listened. I was disturbed by what I heard. As a finance guy, Bob was downright distressed. Bill Valentine was horrified. How had he ever gotten into the position of having to deal with things like this?

The HOK Sport Crisis

The third crisis came soon after. Our colleagues at HOK Sport had become enormously successful in the United States and around the world. They were well-run and made consistently high annual profits. But for many years, those large profits had not generated similarly large HOK Sport bonus pools. Why? HOK Sport profits were diluted by losses in other HOK offices, reducing the bonus pool for Sport and everyone else. The hard truth was that HOK Sport was propping up unsuccessful offices.

HOK Sport leaders knew this and were beyond frustration. They believed they had earned—and deserved—bigger bonuses. Their rumblings of discontent were becoming more like roars. I concluded that they might just pick up and leave HOK. We needed to resolve this issue—and soon. But how could we pay the Sport group a larger bonus? Where would the money come from? For a third time, we faced the identical dilemma: we didn't have the money.

At Bill's request, I teamed up again with Bob Pratzel to tackle the three crises. The root cause of all three was the same: low HOK profits for several years in a row. Despite the rules and metrics I had established as COO, too many offices remained unprofitable, reducing overall earnings for the firm. We concluded that a return to robust profitability was the only long-term solution. Easy to say, hard to do.

> *We concluded that a return to robust profitability was the only long-term solution. Easy to say, hard to do.*

Becoming CEO

Bill Valentine liked being HOK president, but recognized the firm was not just about design. The three crises had made it painfully clear that the business side of the firm needed work. In his mind, I was already acting as CEO, but didn't have the title, which made it hard to get big things done. This was beyond big. Our perilous financial position convinced him HOK needed to fill the CEO position.

During an ExCom meeting shortly after our harrowing trip to New York, Bill abruptly announced, "I think Patrick should be the next CEO of HOK, and we should all support him." Bill seemed enormously relieved by his decision and waited for our reaction. The other four members of the ExCom were surprised by Bill's sudden announcement but quickly agreed. He had not confided his intentions to me earlier, so I was as stunned as everyone else—and pleased. I don't remember much else from that day except wanting to call my wife, Jeanne, with the news.

As I pondered my new role, I thought back to what Jerry Sincoff had told me about his own goal as CEO. He had wanted to work on growth rather than "fixing the business." It seemed to me that we could no longer afford to kick that can down the road. Jerry had always said I should pick my battles, but it seemed my battles had picked me. I needed to reinvigorate HOK's leadership, then fix its offices and Central Services. Most of all, I needed to repair the firm's finances so we could satisfy our investors, our bank, and ourselves. And I needed to restore HOK culture—to make it like a big family where collaboration inside helped us to compete outside. I thought of it this way: Small company, small problems; big company, big problems. Jerry's tremendous success at growth had just made fixing HOK even more critical. If I failed, it is no exaggeration to say that we were doomed.

Chapter 20: To Design a World-Class Firm

1. Never take your investors for granted or assume they will always be satisfied with the status quo.
2. Be calm in a crisis, and if you are unsure about what to do, don't be afraid to ask for more time to solve the problem.

3. Maintain a personal connection with your bank, no matter how big, so that there is mutual goodwill when a financial crisis occurs.
4. Discourage your partners or offices from expecting specific revenue splits. These expectations may seem benign at first, but can become major problems.
5. Maintain a balance between growing your firm and fixing your firm.

SECTION FOUR

THE MACLEAMY ERA, 2003–2016

CHAPTER 21

Communicating Your Vision

I became HOK CEO at age 60, after 36 years at the firm. I had started as a junior designer and worked my way up. How many places can you do that? During that time, HOK had grown to be a firm of 1,700 people in 20 offices in the United States and abroad. We were now a highly diversified design practice, following the strategy established by the founders. HOK had earned a good overall reputation, viewed by our profession and our clients as one of the best design firms.

A Company in Crisis

Yet, while HOK looked good from the outside, it was a mess on the inside. Too many offices were underperforming, and the profitable offices were understandably unhappy to see their profits used to prop up weak ones. I had tried to put good accounting, technology, and operations practices into place over the years, but they weren't enough in the face of our rapid growth. I was a new captain overseeing what could easily turn into a mutiny.

Angry office and market leaders found a variety of ways to test the system. A leader in HOK London wanted to leverage the HOK name to create a European network of offices, but operate it separately from the rest of the firm. Another leader in HOK Canada tried to take advantage of HOK's reputation for airports and hospitals, but refused to collaborate with the HOK aviation and healthcare experts who had created that reputation. Meanwhile, office and market leaders elsewhere stood back from the controversy, waiting to see how things would play out.

People outside of HOK were dissatisfied too. Engineers and other consultants were unhappy that the firm did not pay them promptly, and several even threatened legal action. Kajima was disappointed with the slow growth of HOK stock and had followed through on its demand for annual dividends as a substitute for stock growth. Meanwhile, Bank of America had escalated its allegation that we were in violation of its covenants, threatening to cancel our line of credit and demand repayment of the entire amount. All of this strained our inadequate cash flow.

Everyone around the firm held the ExCom responsible for HOK's troubles. They accused us of ineffective leadership and avoiding tough decisions. I visited branch offices and listened to endless complaints about poor ExCom leadership and weak Central Services. During one memorable trip to Houston, leaders there subjected me to a barrage of complaints. "How can you allow other offices to get away with losing money every year?" "We make great profits every year. When are we going to get the bonuses we deserve?" "Why don't you close losing offices?" "Central Services are a joke—too much money and no service." Tom Robson drove me to the airport after the meeting and described my experience with one of his famous South Texas expressions, "Waal, you got a good 'wire brushin' today!"

HOK was close to breaking apart—and now I was about to take charge of it. How was I going to fix so many disasters, and which ones should have priority? My biggest challenge was to restore HOK operations and finances, to bring HOK back to robust profitability. This was a crucial step so we could mend what I viewed as our broken relationships with the bank, Kajima, and HOK Sport. These goals were a tall order, but I wanted to do more.

As I have said, the original HOK culture—a family in which everyone worked together, helping each other to succeed—had been diluted by the addition of new offices and the influx of new employees. It wasn't their fault. They just didn't know what we were all about. I wanted to restore HOK culture across the firm once and for all. I began to think about how to communicate my goals to leaders from around the firm at the upcoming shareholder's meeting. Charm school had taught me the importance of building a case, of explaining why a strategy was important to our future, rather than just issuing edicts. I believed that regular, consistent communication would be necessary to win the support of HOK's office leaders and then, the entire firm.

Juliette Lam, the leader of HOK interiors and an HOK board member, gave me a book, *Who Says Elephants Can't Dance?* She had written a note on the inside cover saying, "I like the lessons in this book. Perhaps they will be helpful in your new role as our CEO." It's the story of how new CEO Lou Gerstner transformed IBM from a mainframe maker on the verge of bankruptcy to a unified firm offering comprehensive technology solutions to customers. One of Gerstner's biggest challenges was internal—competition between IBM divisions—a situation I also faced. Most of Gerstner's book was about the tremendous difficulty of making cultural change in a company. His solutions for IBM were not directly applicable to HOK, but the challenge of unifying an entire corporate culture certainly was. Gerstner's book inspired me to think about a simple way to communicate my goals for HOK.

Instead of introducing some fancy business plan in a long document no one wanted to read, I developed four goals that were easily demonstrated by a single diagram: a pyramid. Visuals can be powerful. I thought this was fitting since a pyramid is one of the oldest building forms, and I was trying to communicate to building professionals. My pyramid consisted of four successive levels, representing four firm-wide goals. The goal at the bottom was the foundation. Buildings need strong foundations—and so do companies. We couldn't accomplish any of the higher-level goals without our foundation. My plans for HOK built upward from there, with each level depending on the strength of the one below it. Here is the diagram I created:

FIGURE 21.1 Graphic of HOK pyramid strategy.
Source: Image courtesy of Patrick MacLeamy and HOK.

The pyramid of four successive goals was something everyone at HOK could understand and remember. It contained no details—we would work those out along the way. I wanted the strategy—and the firm—to be nimble and adaptable. Different HOK offices had tried creating formal strategic plans over the years, and I learned that those who wrote the most elaborate annual plans were almost always those who failed to make good on them. Their energies went into a pretty plan, not into implementing anything. I was eager to share my nine-word vision with the HOK board of directors. After all, they were the base of the pyramid.

The Election

About 50 people attended the annual shareholder's meeting in February of 2003, which had rotated to HOK Houston. I was on the ballot for reelection to the ExCom, but everyone knew I was also about to become the next CEO. Bill Valentine was also on the ballot and would remain HOK president. St. Louis Managing Principal Clark Davis, CFO Bob Pratzel, and HR Director John Mahon were also up for re-election. I was oddly nervous, even though HOK shareholder elections had historically been uncontested. We had sent paper ballots to every shareholder prior to the meeting, and General Counsel Bob Staed was responsible for counting votes—one for each share of HOK stock. Fortunately, the shareholders elected our proposed slate. Bill Valentine gave a short speech thanking everyone for putting their trust in HOK's leadership. I felt relief that the election was over, but this was replaced by the weight of my new responsibility. Would I be worthy of that trust? Would I be able to restore HOK?

Following the vote, the HOK board of directors met in a large conference room in the Houston office. After thanking everyone for their support, I told them my first job as CEO was to share my thoughts about the state of HOK. I briefly summarized our history of growth and success. Then I listed our considerable challenges, including the problems with cash flow, low profits, internal competition, and nonaligned leadership. Next, I piled on, confiding how both our bank and our investor, Kajima, had threatened to demand full repayment—which we couldn't afford. I wanted everyone in that room to feel the weight of our predicament. However, I concluded by pointing out that our challenges were *internal*. They were all caused by us. We had gotten ourselves into this mess, and we could get ourselves out—but only if we worked together. I paused a moment and asked if everyone understood what we were up against. No one spoke.

. . . our challenges were internal. They were all caused by us. We had gotten ourselves into this mess, and we could get ourselves out.

The Pyramid Strategy

I said, "How are we going to overcome our challenges and restore HOK to the firm we want it to be?" Silence. I began to describe the four broad goals we must adopt, using my pyramid diagram to introduce each objective and how the four fit together. I reinforced my visual, by using four books of different sizes to illustrate the pyramid I wanted us to build. Crude, but effective. I placed the largest book on the table first, representing the base of the pyramid.

Strong Board of Directors

"Our first goal is to create a strong board of directors," I said. "That's you." I explained why I was positioning our board at the base of the pyramid, rather than at the top, as in most organizational diagrams. I used my solid-foundation metaphor. Without a strong foundation—a dynamic, aligned board—HOK would be unable to reach the other levels of the pyramid. The 30-member board must become unified across the firm, not fragmented by office or market practice. The board must support and enable teams of people around the firm to serve clients with great design and service. The board must work for everyone else in the firm—not the other way around. We must lead, not manage. I saw a united board as the foundation for our success.

The original HOK board of directors had not been particularly strong because the founders—and later the ExCom—usually ran the show. I wanted our newly enlarged board to be different. I wanted it to help pull the firm together and get things done. "Suggest, don't tell" no longer worked as a method of accomplishing things. I recognized that I could tap into the HOK board to validate and support my plan for saving HOK, but only if I treated the members seriously and gave them a strong role. I concluded my description of the strong board by saying, "Our strategy begins with each of you on this board. If you do not see yourselves this way, you don't belong here."

Great Operations

I placed the next book on the stack representing the next level on the pyramid. "My second goal for HOK is great operations," I said. HOK had grown large on the strength of its diverse workload and successful marketing, but operations had not kept pace with growth. We were a mix of profitable and unprofitable offices. Some collected fees on time, whereas others struggled to bill and collect, as I have described. Some offices always had a healthy backlog of new work to keep people busy, whereas others struggled to land new projects and earn enough fees. The board needed to hear these facts out loud, in the light of day. Our future depended on bringing operations to a new level across the firm. I had developed financial metrics as COO, and every office had to meet them for us to succeed.

I explained that it was not enough for board members to pledge to support HOK's new financial metrics. Instead, I was asking each to *meet* HOK's financial metrics in his or her own office or specialty. No more talk. I needed action. This was the only way to meet the goal of great operations. I went on to say that I would be sharing each office's financials at monthly board meetings, so everyone could see which were in compliance and which were not. This was a departure from the past, when goals were merely encouraged, and therefore easy to ignore. This was a mandate. I concluded by saying, "Great operations are an imperative, not an option. Great operations will succeed only with support from our strong board foundation. In other words, I'm counting on each of you as individual leaders in your offices."

I knew that despite my strong words, everyone wondered if things would really be different this time. Their doubts were a challenge to my leadership, and I was determined to succeed.

True Collaboration

I placed the third level of the pyramid atop the other two while describing the third goal: true collaboration. This goal meant every office must help the entire firm to prosper, not just look after their local business. It was my way of stating the founders' original belief that "Collaboration inside is the best way to compete outside." People naturally develop a bond with those in their own office, but the goal of true collaboration was for leaders, beginning with the board, to extend their loyalties beyond their local offices to the entire firm. It made no sense for one office to be expanding and hiring new staff while another office was shrinking and laying people off. We needed to embrace working across offices, once and for all, for the greater good of the firm. True collaboration also meant sharing work with the most qualified people, even if they were in another office. Only then would each client and project get the best HOK team. I believed true collaboration was essential to designing a great firm—*and* doing great work.

Once again, the building blocks were key. I explained that we could not achieve true collaboration without first developing the pieces of the pyramid below that. "True collaboration means putting clients first, HOK second, my office third . . . and myself last," I told the people assembled. "Achieving the goal of true collaboration depends on a strong board for support. It also requires that we firmly establish good operations across HOK." A board member asked, "Why should my office give fees to another office? Why shouldn't they win their own work?" I replied, "That is the key question. When your office has plenty of work, you don't want to share. But sooner or later yours may be the office without enough work. Then you will think true collaboration is a great idea!" Everyone laughed, and the point was made, but as with the goal of great operations, everyone waited to see how I would follow up.

Dreams

I placed the top level on my pyramid while describing the fourth and final goal: dreams. "HOK is a large firm with a diverse mix of offices, market practices, and people," I said. "We want HOK to be the firm where dreams are real—part of our company, and achievable—not out of reach." I tried to paint a vivid picture: "Dreams of great designs, big bonuses, the admiration of our peers, being the best in everything we do, can be a reality, but only after we have reached the three goals on which dreams depend." And now I tied it all together:

"Dreams depend on a strong board as a base, great operations to keep us on the right track, and true collaboration, so we all succeed together."

Dreams were by far the most popular part of my presentation that day, and I asked everyone to share their own dreams for HOK. Bill Valentine said, "I want HOK to be the world leader in sustainable design." Chuck Siconolfi, the new leader of the healthcare group said, "I want our hospital design to take a new direction toward patient-centric care." Ken Young, the IT leader, wanted a faster network. Bill Hellmuth said, "I want HOK to become recognized by our peers as the leading design firm in the world." CFO Bob Pratzel spoke last, and said, "I want us to make so much money that we can stack it in the halls and pay off the bank!" Everyone laughed. Bob always wanted to make money, but this time we needed to take his dream seriously. I reminded everyone that dreams are the final goal, not the first goal, and we had much work to do before we earned the right to dream.

Following HOK tradition, the board did not formally vote that day. Instead we adopted the pyramid strategy by consensus, an echo of the mutual respect the founders had tried to instill in the firm. Now that the board of directors had adopted the pyramid, I needed to find a way to reinforce it among our leaders and convey it to the rest of the firm. I brought up the pyramid strategy in weekly ExCom meetings and monthly board meetings so that it was always top of mind. And I scheduled visits with all 20 offices so I could speak with the local leaders and staff and gain their support for a strong board, great operations, true collaboration, and dreams.

I also began a monthly series of pyramid messages to everyone in HOK using our new, integrated email system. The first message described the pyramid strategy and its vital importance for our future. Successive messages always featured the pyramid image and a story about our progress, often celebrating an office achieving good operations. Without regular reminders, people tended to forget, but with this drum beat of positive reinforcement, the pyramid strategy gradually became part of who we were and helped unite the firm.

In fact, the pyramid messages had a bigger, broader goal: to underline our shared journey. I was trying to lead, not manage, as I had learned back when I was a project architect. The message wasn't "Here's what I want you to do." It was "We are doing this together."

Chapter 21: To Design a World-Class Firm

1. Build a case and explain why your chosen strategy is important rather than issuing orders.
2. Use simple graphics to convey your big ideas to your employees—like the pyramid, which was so relatable to building professionals.
3. Don't count on formal strategic plans. So often, companies put all their energies into a pretty plan that nobody reads and that accomplishes nothing.
4. Figure out if your firm's problems are internal or external. If they are internal, that means you caused them, and you can fix them.

5. Think of your leadership group as the foundation of your firm, rather than the pinnacle. This is an extension of leading rather than managing.
6. Back up your requests for change with strong mandates to make change happen.
7. Put clients first, your firm second, your office third and yourself last when prioritizing your work loyalties.
8. Encourage offices to share work by pointing out that it's a good idea to help another office now, because your office may need help later.
9. Make dreams the final reward, achievable only if you and your employees accomplish all the firm's other strategic goals first.
10. Share your journey. The message isn't "Here's what I want you to do." It's "We are doing this together."

CHAPTER 22

Empowering Firm Leadership

Implementing the pyramid strategy took more than communications. The first step in the strategy was to build a strong board of directors, led by a strong ExCom. Remember, the HOK board was now made up of 30 leaders from the offices and market practices, and the ExCom was part of the larger board. I believed that if the ExCom developed strong, unified leadership, the broader board would follow. This is a logical sequence that other firms could follow when retooling.

Invigorating the ExCom

The ExCom consisted of five people when I became CEO. President Bill Valentine and I were in San Francisco, while St. Louis Managing Principal Clark Davis, HR Director John Mahon, and CFO Bob Pratzel were in St. Louis. The members of the ExCom had the advantage of being longtime friends, but since we were separated geographically, I instituted ExCom conference calls every Monday morning with an Excel spreadsheet agenda shared across linked screens. Every ExCom member traveled regularly, but we committed to dial in and share a linked screen wherever we were. Virtual meetings can serve you well, whether your people work in separate cities or are on the road a lot. There is no excuse not to connect.

The ExCom's first priority was to improve operations in lagging offices. As you have heard, some offices were good at winning and designing work, but not generating profits. Some were prompt with billing and collecting, and others were not. The root cause of these problems was almost always leadership. Some offices lacked good leadership in management, marketing, or design. Other offices had good leaders who had not learned to work together.

Instead of just talking about . . . problems as in the past, I insisted that the ExCom agree on a solution for each problem.

Instead of just talking about these problems as in the past, I insisted that the ExCom agree on a solution for each problem. This really is the key to implementing change.

Every agreed-on solution became an "action item" assigned to one member of the ExCom to carry out. My assistant Susie kept a list of action items in the weekly ExCom workbook, and during each Monday call we reviewed them. "Bob, have you gotten the payment that was promised from HOK Dallas?" "Bill, have you hired that new designer in New York?" My colleagues did not like to have their names on the action list! Weekly action-item reviews became a kind of game as ExCom members worked to reduce their action items to zero. Many executives do not know how to conduct an effective meeting and I learned that this is crucial. Don't just sit around and gab! Decide what needs to be done and assign the task. Then make a point of following up on this "to do" list at the next meeting.

The combination of weekly meetings and action-oriented discussions began to shape the ExCom into a truly effective team. But we found we needed to get together in person for longer strategic discussions and began to meet in different HOK offices every quarter. Soon we learned that meeting in an HOK office was less than ideal, as people in the host office frequently interrupted us with some urgent matter. Instead we began to meet in hotel meeting rooms and retreat centers.

Quarterly meetings gradually evolved to last two-and-a-half days, giving us two evenings for dinner together. Dinners were times for bonding, and repairing whatever disagreements or stress were left from the day's meeting. Some of our best ideas emerged in the morning after our shared dinners, when a good night's sleep clarified our thinking from the day before. I've noticed that sometimes you must step away from a problem and let your subconscious brain continue to turn it over, looking for solutions. That's why we instituted "sleep on it thoughts" as the first item on each morning's agenda.

Regular meetings, action-oriented discussions, and in-person bonding transformed the ExCom into a team that got things done. As we began to see positive results, we became even stronger. Now that we had our core house in order, we were ready to welcome new members.

Expanding the ExCom

HOK had outgrown its ExCom, just as it had outgrown the original board of directors. After all, we were now a global firm with offices and people spread across the world. My assistant Susie Becker had a good grasp of how things worked at HOK and said, "Patrick, I don't know what we would do if you got hit by the milk truck. No one else in leadership would be able to pick up where you left off." I was in this unique position because I cared about good design, but also cared about "boring" things like backlog, billing, and collections—and carried a torch for HOK culture. I needed allies and the ExCom needed new thinking if we were going to fulfill our pyramid strategy. Susie's message reinforced my determination to add more firm-wide leaders to the ExCom.

The most urgent priority was to find a new chief operating officer (COO) to focus on firm-wide operations, the second step of our Pyramid Strategy. I had given up my formal COO title upon being named CEO but kept those responsibilities until we could find a suitable person. To get us started, I appointed an operations committee (OpsCom) of four people to work with lagging offices. They were specialists in project management, finance, construction, and technology. With their help, operations and profits improved gradually, but progress was uneven. Some offices became much better at consistent operations, whereas others lurched from profit to loss every few months. One bright spot: The OpsCom helped almost every office improve billing and collections, so at least we were able to pay our core monthly bills. I think every design firm could benefit from having an effective OpsCom.

Naming a Design Successor

As I thought about expanding the ExCom and grooming new HOK firm-wide leaders, the other priority was to encourage Bill Valentine to name a successor as HOK design leader. This priority was not as urgent, because Bill was a very energetic 65 years old, but it was a prudent step for the long-term success of the firm. Architecture firms need to publicly name their next design leader, more than any other successor, since design is at the heart of the firm. Bill was surprised when I proposed he name a successor, and said, "Gee, I haven't even thought about retiring. What's the rush?" I said, "Bill, you are 65 years old. Obata named you as his successor when he was only 59 years old. I am not asking you to retire, just to identify a successor." I was referring to 1972, when all three founders named successors for the long-term benefit of the firm. Bill reluctantly agreed, but because he was so passionate about his work and had not thought of stepping down, no single name rose to the surface in his mind.

A week later, we met to review his progress, and Bill was still mulling a long list of names. "How about Bill Hellmuth in DC?" I asked. "He's an outstanding design leader, has forged a strong relationship with his DC partners, and built a successful practice. I think he would be a great design leader for HOK when you step down." Bill Valentine cautioned me, saying, "You're right, Bill Hellmuth is a talented designer, but he has a strong personality. Let's invite him to join the ExCom first and see how he performs as a firm-wide leader." I countered, "Yes, he has a strong personality—that's precisely why I recommended him. We need strong leaders like Bill to assure our future." Inviting him to join the ExCom was a good compromise. Bill Valentine telephoned Bill Hellmuth with the news. As expected, Bill Hellmuth was elated, and Bill Valentine was relieved to have made progress toward naming a successor.

Many designers tended to be introverts, but Bill Hellmuth was just the opposite—sociable and engaging. He always seemed to make friends with our clients and was a natural leader for his project teammates. He was extremely energetic, never seeming to tire even after a long day of work. At dinner, Bill was the entertainer, telling story after story.

People began to call him "the energizer bunny" after the well-known advertisement for long-lasting batteries. I learned later that Bill gets up very early every morning to run on his treadmill at home before biking or driving the short distance to HOK's Washington office.

In the spring of 2004, one year after I became CEO, shareholders formally elected Bill Hellmuth to the ExCom. As we had done in earlier years with two founders named George, we began to refer to Bill Valentine and Bill Hellmuth as Bill V. and Bill H. Bill Hellmuth fit easily into the ExCom. He was bright, energetic, and quick, with an ability to get to the core of each issue faster than anyone else. He had a strong focus on design and wanted to improve design leadership around the firm. He also had a strong desire to raise all the offices up to a high level of financial performance. I had a new ally to help fix HOK.

Finding an Operations Leader

Even though finding someone to lead operations was my top priority, I did not identify the right person until almost a year after Bill Hellmuth joined the ExCom. Tom Robson, who had come to HOK with the purchase of Caudill, Rowlett, Scott (CRS), was an outstanding success as the managing principal of HOK Houston. Early in my tenure as CEO, I reached out to Tom for help with a difficult project. HOK Los Angeles had designed a major addition to the Los Angeles County teaching hospital, jointly operated with the University of Southern California. The project had fallen behind schedule during construction, and I asked Tom to get it back on track. After several years of dividing his time between Houston and Los Angeles, Tom and his team were able to do just that, earning the respect of the contractor and praise from our clients. Tom was one of my first "fixers" who could parachute into a problem spot—run toward trouble!—and make things happen.

I became convinced Tom was the right person to lead HOK operations and asked him to join the ExCom in the spring of 2006. He was excited by the opportunity to spearhead operations and took over leadership of the four-person OpsCom I had established earlier. Tom was a big guy with a friendly and disarming manner. In his time off, he was an avid hunter and took vacations to hunt pheasant and wild boar with his Texas buddies. He often used his Texas accent and mannerisms to defuse tense situations and get people to work together. When someone was in trouble, Tom would come up with sayings like, "His ox is in the ditch!" He fit in well with the members of the ExCom and his sense of humor helped us through many difficult decisions. Never underestimate how helpful it can be for at least one of your leadership team to have a refreshing sense of humor.

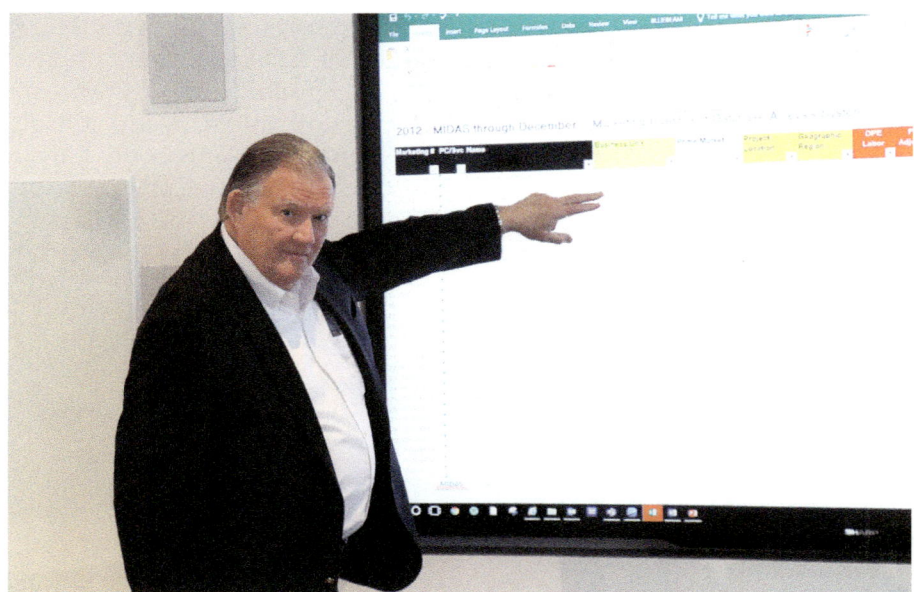

FIGURE 22.1 Tom Robson teaching a course at HOK, 2019.
Source: Photo courtesy of HOK.

Removing Office Leaders

The challenge of getting every office leader to support and fulfill the pyramid strategy fell to the ExCom. During Monday calls and quarterly retreats, the newly expanded ExCom discussed individual office leaders who led underperforming HOK branches, or who did not embrace the pyramid strategy. As usual, I insisted we make a decision for each leader, not just talk about them as we had in the past. Some leaders needed a private conversation. I continued the founders' tradition of sharing compliments publicly and criticisms privately. A discreet conversation can be very effective, but only if your personnel problem is relatively mild.

Sometimes those talks happened on the phone. I preferred the speakerphone for calls when I was in my San Francisco office because it was easier than keeping a handset against my ear. From boyhood, I had been a doodler when listening to my teachers at school. Sketching somehow helped me listen better, and during HOK speakerphone calls I doodled when no one could see me. My office had been paperless since the late 1990s, and the only available paper was a tray of 4 × 6 note paper I kept for jotting down quick notes. I ended up doodling more than writing on those slips of paper.

My assistant Susie noticed a pattern: When my conversation was difficult—like a shape-up-or-ship-out talk with an office leader—the doodles were very geometric with hard edges and angles By contrast, when my conversation was positive—something like winning new work or collecting an overdue bill—my doodles were soft-edged and free-flowing. Regardless, doodling seemed to help me think and cope. I always threw the doodles away after a call, but Susie started secretly saving the ones she found most interesting, noting the person, the topic, and the date of the call. She made a scrap book of my doodles and presented it to me on my last day in the office. Only then did I learn Susie had been collecting them for years.

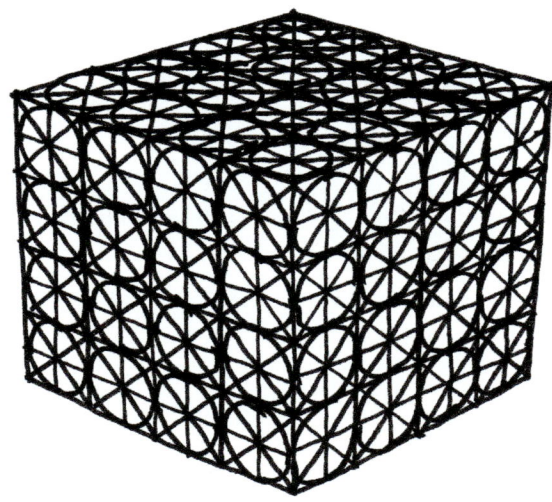

FIGURE 22.2 MacLeamy Doodle during a difficult conversation.
Source: Image courtesy of Patrick MacLeamy.

Sometimes a firm talk was not enough, and we needed to remove an office leader. Getting the ExCom to agree to this more drastic action was always difficult. If I was hard-headed, Bill Valentine was soft-hearted. Here we were, HOK's two top leaders, with very different approaches. Bill chose to see the good in everyone and overlook the bad. "Remember, sometimes good people do bad things," he would say. During one of these difficult discussions, Bill removed his glasses, held them up to the light, and said, "I'm an incurable optimist. I see the world through rose-colored glasses!" Bill was always the last one to agree that someone had to go. My response was usually something like, "Bill, you are driving with the parking brake on. We need to move faster!"

I felt a real sense of urgency to fix HOK, and had to dismiss a number of people over the years. Each dismissal was always in person—never by phone—because our leaders deserved respect even when being dismissed. I never got used to letting people go, and told our HR leaders many times, "If I ever get to the point where this doesn't bother me, take me out and shoot me." Never fire people lightly, but when you must, do it without looking back.

FIGURE 22.3 MacLeamy Doodle during a positive conversation.
Source: Image courtesy of Patrick MacLeamy.

The ExCom began to lead HOK with more confidence as we replaced problematic office leaders and rooted out sloppy operations. Bill Hellmuth and Tom Robson proved to be outstanding additions and helped us build a strong team. The ExCom was the first part of the first step in the pyramid strategy, and people around the firm were becoming more confident in our leadership.

Empowering the Board of Directors

As we were reinvigorating the ExCom, we were working to transform the larger HOK board of directors into an effective, influential body at HOK. Every major office and market practice was now represented on that board, as were the leaders of the design disciplines—architecture, interiors, engineering, planning, landscape architecture, and more. Our goal was for board members to bond together to lead the firm, and for board members to convey and follow our agreed strategy in their offices, market practices, or disciplines. It was a ready-made group that I could build into a team to support my strategy—if only I could convince them.

Positive Peer Pressure

Now that I was officially CEO, I had the mandate to try an experiment in positive peer pressure. This was something I had wanted to do when I was COO but did not have the mandate. Remember those simplified financial reports that Bob Pratzel, Tim Tynan, and I had created? They didn't do HOK much good buried in a computer somewhere. Their true power would come from bringing them into the light, so I made side-by-side financial reports a central feature of HOK board meetings. Everyone on the board was able to compare results among offices, because they were shown right next to each other in one Excel workbook. We displayed fees, backlog, collections, profit, and more for everyone to see. We showed noncompliant office results in red to make them impossible to ignore.

We began to emphasize the importance of meeting financial metrics at every board meeting. The most challenging metric was the 50 Percent Rule governing the amount of staff each office was able to afford. Unprofitable offices consistently violated the 50 Percent Rule, meaning they must increase fees or reduce staff. It was painful. We soon learned that showing a single month's metrics was not enough, because it's easy to mask weaknesses over a short period. Thus, we began showing 12 consecutive months' worth of results to get the real story. Positive peer pressure grew on underperforming offices to work toward compliance with HOK's metrics. Positive peer pressure is a tool any firm can tap into for a variety of purposes.

CFO Bob Pratzel or I put board members from underperforming offices on the spot, asking them to describe their strategy for returning to profitability. It sounds harsh, but HOK was not going to survive without this kind of accountability. Board members from profitable offices became activists, questioning underperforming office leaders about their lack of success and offering advice about what had worked for them. Positive peer pressure became a regular part of our board meetings and had its intended effect. No one liked to be the center of attention for underperformance, and results gradually improved. More consistent profits meant less grumbling around the board table and more shared success.

As HOK's operations gradually improved month after month, we began to generate consistent firm-wide profits. I asked Bob Pratzel to begin making payments to Bank of America to pay down our line of credit. I decided that it was only fair that we make good news a part of the financial reports we shared with the HOK board every month, so Bob added a line item showing our loan payoff progress. Everyone began to look forward to the day when we paid off the bank. Our ability to make regular payments became another indication of our growing strength as a firm, a tangible sign of: "We can do this together."

Replacing Board Members

I wanted board membership to be a privilege, not a right. After all, if we wanted HOK's board of directors to be an influential force at HOK, we needed the right people. Board members should be leaders who met HOK's financial metrics and worked for the good of the entire firm. This was even more important now that our board had expanded to include 30 people. Big boards can be unwieldy and counterproductive if they're not aligned.

The ExCom was responsible for electing a new board every year, and we began to replace board members from underperforming offices. We also added more leaders from the various market practices and professional disciplines, so that the board reflected our diversified company. Bill Hellmuth asserted himself, arguing, "We are a design firm and need more designers on our board." Design principals began to replace some managing principals. Replacing board members signaled the board was a serious responsibility, not a right. The board began to function as a *strong board*, becoming our rock solid foundation. The first level of our pyramid was in place.

Chapter 22: To Design a World-Class Firm

1. Work on your top leadership first, so improvements there will filter out to your broader leadership team.
2. Meet with top leadership regularly to keep them focused on your goals.
3. Don't just talk about problems. Agree on solutions. Then assign those solutions to specific leaders as "action items." Follow up weekly until they are done.
4. Publicly name your next design leader. Architecture firms need to communicate this successor very clearly, since design is the heart of the firm.
5. Never underestimate the value of humor to help teams smooth out their differences.
6. Try discreet shape-up-or-ship-out conversations with problem personnel, but only if the issue with them is relatively mild.
7. Replace key leaders if necessary. Never do this lightly, but when you must, be decisive with the future of the firm in mind.
8. Share financial reports openly with firm leaders so they become a force for improvement.
9. Use positive peer pressure to motivate your firm's leaders, offices, and operations to improve.
10. Make board membership a privilege, not a right. Replace board members who do not meet your goals or do not work for the good of your entire firm.
11. Appoint a board of directors that reflects all locations, disciplines, and specialties at your firm.

CHAPTER 23

The Effort Curve

In late 2003, less than a year into my tenure as CEO, I was forced to take a brief break from the urgent task of climbing up HOK's pyramid of goals—a break that ended up benefiting the firm in the end. I received a call from Gertraud Breitkopf of the federal government's General Services Administration (GSA), the agency responsible for buildings. Gertraud got right to the point. "GSA is a member of the Construction Users Round Table (CURT), an organization of very large companies with extensive real estate holdings," she said. "I chair a CURT committee created to find out why our member companies have so much trouble with building construction. Our committee requests your presence next week to understand our concerns."

The CURT Summons

It sounded like a summons, and it was. The GSA was a crucial HOK client. It is the largest landlord in the country, responsible for managing most federal civilian facilities. I agreed to change my schedule and attend. CURT held its meeting in a windowless conference room at a hotel near the Houston Airport. I saw some old friends and colleagues from design, engineering, and construction firms, as well as Phil Bernstein from Autodesk and representatives from other software companies. One person I knew by reputation and met for the first time was Carl Galioto, the highly regarded Technical Partner at SOM, New York. CURT members in attendance included Gertraud from GSA plus representatives from Shell, Johnson & Johnson, General Mills, General Motors, and other big companies.

Our CURT hosts were responsible for building refineries, power plants, assembly lines, power grids—and an occasional building. The representative from Shell described the frustration he and his CURT colleagues felt by showing us an aerial photo of a recently completed refinery. He said, "Our new refinery is spread across many acres and contains thousands of pipes, valves, processing equipment, pumps, sensors, and storage tanks." Then he pointed to a tiny building almost lost in one corner of the refinery. "See this building? It contains offices for the refinery manager and his staff," he said. "We had more change orders for this little building than we did for the entire refinery!" Change orders are requests to alter a building once construction has already begun. "We want to know why this happens," he demanded. "And we want you to help us fix it!"

We all looked at each other. This was important. We all worked for the GSA, and many of us worked for the other CURT members in the room. We had to find ways to improve the design and construction process to reduce avoidable change orders. Our CURT clients made it clear that if we couldn't improve things, they would find a way to build their facilities without us.

The change orders our CURT hosts described were not new to anyone in the meeting, including me. They reminded me of something from my childhood. As a boy, I had done woodworking projects with my grandfather, Pop Hogue, who was a carpenter. Pop taught me the old adage, "Measure twice, cut once." When I asked him why, he said, "Wood is expensive. If you cut wrong, you will waste the wood and it will cost more time and money to replace—so measure twice!"

> ... it's cheap to make changes early, while a project is still on paper or on a computer. It's expensive to make changes later, when the project is being built of concrete or steel.

As a young project manager, I had learned that my grandfather's wisdom is even more true when designing a big building instead of a small woodworking project. After all, it's cheap to make changes early, while a project is still on paper or on a computer. It's expensive to make changes later, when the project is being built of concrete or steel. I thought back to that too-skinny ramp at the San Bernardino Courthouse in California, the one where the buses got stuck. It sure would have been easier to widen it on paper instead of jackhammering out the concrete after it was built.

Traditional architects tended to wait too long to consult with engineers and other specialists, making coordination more difficult and expensive. I believed architects should coordinate early with other design team members, and I remembered Obata brought in the best engineers he could find to lend their expertise early in the design process.

A second giant improvement would be for the design team to coordinate with the contractor during design, an idea gaining acceptance around the building industry. I recalled how helpful it was to work with Turner Construction during design of the Moscone Convention Center in San Francisco, when they provided early advice about cost and "constructability."

Clients have a responsibility, too. They need to make key decisions about the project in a timely way to keep the project on track. If architects, engineers, contractors, and clients could begin this vetting process as early as possible—the equivalent of measuring twice—our projects would run more smoothly with fewer change orders.

The Effort Curve

On the second day of the meeting, I asked for some time and drew a diagram on the flip chart—another instance where a simple graphic helped me get my ideas across. The diagram showed the time and effort involved in seeing a building through from the beginning of design through the end of construction.

Chapter 23 The Effort Curve

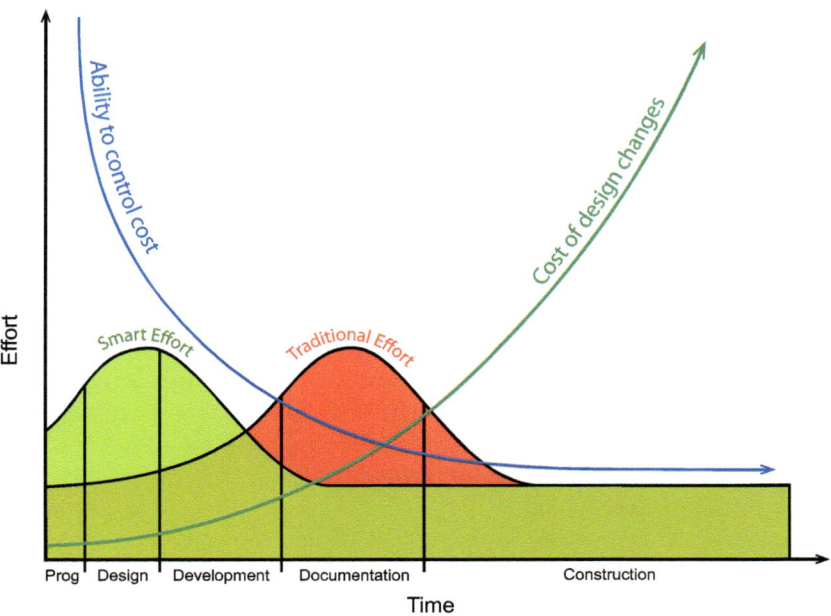

FIGURE 23.1 Effort Curve diagram showing the benefits of early collaboration and decision-making. Source: Image courtesy of Patrick MacLeamy.

Traditional Effort Curve

First, I drew a red curve I called the traditional Effort Curve. It showed that architects and engineers traditionally assigned a small team and put in a modest amount of work during schematic design, then increased their efforts slightly during design development. Efforts and staffing rose to a peak during the documentation phase, during which architects and engineers prepared construction drawings and specifications for the contractor. In the days of drafting by hand, preparing drawings for the contractor took a big team and a Herculean effort. After bidding, firms usually reduced their teams and efforts for the construction phase.

The traditional Effort Curve grew out of a time when architects needed large teams of draftsmen to prepare construction documents for the contractor. Remember, when I first joined HOK, Kassabaum's production team was larger than the design and marketing teams combined. They were the ones who prepared those construction drawings, the fattest part of the traditional Effort Curve.

Ability to Control Cost

I drew a blue line high on the left, at the beginning of design, but descending in a steep curve to become almost flat by the bidding phase on the right. This line represented the design team's ability to control the cost of the building. We had the most control over the price tag at the very beginning of design, but that control rapidly diminished as we made design decisions and locked in more choices. By the time of bidding, the ability to control cost was almost zero. If the bids came in over budget, we only had two ways to reduce the construction cost: redesign the building or "strip the finishes"—which means replacing the planned finishes, inside and outside the building, with less expensive materials of lower quality. Redesigning the building was impractical; stripping the finishes cheapened the building—literally and figuratively.

Cost of Design Changes

The second problem with the traditional Effort Curve also involved cost, this time the cost of making design changes later in a project. I drew a green line sloping steeply up from left to right. Changing the design was cheap at first, but grew exponentially more expensive as the project progressed. Remember, we're basically talking about the difference between making changes on a computer versus making changes in concrete. Of course, making changes during construction is the worst of all, since it might even necessitate demolition.

But even making changes in the middle, during the documentation phase, is pricy because we must reconcile so many different parts of the design. Say the client wants to change the location of a conference room late in the game. That one change, made out of sequence, has a ripple effect: the mechanical engineer might be forced to re-route ductwork through steel beams, forcing the structural engineer to strengthen those beams . . . and on and on. Finally, everything must be re-coordinated on the drawings and specifications.

As I spoke, I saw heads nodding with recognition. We had all lived this nightmare.

Smart Effort Curve

I posed a question: Why can't architects, engineers, clients, and contractors coordinate with each other early, when our ability to control cost is greatest and the price of design changes is smallest? If clients would articulate their needs and wants early, we would have better guidance. If engineers would vet design concepts early, we would optimize the engineering systems. And if contractors weighed in with their cost information and practical knowledge early, we would have better control of cost and constructability.

All these efforts could be supported by the newest Building Information Modeling (BIM) software. Modeling buildings in three dimensions made it possible to check and test design decisions much earlier. Even if architects, engineers, clients, and contractors missed it, a computer might just catch the fact that our courthouse ramp was too skinny—and warn us before it was too late.

With an early, interdisciplinary effort like this, the construction process was bound to be smoother, with fewer change orders. I sketched another Effort Curve, this time in green, with a peak of effort much earlier, during the design and development phases. I called it the Smart Effort Curve and suggested it could begin to answer the CURT questions.

As I finished drawing and speaking, the mood in the room felt electric. Phil Bernstein of Autodesk rushed up to the diagram to study the different curves. Everyone began talking at once, relieved to see an approach with the potential to reduce expensive last-minute change orders. My new friend, Carl Galioto of SOM, liked the Effort Curve and realized his thinking was aligned with mine, even though we represented competing firms. By the end of the session, we had decided to adopt the Effort Curve as the centerpiece of our CURT committee report. All of us recognized that early teamwork between the owner, design team, and contractor, supported by the latest software, could improve the design and construction process and reduce change orders. It was not a guarantee of perfection—but it was a step in the right direction.

The representative from Shell—the one who had shown us the aerial photo of his new refinery—said, "What you just described is the way we built our refinery. We hired a design–build contractor who designed and built the refinery—and we were heavily involved as the owner from the beginning . . . I guess we should have built that little office building in the corner of the refinery the same way!"

CURT published our work in August 2004.[1] By that time the American Institute of Architects had gotten interested and invited our CURT committee to present its findings at a plenary session of the 2005 National AIA Convention. I was part of the CURT presentation team and described the Smart Effort Curve at that session. Our concept was enthusiastically received and led to formation of the AIA Committee for Integrated Project Delivery. Eventually the AIA committee published a new contract form called the Integrated Project Delivery (IPD) form of contract, linking the owner, architect, and contractor into one team based on the CURT recommendations and the Effort Curve.

The Effort Curve at HOK

After the AIA convention, I hustled back to HOK and got busy formalizing HOK's own commitment to the Smart Effort Curve. Of course, we could only realize the full benefits with willing design team partners, contractors, and owners. But we could prepare for early coordination by learning to use new BIM software. BIM software was a leap forward from Computer-Aided Design (CAD) software because it supported three dimensional design, allowing architects to see and design buildings as virtual models. Better yet, BIM software had the capacity to carry digital information for each building component. It was a game changer. The HOK board approved the move to BIM software in early 2005, and we began to distribute the new software to all the offices.

Next came the challenge of training people to use the new BIM software. As usual, the results were uneven across the offices. So, in 2006, I recruited a specialized team of technical experts to train HOK employees on the new BIM software, and I gave them the not-so-creative name buildingSMART@HOK. This was my version of "bringing in the pros,"

---

[1] The Construction Users Roundtable, "Collaboration, Integrated Information and the Project Lifecycle in Building Design, Construction and Operation," Architectural/Engineering Productivity Committee of The Construction Users Roundtable (CURT), WP-1202, August 2004. Accessed April 21, 2019. https://kcuc.org/wp-content/uploads/2013/11/Collaboration-Integrated-Information-and-the-Project-Lifecycle.pdf.

just as HOK had hired professional finance and HR people years before. I'm a firm believer in hiring experts to help your people get up to speed technologically, so your people can stay focused on their core design competency.

HOK and I were still heavily involved in buildingSMART International, so this was a natural extension of those efforts. In addition to training our people, the HOK buildingSMART team began testing more advanced software that could alert us to conflicts in our designs. The software was automated to give the design team results in real time, allowing them to double check our designs for compliance with client programs, budgets, energy efficiency goals—and more—as we went. It wasn't perfect, but it was a giant step in the right direction.

As the new BIM software became established around the firm, our teams began to experiment with a few owners and contractors who saw the benefits of early decisions and coordination. We did not know it yet, but the pieces were falling into place just in time for the biggest, fastest, most challenging project in HOK history.

Case Study: KAUST

King Abdullah bin Abdulaziz Al Saud of Saudi Arabia was in failing health and wanted to cement his legacy before he died. He envisioned something revolutionary for Saudi Arabia, a huge new university that would educate both men and women for careers in science and technology, to be named the King Abdullah University of Science and Technology, or KAUST. He wanted it to be a beacon of knowledge in the Middle East and a leading world university. King Abdulaziz asked the Saudi Ministry of Education how long it would take to design and build a new university and he didn't like the answer—it was going to take too long.

The King turned to Saudi Aramco, the national oil company, for help. Aramco knew how to build to support its oil business—and knew how to move fast. The people at Aramco told King Abdulaziz they could design, build, and equip a major new university of five million square feet—plus an entire town where the faculty would live—in 32 months. It was incredibly ambitious. Saudi Aramco assigned the project to its large Texas office, not far from HOK Houston.

Tom Robson, Jay Tatum, and Roger Soto heard Aramco needed a master plan for a new university and submitted a proposal. HOK was well-qualified for the work, having designed many university projects. Not only that, HOK had already designed a university in Saudi Arabia itself: King Saud University in Riyadh, the dream project founder George Hellmuth had snagged for us years earlier. Tom Robson received a phone call from an Aramco representative on a Thursday. "Congratulations," the man said. "You have been selected as the master planner for the new university . . . uh, can you be in London this Sunday for a kickoff meeting?"

Tom Robson, Roger Soto, and others managed to get there in time for the meeting. When a project is this promising, you make it happen. It's a good thing they made it, because they learned at the meeting that the commission was for much more than just a master plan. Aramco wanted HOK to lay out the entire campus and town—plus design every building on that campus! We're talking about five million square feet of buildings. This was the first HOK had heard that the project had to be complete in just 32 months. Robson raised his hand and asked, "Do you mean design *and* construct the university in 32 months?" The answer was yes. Because the King was in such a hurry, Aramco had made this a fast-track project, in which construction is already underway as the designers work out the details.

For this, HOK would need a much larger team than was available at HOK Houston. In fact, Robson and his Houston colleagues eventually received help from 900 different HOK people working at nine other HOK offices. The KAUST project challenged the Advance Technology Group and the buildingSMART@HOK group to equip and support a sprawling team of people across multiple offices. They placed all electronic files for the project on the HOK network for collaboration by team members anywhere.

The fast-track strategy adopted by Aramco meant the usual phases of the Effort Curve were even more compressed. The aggressive schedule meant the design team was under pressure to get things right the first time. The project team couldn't fix mistakes during construction because there was limited time to do all the work required. As design continued on the buildings, the buildings themselves were already rising from the desert like a mirage. There was only one way to get this massive job done: Front-load our work on the Smart Effort Curve with BIM. It was an extreme test of BIM technology and of the Smart Effort Curve—and both passed with flying colors. King Abdulaziz dedicated the new university in 2009, only 32 months after we began design, just as Aramco had promised.

FIGURE 23.2 King Abdullah University of Science and Technology, Thuwal, Saudi Arabia.
Source: Photo by: Sam Fentress. Image courtesy of HOK.

When the sand had settled, King Abdullah University of Science and Technology was a success on many fronts. KAUST was Saudi Arabia's first certified Leadership in Environmental Energy and Design (LEED) Platinum project, the highest globally recognized level of sustainability. In fact, at the time, it was the largest single project ever to earn a LEED Platinum rating for green design. KAUST also won Lab of the Year and Library of the Year awards. Internally, it was a huge victory for *true collaboration*. When it was do-or-die time, multiple HOK offices and market practices had come together to get the job done. We had used BIM to coordinate our efforts and the Smart Effort Curve to make sure our design was sound before construction.

The MacLeamy Curve

As you can see, the Smart Effort Curve and BIM became interconnected. Many other people have referenced the Smart Effort Curve in presentations over the years. I later learned a similar curve had been discussed in civil engineering circles, but as far as I know, the idea had never made it into the more creative world of architecture. It wasn't rocket science, but it resonated. Eventually people—not me—began calling it The MacLeamy Curve, which I have found alternately gratifying and embarrassing. To me it is a natural extension of "measure twice, cut once," taught to me years before by my grandfather. Today, I am amazed—and amused—to report that young architects all over the world approach me at conferences and say, "You're the MacLeamy of the MacLeamy Curve! Can I take a selfie with you?"

Chapter 23: To Design a World-Class Firm

1. Measure twice, cut once. It's cheap to make changes on paper or on a computer. It's expensive to make changes in wood—or concrete or steel.
2. Shift your efforts earlier in time to solve problems at the beginning of a project, when costs are low, rather than later, when costs are high.
3. Coordinate early with engineers and other consultants, rather than waiting until a time when changes are more difficult and expensive.
4. Coordinate early with the contractor for best results later.
5. Get timely decisions from the owner for a more successful design and construction process.
6. Hire experts to help your people get up to speed technologically, so your people can stay focused on their core competencies.
7. Use BIM to coordinate the work, especially when you undertake a giant, sprawling project,
8. Use BIM to keep up with fast-track or design–build projects in which the usual phases of the Effort Curve are even more compressed.

CHAPTER 24

Fixing Offices

Back to HOK's pyramid strategy. Our second goal of achieving great operations was going to take more than commitments by the ExCom and board. We needed this hard work to happen in every office, too. The real challenge was fixing underperforming offices, first getting them to profitability, then to constantly improving performance. HOK had grown by adding offices since its founding, but when I became CEO, expansion was not on my mind. For the firm to get back on track, we needed to focus on fixing offices, not adding more. Fixing offices meant finding the right leaders.

Finding New Leaders

Sometimes good people are still not the right people to lead an office. And sometimes good architects are terrible managers. As I have mentioned, occasionally the ExCom made the difficult decision to dismiss an office leader. Of course, that meant we had to find a replacement leader. We preferred to promote someone from within HOK to a vacant leadership position, which often meant transferring a leader from one office to another. In our quest to reclaim our culture, the wise move was to choose somebody who knew what we valued.

On the other hand, we had the same problem as the one that had confronted Obata years before: If we mined a successful HOK branch too aggressively for talent, we might undermine that office's future fortunes. That's when we would work to recruit a leader from another firm to fill a leadership position, hoping to find a good fit and "vaccinate" the new hire with HOK culture once they arrived. Here is one successful example of each —a transfer and a recruit—who became third generation HOK leaders. Both had what I call "fire in their eyes," a combination of curiosity and ambition that seems to shine forth from the most promising leaders.

The Fixer

Remember Riccardo Mascia, who first joined the Mexico City office? By now, Riccardo had been with HOK for many years and was one of us. For a while, he was content to lead HOK Mexico City and enjoyed living there with his wife, Sofia, and their young daughter, Sofia-Marie. Riccardo had built the office to a staff of 55 with work in Mexico and Latin America, and had earned a good reputation for leadership around the firm.

FIGURE 24.1 Riccardo Mascia in his HOK Chicago office.
Source: Image courtesy of HOK.

But for some reason, Mexico City had become a much more dangerous place. I don't know why. Riccardo's wife was robbed at gunpoint—twice—while stopped in traffic. The thugs tapped on her window and demanded money. Then, even though she handed over her cash, they hit her in the head with a pistol for good measure. The last straw was when thieves burglarized the Mascia home while they were sleeping. "Sofia and I realized we were prisoners in our home, not even letting Sofia-Marie ride her trike on the sidewalk," Riccardo told me later. "That's when Sofia and I began to seriously consider leaving Mexico."

HOK London had won a project to design a new headquarters for Telefónica, the Spanish telephone company, and needed a Spanish-speaking HOK representative in the Madrid project office. London Managing Principal Ralph Courtenay asked Riccardo if he would be interested in moving to Madrid. Riccardo accepted the offer and moved with his family to Madrid in 2002, the first of many moves he would make for HOK.

Riccardo left behind a good leadership team at HOK Mexico City, and they ran the office for several more years after his departure. The difficulty of doing business in Mexico, coupled with a poor local economy, prompted us to sell HOK Mexico to the office leadership in 2009.

I was not happy with Riccardo's move to Madrid. He had only gone there because things were so bad for his family in Mexico. His talents were wasted in a project office when several large offices lacked an effective managing principal. That included San Francisco, where Ed McCrary, who had replaced me as managing principal, said he was close to retirement. I called Riccardo with an offer to move to San Francisco and fulfill that role. Riccardo listened, then said, "Let me think about it and talk to Sofia." I replied, "Talk to Sofia, but I'm not taking no for an answer. I'll call you tomorrow for your 'yes'." I called Riccardo the next day and he said . . . "yes." Since I was based in the San Francisco office, I met with Riccardo every couple of weeks to see how it was going. Turned out, he did not have the challenge he had expected. Ed McCrary was still enjoying the job and delayed his retirement, so Riccardo needed another challenge.

Our Hong Kong office was struggling to establish itself and become consistently profitable, so I asked Riccardo to figure out what HOK needed to do to make that key Asia office successful. Riccardo made several trips to Hong Kong and agreed the office needed a new leader. He recruited Toby Bath, an English architect who had worked for SOM in Asia, as the new leader. Riccardo continued to divide his time between Hong Kong and San Francisco for two years. His efforts contributed to HOK San Francisco, but Ed McCrary was still going strong. And now Toby Bath was asserting himself in Hong Kong. Riccardo was ready for yet another challenge.

I asked Riccardo to move again, this time to Los Angeles which was floundering under poor leadership. Riccardo agreed and moved with his family to Los Angeles in 2005, his third move for HOK. Thanks to the efforts of our most well-traveled fixer, we learned that it took about two years to get a stumbling office on its feet and running well. This is a good benchmark for other firms to keep in mind. That includes changing out leaders, if necessary, and reorganizing for success. Sure enough, after two years, the LA office was well on its way. Riccardo and his family got a little bit of a breather, remaining there for five years.

Meanwhile, Toby Bath had aggressively expanded HOK in Asia, opening branch offices in Beijing, Shanghai, Singapore, and Ho Chi Minh City. I admired his initiative, but the operation was stretched across too many countries and became almost ungovernable. It was already a challenge for HOK Hong Kong to make a profit every year, and the addition of so many branch offices made it impossible. Toby eventually resigned, and in 2010, I asked Riccardo to move to Hong Kong. Visiting frequently had helped before, but this time the region needed a real presence. Riccardo agreed, and moved his family for the fourth time.

Riccardo told me Hong Kong was his most challenging assignment. Over the next several years he closed offices in Singapore and Ho Chi Minh City, and reorganized Hong Kong as a leaner and more nimble office. He learned not all projects proposed in Asia were realistic, and focused marketing efforts on the most promising clients and projects. There is an idea called the Pareto Principle,[1] which suggests that 80% of your business comes from just 20% of your clients. The exact ratio may vary, but Riccardo found this to be true in Asia. HOK Hong Kong eventually became modestly profitable, but by then the firm needed Riccardo elsewhere. The fixer was set to move again.

---

[1] Kevin Kruse, "The 80/20 Rule and How It Can Change Your Life," *Forbes*, March 7, 2016. Accessed July 27, 2019. https://www.forbes.com/sites/kevinkruse/2016/03/07/80-20-rule/#6a7e97903814.

The Recruit

Now, let's look at the case of the ultimate recruit. Carl Galioto and I had stayed in touch after our shared CURT adventure. Carl's best friend was Robert Chicas, a colleague who had left SOM New York to join HOK New York as an aviation market-practice leader. Robert let me know Carl was not satisfied with his career at SOM and would be interested in talking with me. Oh, was I interested! I knew from collaborating with Carl on the CURT committee that he would fit in well with HOK culture, not to mention that Carl was the highly regarded technical partner of SOM New York.

For readers from outside the field, a technical architect is the same as a production architect or project architect. The terminology has evolved over the years. Good technical architects are prized for their understanding of how to put buildings together in the real world. They know how to turn designs into buildings. Technical architects understand "building physics," like the right kind of steel to use and how to make mechanical equipment fit above the suspended ceiling. Today, technical architects are also masters of BIM, using 3-D modeling to assemble a virtual building before the contractor assembles a real building of concrete and steel.

Founder George Kassabaum fulfilled two roles at HOK, leading both production and management. His production role was not optimized because he did not have the time to devote to what is today called technical architecture.

For years HOK offices had been modeled after the founders, with three leaders in marketing, design, and management/production. It was high time that HOK split the Kassabaum role into two parts and add a technical architect as a leader in each office, and I knew just the person to lead technical architecture at HOK. I wanted Carl Galioto.

FIGURE 24.2 HOK President Carl Galioto speaking at the 2019 National Organization of Minority Architects in Brooklyn.
Source: Image courtesy of HOK.

To give you an idea of his level of accomplishment, Carl's project at the time we started our dialogue was the Freedom Tower at One World Trade Center. At 1,776 feet, it was the tallest building in the United States, overlooking the site of the World Trade Center's fallen twin towers designed by founder George Hellmuth's former partner Minoru Yamasaki years before. After several months of private discussions and with the support of the ExCom, I offered Carl the position of managing principal of HOK New York, plus leadership of the HOK buildingSMART group, technical leadership of the entire firm, and a seat on the HOK board of directors. Carl accepted our offer and joined HOK in September 2009.

Carl Galioto was born in Brooklyn and remembers when the Dodgers still played there. Later his family moved to Queens, which seemed bucolic by comparison because they had a yard and a tree. Carl always knew he wanted to be an architect and attended the Pratt Institute. After an early job at a small New York firm specializing in preservation architecture, Carl wanted to work on new buildings. In 1978, he joined the production department of SOM on Park Avenue. Carl loved the technical work and rose to become technical partner. Although Carl enjoyed the dedication to design and technical excellence at SOM, he felt typecast within the partnership and was eager for new experiences and growth. Carl was to find that opportunity for growth and a respectful environment for collaboration at HOK.

It's a small world, and it turns out that Carl Galioto and Bill Hellmuth overlapped in their SOM careers. As Carl was considering joining HOK, he asked Bill Hellmuth what the firm was like. Bill said, "HOK is different from your experience at SOM. All of the principals at HOK actually want the others to succeed." Carl couldn't bring himself to believe it, but after joining HOK he found out it was true. "There is an absence of negative energy here. HOK has created an environment where people are supported," Carl told me later. "You have done it—without a hidden agenda—simply for the sake of improvement. I realize that this is where I was meant to be, and I feel like I've come home."

Case Study: HOK New York

When Carl joined HOK, our New York office was in an old department store from the 1800s on Eighth Street in Manhattan's Chelsea District. There was not enough natural light, the wooden floors creaked—and there were mice. Within a few months, he leased offices facing beautiful Bryant Park on Fifth Avenue in Midtown. Carl wanted an office that would inspire staff. It also ended up reassuring clients, a good lesson. "If we were not in the Bryant Park office, we would never have gotten the LaGuardia Airport project," Carl told me later. Sometimes you have to look world class to play with world-class partners, just as Jerry Sincoff had discovered years earlier.

HOK was part of the LaGuardia Gateway Partners team to bid on the $4 billion LaGuardia Terminal B redevelopment project, along with Vantage Airport Group (operations), Skanska (construction), Meridiam (financing), and WSP (engineering). The LaGuardia Gateway Partners design envisioned two new island concourses connected to the terminal by bridges that soar over aircraft taxiways, giving passengers a glimpse of the famous Manhattan skyline as they move through the airport. A daunting requirement: the existing airport had to remain open during construction. "This is a difficult technical project," Carl explained, in his element. "Construction is being done in phases."

FIGURE 24.3 Rendering of LaGuardia Airport with New York skyline in the distance.
Source: Image courtesy of HOK and WSP
Design Credit: HOK and WSP + LaGuardia Gateway Partners
Image Credit: HOK and WSP + LaGuardia Gateway Partners

Carl was the right person for the job and helped HOK earn the confidence of the client, the Port Authority of New York and New Jersey. "One day, they called and said, 'We need a master plan for the entire airport,'" Carl recalled. "Meet us at Governor Cuomo's office." HOK also landed that master plan project, meant to connect LaGuardia to the New York transit system. Many of Carl's SOM colleagues followed him to HOK for the chance to work with him on exciting projects like this. With his leadership, HOK finally became a highly visible and trusted design firm in the Big Apple. You know what they say: "If you can make it there, you can make it anywhere," which was exactly what we were trying to do.

Tweaking the Bonus Program

... I wanted to restructure the annual bonus program to reward leaders for collaborative behavior, not just for profitability.

Once the right leaders were in place, we needed to reward them and retain them. Bonuses were a big part of that. Remember, keeping talented people was part of George Hellmuth's depression-proof-firm plan. However, I wanted to restructure the annual bonus program to reward leaders for collaborative behavior, not just for profitability. I saw this as a crucial step in achieving true collaboration on our HOK pyramid strategy.

Like most firms, HOK distributed a large portion of annual profits to employees through its annual bonus program. In the original St. Louis office, the founders determined the size of the overall bonus pool based on profits for the last fiscal year, then divided the pool into individual bonuses, with the most senior employees receiving the biggest bonuses and other employees receiving smaller amounts. In a good year, everyone in the office received a bonus, including accountants, secretaries, and the people who ran the print machine and made our coffee. If you can achieve this, it is a wonderful precedent that will earn employee loyalty.

As HOK grew into a large firm with many offices, the size of the annual bonus pool continued to be based on profits for the preceding fiscal year. That overall pool was then divided into individual office bonus pools based on the contribution of each office to firm-wide annual profits. This bonus system functioned reasonably well when the firm had just a few offices and each was profitable. As HOK added more offices—and some failed to make money—the bonus system became an annual controversy.

The biggest problem with the bonus allocation system was that it was purely mathematical, based on profits. It became an incentive for individual offices to win and keep as much fee as possible, supporting office-centric behavior and undermining collaboration or quality.

The ExCom had many discussions about how to change the bonus allocation from purely profit-based to a system where market practices, design quality, client service, and collaboration would be considered alongside profits. The discussions were earnest, difficult—sometimes even heated. Eventually we created a second bonus pool for about 80 office and market practice leaders that was separate from the office-based bonus pools, something other firms could adopt.

The ExCom awarded bonuses from this separate pool to each individual leader by considering profits, but also looking at qualitative metrics such as support for great design, collaboration with other offices, and client service. After determining individual leader bonuses, we conducted a fairness check by comparing leader bonuses with each other. For example, we reviewed the bonuses of all design principals side-by-side. Evaluating leaders in this new way required judgment. Members of the ExCom needed to know each leader well enough to judge performance, so we assigned each of the 80 leaders to an individual ExCom member for an annual performance review. The ExCom member had the additional responsibility to inform the leader of his or her bonus. This system is much more complicated, but I recommend it to anyone who wishes to encourage positive behavior in addition to profits.

In 2011, the ExCom delegated the work of establishing leader bonus amounts to a subcommittee, the Compensation Committee or CompCom. (We love our committee abbreviations at HOK!) The CompCom consisted of several ExCom members supported by the HR and legal departments. The committee made the first pass, establishing leader bonus amounts, for review and approval by the full ExCom. Bill Hellmuth was an early supporter of the new bonus system for leaders and became a strong force on the CompCom.

The effect of the leader bonus changes was gradual, but eventually everyone got the idea that other factors besides profits were important. Actually, the factors were intertwined: We believed that support for great design and true collaboration among offices and disciplines would *yield* higher profits for the firm. The tweak to our bonus program helped firm leaders begin to think of themselves as leaders in HOK, not just their office. The other benefit was the reinforcement of ExCom leadership as the anchor for a strong board and the strong board as a foundation for the entire firm. By 2007, every office was profitable for the first time in decades. In future years some offices would occasionally slip back into the red, but the era of chronic unprofitability was over.

Chapter 24: To Design a World-Class Firm

1. Recruit candidates with "fire in their eyes," a combination of curiosity and ambition that seems to shine forth from the most promising people.
2. Choose new office leaders from a combination of talented internal candidates and promising external ones.
3. Identify your own "fixers" who can parachute into problem spots in your firm and get them running smoothly.
4. Keep in mind that it takes a minimum of two years to get a stumbling office back on its feet and running well.
5. Focus on the 20% of clients that generate 80% of your business.
6. Recruit and value skilled technical architects who know how to translate designs into concrete realities.
7. Reshape your bonus program to reward not just profitability, but other factors you value, such as collaboration, quality of design and client service.
8. Award bonuses to everyone in your office, including support staff, if you can, to earn lasting employee loyalty.
9. Cross check the bonuses you are awarding to each category of leader to make sure they are fair.

CHAPTER 25

Fixing Central Services

We began to fix Central Services—Central Accounting, Legal Services, Marketing, Central HR, and the Advance Technology Group—in parallel with fixing the offices. This challenge required years of unglamorous hard work, but was an essential part of great operations, the second step in our pyramid strategy. Three departments in particular needed rethinking.

Consolidating Accounting

As HOK grew from the founding office to a network of many offices, each office developed a local accounting staff for office and project budgeting along with billing and collecting. Local accountants reported to the managing principal of that office. This arrangement created conflicts with Central Accounting, and those conflicts only grew worse as the firm added more offices. Some local accountants were under pressure from their offices to inflate monthly accrual income, leading to skirmishes with Controller Tim Tynan. Despite the 90-Day Rule, every month some local accountants tried to negotiate with Tim to give them credit for fees earned, even if the 90-day deadline for collecting fees had passed.

Sometimes managing principals relied on their own accountants instead of the firm-wide financial report. During one board of directors meeting, CFO Bob Pratzel reported London had suffered a loss. The managing principal for London disagreed, saying, "Bob, your figures are wrong. My accountant provided me figures before the board meeting and they show a good profit." It turned out the London accountant furnished figures that excluded Central Services overhead. Perhaps it was wishful thinking!

I proposed we consolidate accounting across the firm. Local accountants would remain in their host HOK offices and continue with project accounting, billing, and collecting as before, but report to Controller Tim Tynan, not to their managing principal. I believed this step would remove confusion—as in the case of HOK London—and result in a more cohesive, efficient operation. No one liked the idea at first. Managing principals had become accustomed to semi-autonomy and did not want to give up their authority. Board members complained that Central Services were already too expensive, and the addition of new people would drive up central overhead further. I explained overhead would be the same, just moved from the offices to Central Services.

The ExCom agreed with my idea of consolidating accounting, and the board of directors eventually fell into line. By the end of 2009, accounting consolidation was complete and the benefits became obvious to everyone. The accountants worked well as a single team and became more efficient at handling their workload. After the consolidation, everyone had difficulty imagining how we had functioned with fractured accounting departments in the past. It's a step I would recommend for any design or creative firm with multiple branches.

Fixing Advance Technology

By the time I became CEO, technology was widespread across HOK. But our Tech 2000 initiative had turned from vision to chaos because we did not follow through with an operating strategy. Every office connected to the firm-wide network, allowing people to communicate and share work. But, just as accounting had been structured, each office was responsible for its own information technology purchases and local IT staff. This meant technology in the offices was uncoordinated and in conflict with the central Advance Technology Group. The name Advance Technology Group was supposed to be a positive play on words—advancing HOK toward the newest and best technology—but because the ATG and office tech efforts were separate, it wasn't working.

Some offices purchased computers, whereas others leased. Financially stressed offices kept computers too long instead of buying upgrades, making their computers too slow or unable to run the latest CAD programs. Each office was responsible for keeping software up to date, but not everyone did. Some offices neglected to upgrade AutoCAD software, whereas others, in unprofitable offices, resorted to illegally copying AutoCAD software instead of buying more copies. One IT manager in the small Tampa office refused to configure his network to be compatible with the firm-wide network because he thought his configuration was better. His boss, the managing principal for HOK Tampa, was unaware that his small office was delaying adoption of a common network across HOK until I called and told him about it. It was a mess.

I proposed that we consolidate Advance Technology in the same way we had unified accounting, making IT specialists in each office employees of the Advance Technology Group (ATG). This time, after our experience with consolidating accounting, the ExCom and board of directors accepted the need for change more readily. ATG consolidation was complete by the end of 2009 and the benefits were immediate. CIO Ken Young and his top assistant, John Bartolomi, developed an HOK-wide master lease program for computers and software, and soon everyone in the firm had the latest equipment. The ATG updated the HOK network, making it faster and more reliable. Differences of opinion about how to configure the network became a thing of the past. As with accounting, once the changes were made it was hard to imagine how we had functioned the old way. Sometimes, you must shake things up to get the best result, even if there's a painful transition period.

Fixing Advance Technology made progress on two of our pyramid goals: great operations and true collaboration. People in any HOK office were able to seamlessly work on projects in another office, thanks to a consistent technology approach. And that technology was top notch. This anticipated our future: higher levels of collaboration between different offices to win work and serve clients. As a result of our tech consolidation, the Advance Technology Group and HOK are regularly recognized as leaders in the application of information technology. *DesignIntelligence* magazine consistently ranks HOK as the number-one professional design practice for information technology innovation.

Streamlining Human Resources

Human resources (HR) initially operated in the same way as accounting and technology, with employees divided between central HR and the offices. Local HR representatives supported the staff in their individual offices and answered to their own office leadership. They were responsible for local recruitment, training, promotions, raises, performance reviews—the works. Architecture is a service business, so our employees are our lifeblood, and they were being treated differently in every single office. It didn't make sense and it wasn't fair.

Meanwhile, this wacky system effectively relegated central HR to a department that only managed the employee benefit program and a recruitment program for leaders. We had to do better. Over several years, central HR set a goal of becoming professionally organized and completely digitized. The most difficult challenge was getting each office to adopt the same standards for annual reviews, promotions, and raises. As always, each office believed its system was the best and resisted change. If employees were our most important resource, HOK needed a firm-wide system and policies to match our growth. Eventually we coerced and cajoled every office into adopting an integrated system. Then we placed useful HR information on that integrated system for easy firm-wide access.

Central HR established consistent policies for recruitment, onboarding, and training of new employees. HR Director John Mahon worked with each office to recruit new graduates from nearby universities. Central HR established a summer internship program in cooperation with the offices, enabling students to gain real work experience. We paid our interns—we believed it was the right thing to do—well before this became the norm. I was proud of our program, partly because I still remembered being offered an unpaid internship myself years ago. I recommend that all firms pay their interns. Paying our interns attracted higher caliber people and created a pipeline for many summer interns to become full time HOK employees after graduation.

Of course, we needed to attract senior people too, so we also built up our protocol for recruiting leadership-level employees from outside of HOK. The key was to be on the lookout for bright lights well before we needed them. Strong leaders are always difficult to find, and as I searched for someone to fill an empty leadership position, the three things that mattered were: Can the person do the job? Does the person have integrity? Can the person work as part of a team?

... the three things that mattered were: Can the person do the job? Does the person have integrity? Can the person work as part of a team?

We wanted not just big talents, but big talents who would integrate well into our HOK culture. That effort is ongoing today, managed by central HR in partnership with the ExCom. Central HR also helped us transfer HOK leaders from one office to another, our other method of growing and strengthening the firm. In fact, the ExCom transferred so many leaders between HOK offices that HR developed a uniform protocol to help employees and their families move from one city to another.

Diversity was also important to HOK. In the early years, the firm was predominantly white, male, and Midwestern, but incredibly proud that a Japanese-American designer was one of our founders. My wife, Jeanne, was one of just a handful of female architects at HOK when she joined the firm in 1974, but today about half of HOK people are women. Women and minorities are moving into leadership ranks around the firm, with even more leadership diversity as our goal.

Chapter 25: To Design a World-Class Firm

1. Maintain strong support services like accounting, HR, legal, and IT. Well-oiled non-design departments will help your firm be world-class.
2. Have all your accountants report to a central leader, rather than to their separate office leaders, for more streamlined, accurate, and harmonious accounting.
3. Consolidate your technology efforts under a central leader, too, rather than letting each office or department manage its own tech program.
4. Treat your employees consistently across offices by aligning your HR policies.
5. Pay your interns even if they are earning school credit for the work. Paying interns will help attract top candidates and create a pipeline for recruiting future talent.
6. Be on the lookout for bright lights well before you need them. Look not just for big talents, but big talents who will integrate well into your company culture.
7. Strive for diverse employees, who will, in turn, better understand your diverse clients and leverage that understanding to do great work for them.
8. Ask yourself three questions when recruiting top leadership: Can the person do the job? Does the person have integrity? Will the person work well as part of a team?

CHAPTER 26

Reclaiming Company Culture

We were still working on the first two goals of our pyramid strategy when we began addressing the third: true collaboration. We could not afford to wait. If it seems like I keep circling back to this point, you are right. I harped on it then, too, because that's what it took. As the founders had said, there was plenty of competition on the outside. We needed to be unified on the inside and help each other to succeed. The ExCom took advantage of every meeting between different HOK offices as an opportunity to help people become friends and foster a spirit of teamwork. And when the offices did not have a reason to come together, I went to them.

Visiting the Offices

In-person communication was a key part of the effort to restore HOK culture around the firm. What are our goals? Why are they important? What's HOK all about? The monthly pyramid messages were a first step, but I needed to speak to people face to face. Any leader in this situation does. I made it a goal to travel to each of our 20 offices at least once a year. Each visit lasted about 24 hours, and included meetings with individual leaders, a large meeting with everyone in the office, and dinner with office leadership.

My favorite meetings were with everyone in the office. I always began by encouraging people to ask questions at any time, not wait until my remarks concluded. I also encouraged people to "ask me anything," saying we had to be open and honest with each other to become the firm of our dreams. In fact, these meetings came to be called Ask Me Anything talks, a concept other firms could adopt.

Next, I drew a pyramid on a flip chart or white board, then described each of our four goals and why they were important. I shared news from around the firm, summarized our progress toward regaining profitability, and spoke about paying down our line of credit with the bank.

While traveling and meeting with employees, I was struck by the fact that I could tell if I was in a well-run office with good leaders. Well-run offices always had a buzz of energy. People in Ask Me Anything meetings were comfortable speaking up and expressing themselves. They were eager to learn and asked lots of questions. This is a good gauge that all firm leaders should be on the lookout for. Young people asked the most questions of all, so I began holding separate meetings with them.

Struggling offices did not have a buzz. They were unnaturally quiet for places where everyone was doing creative work. If an office was not well-run, staff would sit stiffly through these meetings, afraid to put their hands up or ask questions. When leaders do not engage with people, then people do not engage with each other, and nobody knows how a firm is really doing. Often senior people were the ones least willing to take a chance and ask me a probing question, even though I really meant it when I said, "ask me anything." The contrast in individual office vibes was striking, showing how much more work we had to do.

During one visit to HOK Toronto, I encouraged people to ask questions as always, but no one interrupted my remarks. I stopped speaking and called for questions. Silence. No one spoke. I asked again, and still not one person stirred. I took a looney—a Canadian dollar coin with a loon on the front—from my pocket and said, "The first person to ask a question gets this looney." A young woman finally asked a question. I thanked her for her bravery and gave her the looney while answering her question. Then a young man asked, "Do I get a looney for my question, too?" "Well, that one is gone," I replied. "Maybe you'll speak up first the next time!" There was a refreshing burst of laughter. Thank goodness. That looney had broken the ice, and more people began to "ask me anything."

I continued those important in-person office visits throughout my years as CEO. I explained and re-explained the pyramid strategy, adding new details of our progress with each successive visit. This simple, nine-word strategy and graphic became well-known and understood as a way of reinforcing HOK culture—and eventually the pyramid strategy itself became part of HOK culture.

Explaining HOK Stock

The more profitable we were, the more HOK stock rose in value, but we found that new employees did not understand how our stock worked or why they should invest. HOK had been shareholder-owned from the beginning, when the three founders set the firm up as a corporation rather than a more traditional partnership. At first, the founders owned all the stock. As they retired, HOK depended on new leaders to purchase stock, and maintain the viability of the firm. I had bought every share of HOK stock offered to me, as had many others. Everyone on the ExCom was a shareholder, as were most of our board of directors.

By contrast, most emerging leaders in HOK offices were not shareholders, did not understand much about HOK stock, and were not motivated to buy stock when given the opportunity. Why? During visits to the offices I learned people had a poor understanding of HOK stock. I heard questions like, "How does stock ownership work? Who can buy HOK stock? Is stock ownership important for advancement?" Clearly, we had not provided enough information about HOK stock or becoming a stockholder, and employees did what people everywhere do: they filled the void with rumors—and always to the negative. It's human nature, I guess.

The reputation of HOK stock had also suffered because people worried it was a poor investment. Since HOK's profits had, indeed, been flat for several years, and the value of each share is directly linked to profit, the stock had underperformed for quite a while. Others worried about HOK's stability. What would happen to HOK's stock value if we went out of business? Or even if HOK was stable, wasn't the work of architects inherently risky? After all, during recessions, the first thing clients do is stop building buildings. With worries like this, many employees who were eligible to be shareholders avoided buying HOK stock, preferring to invest in real estate or the stock market instead.

I began to describe how the HOK stock program worked during office visits, something I urge all leaders in employee-owned businesses to do. Stock sounds like a cold, hard financial tool, but it can become a tool for reclaiming your company culture. The most frequent question I heard was always, "How is the price of HOK stock determined?" The answer was very simple, something all firms should strive for. HOK stock value is based on the net worth of the firm:

$$\text{HOK assets} - \text{HOK liabilities} = \text{HOK net worth}$$

and

$$\text{HOK net worth} \div \text{number of HOK shares} = \text{value per share}$$

I shared this simple calculation with each office by writing it on a flip chart or white board. Then, I answered every question about stock as simply and honestly as I could. CFO Bob Pratzel was a member of an architecture industry group called the Large Firm Roundtable and told me almost no other firms were disclosing their financial results or their stock value to their employees like this. "Many firms did not let their people know how they were doing, but HOK was just the opposite," Bob told me later. "We were very transparent about almost everything." People gradually began to understand how the HOK shareholder system works. But many still asked, "Is HOK stock a good investment?"

HOK had become consistently profitable from my first year as CEO. However, the reputation of our stock had not caught up to this reality. The truth was, even after paying annual bonuses to staff and paying taxes on the remainder, we were now able to retain an after-tax profit each year. Retained profits made HOK's net worth increase annually, whether we used the money to pay down the bank loan (to reduce liabilities) or saved it as cash (to increase assets). Bottom line: HOK's stock was growing in value. By the end of my first year as CEO, thanks to the hard work of so many, HOK stock rose in value. The next year it increased again. In the following years, HOK stock almost always increased.

I began thinking about comparing HOK's stock to investments someone might make in the stock market, and selected the Dow Jones Industrial Average, the most commonly used measure. I asked controller Tim Tynan to create a chart comparing HOK stock growth with the Dow's average, beginning in 2003, the year I became CEO. We began to show the comparison chart at shareholder and board meetings and during visits to HOK offices, a tactic others could try. Over the next several years, HOK stock grew faster than the Dow. With this information, people began seeing stock ownership as more than a way of participating in the growth of HOK. HOK stock was a great investment.

I asked Tim to lengthen the comparison with the Dow every year, and after five years, he began showing one- and five-year comparisons. Later, we added a 10-year chart. HOK stock grew faster than the Dow most years and positively thrashed the Dow in 5- and 10-year comparisons. The results were striking, especially during years when the Dow declined. We were not rich like some of the huge consumer corporations we were comparing ourselves to. Architects usually have thin margins. But we were *growing* our profits, and thus our share price.

Sharing these comparisons built interest in how we performed as a business. Current HOK shareholders began asking how they could buy more stock. Emerging HOK leaders became interested in becoming HOK stockholders. And younger staff started asking how they could qualify for stock ownership. Suddenly we had a brand new question to answer: "How do I get more stock?" Our reply was simple: "Do more for the firm, and we will offer you more stock." Stock ownership grew around the firm until one in every six employees was a shareholder.

As shareholders saw their HOK stock value go up and learned more about the business side of the firm, they began to take an interest in whether other offices were profitable—and if not, what was the leadership of that office going to do about it? Stock value is tied to the health of the entire firm, not the individual offices, so this reinforced our goal of helping people view HOK as a whole. Stock became an important factor in binding us together and it can do this for other firms as well.

None of this happened quickly. It took many Ask Me Anything talks to raise the level of understanding about how our profits related to stock valuation. These conversations were not just about stock, but also about how the firm fit together. As HOK grew and expanded into other cities, states, and countries, the HOK stock ownership model helped glue everyone together. Whether shareholders are in Houston or Hong Kong, they own part of every office, not just their office. Collaboration inside to compete outside is not just a nicety; it's a way of making the stock you own more valuable! HOK stock ownership gave people a deep interest in the success of the firm. For shareholders, HOK comes first, their office second, and only then comes self-interest. HOK stock had become an important part of keeping the firm together and of people helping one another to succeed.

Posting Staff Photos

A small but helpful step I took to bind the firm together was to ask each office to photograph every member of their staff and upload the photos to our internal website. At first, some offices resisted, saying "We shouldn't do that. Some of our people don't want their pictures taken. We might be violating their personal privacy." I explained why the photos were important to HOK, just as my charm school coach had taught me, and insisted, "As long as they work at HOK, this is our policy. We will take their picture and post it." We used a standard format for the photos: color head shots against a uniform gray background.

When we posted employee photos on the internal HOK website, we also included information about them—things like where they went to school, their degrees, professional registrations, project experience, and languages they spoke. Having the photos on our website in a uniform format helped make HOK feel like one big firm instead of a collection of offices. Employees could look each other up and put a face to a name. Objections to this practice faded away fast, and I can confidently recommend posting employee photos to your company intranet as a helpful practice.

Plus, there was an unforeseen benefit. Marketers from around the firm began to use the photos and biographical information about people for their proposals. As those marketers began to realize the value of placing the very best experts on teams when going after work, they began to include people from multiple offices in their proposals. It was another small victory for true collaboration. We were climbing closer to the top of our pyramid.

Reviving Core Boards

Remember how the founders encouraged employees with similar roles—marketers, designers, project managers, and project architects—to meet and share their expertise with one another? As HOK expanded, these groups had welcomed members from new offices in order to spread the wealth of knowledge. Eventually, the firm formalized these groups, calling them Core Boards. There were Core Boards for design, management, marketing, and production, and they were supposed to be constantly improving the four core competencies of our architecture practice. Core Boards also advised the board of directors on measures needed to strengthen and improve HOK work in each office and market practice.

Unfortunately, the Core Boards had lost their effectiveness by the time I became CEO. They had become discussion forums with hazy goals and were no longer even advising the board of directors or the ExCom. I brought this up and everyone agreed that we should restore the Core Boards to their original purpose. The ExCom appointed a new chair and new members to each Core Board, then asked them to develop goals to improve their core competency. The Core Boards also resumed their regular reports to the board of directors.

It took a few years, but eventually each Core Board was doing important work in its respective area. For example, the Marketing Core Board developed an initiative to leverage the firm-wide communication team—PR, social media, website, and print media—to increase HOK's profile. They have also fostered better collaboration and sharing between marketing principals and market practice leaders to win more work.

The Management Core Board has initiated a Quality Improvement Project Management Initiative, an ongoing live training program with monthly classes for project managers around the firm. The initiative is in response to changes in the building industry including a more litigious environment and the increasing scale of HOK projects. The goal is to increase the number of repeat clients, improve project profitability, better support the design process, and improve project quality.

The Technical Core Board recently began an initiative to revamp the way quality management is done at HOK. Program components include rewriting all project manuals, creating quality checklists for each discipline and each phase of work, and special checklists for each type of project. Soon they will manage the program using software called Smartsheet, which has dashboards for the project, office, and firm-wide levels.

The Design Core Board began organizing and publishing the *HOK Design Annuals*. Each year the annual is full of photos and descriptions of the best HOK design work across the firm. It helps everyone across HOK have pride in our work and it's become an annual tradition.

These are all highly visible contributions, that have made us better, but I had a stealth benefit in mind: The reinvigorated Core Boards helped HOK make real progress toward not one, but two, of our pyramid goals: great operations and true collaboration.

Celebrating 50 Years

As HOK approached its fiftieth year of practice . . . we had survived—not broken apart or gone bankrupt . . . in fact, we were thriving.

As HOK approached its fiftieth year of practice in 2005, we had survived—not broken apart or gone bankrupt—and, in fact, we were thriving. The ExCom designed a series of celebrations to engage the entire firm. First, we connected all the offices to our videoconference system for short remarks by Bill Valentine, Bill Hellmuth, and me. Then we shared a firm-wide champagne toast. It was late in the evening in London and the middle of the night in Hong Kong, yet no one seemed to mind. But that was just the beginning.

Bill Valentine wanted to do something special to celebrate our anniversary. "Most firms throw a big party and showcase their work. It's all about them," he said. "I think we should do the opposite—celebrate our service to others by donating to a worthy cause." Bill identified a project to establish a medical clinic in rural Kenya. We had built up a cash reserve by this time and donated a substantial amount of money to get the clinic going. People around HOK were impressed and pleased to be part of HOK. I was proud of our contribution—and proud that we had the money to do it.

Finally, we could not help it. We had to throw a party—a small one, just for us. This was a major milestone for HOK. The board of directors deliberately rotated its next meeting to St. Louis and followed it with an anniversary party at the St. Louis Art Museum. Gyo Obata attended, as did George Hellmuth's widow, Mimi, escorted by her nephew Bill Hellmuth. Jerry Sincoff was in attendance, and original attorney Paul Watson too. Many others who worked in the founding office joined us, along with the ExCom, HOK board members, and St. Louis leaders. In his remarks, Obata expressed wonderment

FIGURE 26.1 The updated HOK logo.
Source: Image courtesy of HOK.

that the firm he had helped to found had grown so large and now had a global reach. He said he was proud of us for keeping HOK strong. I'm not sure if he knew the blood, sweat, and tears it had taken to make that a true statement, but I was glad that he was right.

In 2008, we revised the HOK logo, printing the H, O, and K on a red background. Deepening the color scheme from orange to red gave our logo a more established look. All of this seemed fitting for a firm that was now more than 50 years old. It was around this time that we also began referring to the firm simply as "HOK," rather than spelling out the founders' names. That's one way to avoid misspellings!

A Different Kind of Retreat

As we headed into our second 50 years, the ExCom continued to press every opportunity for HOK people in different offices to work together and get together. In 2007, Bill V. and Bill H. proposed that we embark on another firm-wide retreat of leaders from around HOK to plan our future together. The ExCom delegated responsibility for planning the event to Riccardo Mascia and other young leaders from around the firm. Planning the event and the event itself would both be chances for people in different offices to connect.

Almost 200 HOK leaders and emerging leaders participated in the retreat, held in October 2007, at the Grand Velas Resort in Puerto Vallarta, Mexico. I welcomed everyone to the retreat and asked a series of questions meant to recognize everyone. "Who are we?" The participants called out their answers: "Architects! Interior designers! Planners! Aviation specialists! Healthcare specialists!" By now HOK was incredibly diverse and this went on for quite some time, until we had identified the breadth of all our contributors.

Next, I wanted to acknowledge depth. I asked people to stand up if they had been with HOK more than five years. Almost everyone stood. "Ten years?" Most remained standing. HOK was blessed with loyal employees. "Twenty years?" Some sat, but many remained standing. "Thirty years?" A smaller group still stood tall. "Forty years?" Bill Valentine and a few others were still on their feet and enjoyed a wave of applause. I posed my last question, asking, "Who has been here *less* than five years?" A sizable group of young, emerging leaders leapt to their feet to a new round of applause. The exercise was a reminder that HOK was all about people, a diverse mix of talents and ages working together to serve our clients.

One of our offices had created a large, three-dimensional pyramid representing our pyramid strategy, and carted it to the retreat, with the four levels temporarily covered. Yes, 50 years later, model-making was alive and well at HOK. We worked our way up the pyramid as a group. First, I asked board members to come to the outdoor stage. As they uncovered the base of the pyramid, revealing the layer labeled Strong Board, I thanked them for being our foundation, supporting everything we do.

Office leaders and project managers mounted the stage next. They peeled away the paper covering the second layer of the pyramid representing Great Operations, and I thanked them for keeping offices and projects running smoothly, which was so crucial to our success.

FIGURE 26.2 Author at left unveiling the pyramid strategy, Puerto Vallarta, Mexico. Source: Photo courtesy of HOK.

HOK's marketing leaders and market-practice experts were up next. I thanked them for collaborating across the firm to win the work so vital to our success as they pulled the cover from the third level of the pyramid with a flourish, revealing True Collaboration.

I invited the young, emerging leaders to the stage last. As they whisked the cover from the top of the pyramid, revealing the word *Dreams*, I described dreams as our ultimate goal, and reminded everyone that they were only possible if we met the first three goals. The young people left the stage to great applause. Everyone had heard the pyramid speech before, but never as a shared experience with people from every corner of the firm. It felt more like a pep rally than a meeting. Any executive would be lucky to preside over such a spirited event.

After the pyramid kickoff, we boarded buses for a trip to a remote village in the foothills of the Sierra Madre mountains, once again trying to give back. Riccardo and his planners had identified a kindergarten in need of help, and we formed teams for each job. One group built a new classroom addition with prefabricated materials, another planted a maze garden for the children, and a third painted murals. My team assembled playground equipment. The village children watched eagerly from behind a fence nearby. Some of the parents worked with us, and the village women brought lunch. They spoke no English and only a few of us spoke more than a small bit of Spanish, but we worked together toward a shared goal.

By the end of the day, we were hot, tired, and dirty—but happy. The most senior people at HOK had worked alongside our youngest recruits and village strangers—as equals—all in the interest of doing a good job. We relished the moment when the teacher opened the gates and the kids raced in to play with the new equipment. All of us learned a valuable lesson about teamwork that day, a lesson we would remember for the rest of the retreat and beyond. Working with that village was a perfect illustration of true collaboration, and a unique way of rediscovering our original HOK culture: helping one another to succeed.

FIGURE 26.3 Children on new playground installed by HOK volunteers, Near Puerto Vallarta, Mexico. Source: Photo courtesy of HOK.

We got back on our buses and transitioned from the rural world of the village back to the rarefied world of our hotel. I went up to my room, decided to lie down for a minute, and slept right through the beginning of dinner, contentedly exhausted. Someone finally came looking for me. The Puerto Vallarta trip ended up not being about the fancy resort or even that hard-working village. It was about *us*, a bonding experience for everyone who attended, which became legend around the firm. It occurred to me that real-world team-building activities like these were far more effective than the goofy blindfolded exercise with the ropes that we had tried years before. Those who were there could just say "PV" and others would respond, "Now that was a *great* experience."

Chapter 26: To Design a World-Class Firm

1. Visit with employees in-person if you need to reclaim your company culture. Regular, face-to-face communication is key.
2. Hold Ask Me Anything talks to foster open and honest communication between leadership and staff.
3. Observe whether your offices have a buzz of energy, with employees who are comfortable asking questions. This is an indicator of a healthy, happy office.
4. Take note of offices that are unnaturally quiet with employees who are afraid to speak up. This indicates a poorly run office.
5. Explain your company's stock to your employees, so they understand how it works and are motivated to buy it.
6. Highlight your company's stock growth by comparing it to something well known, like the Dow, if you want to encourage employees to buy stock.
7. Reward employees who contribute the most to your firm with the right to buy stock.
8. Leverage employees' collective interest in seeing their stock value go up, as a way of encouraging people to pull in the same direction.
9. Post employee photos to your company intranet to make your company feel like one big firm and to help employees put a face to a name.
10. Establish Core Boards responsible for improving your core competencies. Hold them accountable for helping you make real change.
11. Try real-life team-building experiences, like doing service projects together, rather than goofy artificial team-building exercises, like rope games and "trust falls."

CHAPTER 27

Buying Your Freedom

With a strong board, better operations, and real progress toward true collaboration, our profits and cash flow were improving. I cannot emphasize enough how crucial this transformation was to our future. It allowed us to tackle what I viewed as our three big relationship issues: Bank of America, Kajima, and HOK Sport. Each relationship issue was rooted in our period of unprofitability, made worse by uneven collections and spotty cash flow.

Bank of America continued to be a constant source of pressure to pay down our line of credit. Kajima no longer thought of HOK as a strategic partner, instead downgrading us to a mere financial investment and continuing to demand dividends. The relationship with HOK Sport was the most difficult of all, ironic since they were part of the firm.

Paying Off the Bank

The first job was to fix the relationship with Bank of America. Shortly after I became CEO, Bob Pratzel brought me to the Bank of America offices in St. Louis to meet our bank representative. I expected to meet a senior bank official, but our representative was a junior banker about half my age. He was not interested in me, or in my new strategy for HOK. He was interested in one thing only: getting us to pay down our line of credit. "I don't know what kind of operation you have at HOK, but it's not working. You have to begin making regular payments to reduce your line of credit or we will raise your interest rate," he threatened. "If you continue not to pay, we may cancel your line of credit altogether and demand immediate repayment. Now, what are you going to do about this?"

I was angry that we were in this situation and frustrated by the fresh-faced banker's tone. "We will begin to pay off our line of credit as soon as we are able," I said. "Once we begin to repay, we will continue until we pay it off—down to the last penny." The meeting was over. Bob was worried that we may have upset our banker, but I was the one who was upset. I had never been treated so abruptly, and was determined to pay our way out of the relationship with that banker and his bank ASAP. I never saw the young banker again, but any time would have been too soon. I now had an additional reason for fixing HOK's finances. I prefer positive motivation, but sometimes negative motivation sure is powerful.

A few months later, Bob Pratzel informed me that our cash flow had improved enough to allow us to make our first payment on the line of credit. Maybe we could have spent the money on something else, but it was the right choice to make this a priority. From that point on, every month or two we made another payment. After about a year, the banker contacted Bob Pratzel. He was happy to see that we were paying steadily on our debt. Would HOK like to raise the borrowing limit on the credit line? I told Bob, "Tell that guy we don't want a larger line of credit. We want to pay off the line entirely."

After three years of focused work, we did it. We made our final payment on the line of credit with Bank of America. It was 2006 and I will never forget that day. I was thrilled to be free from debt, and happy to share the news with the ExCom and the board of directors. I told Bob we should have a drink together to celebrate, but he was in St. Louis and I was in San Francisco. We postponed our drink until the next quarterly ExCom meeting, when everyone toasted our achievement.

A quirky aside: When Jerry Sincoff had been CEO, we all drank wine when we ate dinner together. When I took over, we all switched to scotch, which I had learned to love after breaking my ankle in that car accident in Hong Kong. It just goes to show that when you're the CEO or a top firm leader, you influence your colleagues in ways large and small —and it's important to use that power for good, not evil!

When we paid off the line of credit, our young Bank of America representative contacted Bob Pratzel with an offer to host us for a fancy lunch the next time I was in St. Louis. Thanks, but no thanks. I told Bob to decline the lunch and begin a search for a new bank. After a few months, we selected Wells Fargo as our replacement banking partner—and I do mean partner. Our new Wells Fargo representative was highly placed, about my age, and extremely helpful. He treated us like clients, not deadbeats. Wells Fargo headquarters is in San Francisco, and early in our new relationship, our banker invited me to meet the bank's CEO. He was very interested in our business and later arranged for us to design new Wells Fargo regional centers in several cities.

Yes, Wells Fargo extended us a line of credit as part of our relationship, but I was interested in building up our resources, not borrowing money. We continued with regular payments to Wells Fargo Bank—except these were deposits into a strategic cash reserve instead of loan payments. We needed that reserve to manage our regular operations, to smooth out cash flow, and to make payroll—all of which we had formerly done on a credit basis. I also wanted the cash to buy our freedom from Kajima and HOK Sport. Later, we would need cash to take advantage of strategic opportunities, like buying another firm or investing in more technology. I believe every business can benefit from a healthy cash reserve.

Our ability to pay down our line of credit was more than a morale booster. It was liberating, a demonstration of our ability to chart our own course, not to be at the mercy of others outside our firm. Two more big relationship problems remained, but we approached those with renewed confidence.

Buying Out Kajima

After we paid off our bank, I was determined to buy back our stock from Kajima, which was still demanding dividends. But remember, Kajima owned 15% of HOK stock, so this was not a trivial goal. Would Kajima even want to sell? When we asked, Kajima's leaders said they would be interested, but there was a condition: They only wanted to sell if the stock value was higher than they had paid in 1990. In other words, not only did we need enough cash to pay off Kajima, we needed to work to raise our share price high enough to make it worth their while.

It was a tall order, but I understood their motivation. When Kajima had bought HOK stock in 1990, things were booming in Japan. The Nikkei index was at an all-time high of 39,000, and real estate in the Ginza district of Tokyo sold for the unbelievable price of $139,000 per square foot. Japanese companies had money to invest. The amount Kajima paid HOK for stock was far in excess of the book value, but they considered it an affordable long-term investment. However, just as Kajima finalized its purchase of HOK stock, the Japanese economic bubble burst. The Nikkei index declined to 7,600 by April 2003, and the Japanese economy dove into a devastating deflation, later called "the lost decade."

As everyone at HOK now knew, our stock value was based on our net worth, and as we worked to pay down the line of credit from Bank of America, both our net worth and stock value rose. Our stock value rose even further after we paid off our old line of credit and began to make regular deposits into our Wells Fargo strategic account. In 2008, HOK stock value finally exceeded the original Kajima purchase price. Bob Pratzel asked the people at Kajima USA if they would be interested in a discussion about re-purchase. They wanted to talk, and Bob and I arranged to meet Kajima USA leader K.C. Koshijima and his CFO at their Santa Monica, California offices.

K.C. had been in the United States for some years and spoke perfect English—much more than I can say for my Japanese. He was sharp, but friendly. We began our meeting in an office high above the Pacific Coast Highway with a spectacular view of Santa Monica Bay. Each of us expressed thanks to the other for our long partnership, which was not as successful as we wished, but had led to some significant project work and genuine friendships. I was mindful that Japanese culture puts a high value on "saving face," as we waded into this fraught discussion.

Bob had done a detailed analysis of the rate of return for Kajima's investment in order to arrive at our opening price. It was my job to make the offer. "K.C., we are prepared to buy back Kajima's stock at this month's HOK stock price," I said. "And we will pay you in 30 days." K.C. looked at me for just a moment. "We would like to sell at a premium above stock value," he countered, then gave me a figure. After a moment of reflection, I offered to pay Kajima more than book value, rounded to an even number. We could both save face by compromising. K.C. looked at me, smiled, and put out his hand. I shook it, and the deal was made. We promised payment within 30 days, and after mutual thanks, the meeting was complete. It took less than 30 minutes.

Bob Pratzel and I were elated! We found a nearby restaurant and had a celebratory lunch. Normally we did not drink at lunchtime, but we did this day—more than one glass apiece, as I recall. We shared a taxi to Los Angeles International Airport and caught separate flights to St. Louis and San Francisco. It was a grand day.

Our relationship with Kajima was always good, and still is. We never forgot that the big Japanese company took a chance on us when we needed it. Many of us maintain friendships with Kajima people, including me. My wife and I have even vacationed with close Kajima friends in Japan. We always look for project opportunities to share with each other and have been successful on a number of occasions.

Spinning Off HOK Sport

After buying back our stock from Kajima, I was emboldened and began to bring up our strained relationship with HOK Sport during ExCom meetings. My colleagues and I were not aligned. "Patrick, we just can't afford to lose HOK Sport," Bill Valentine argued. "Those guys enhance our reputation so much that we would lose big-time if we gave them up. Besides, they bring in lots of profit." John Mahon countered, "HOK Sport has to be worth a lot of money, so we should sell them for the highest price we can get." No consensus existed about what to do with Sport. Meanwhile, the relationship continued to deteriorate.

I believed keeping HOK Sport was a greater risk than letting it go. "They were willing to walk away from us before and they can do it again," I argued. "Think what would happen if they left HOK tomorrow and formed their own firm." I told them the HOK Sport leaders were so specialized that they were likely to take their clients with them, so HOK would effectively be out of the sport business. To complicate matters, the HOK sport leaders owned HOK stock just like other HOK leaders, and we would have to buy it back from them at the same time we were absorbing the loss of the sport business. "That's a *real* risk!" I warned at one ExCom meeting. Suddenly, my ExCom colleagues began to see the folly in keeping things as they were and gave me their support to open a dialogue with HOK Sport leadership.

Ron Labinski, HOK Sport's original visionary, had left the firm a few years before. To me, it was a shame, because he had fit perfectly into HOK culture, whereas the other Sport leaders didn't seem to appreciate what we were all about. I called Rick Martin, the current top HOK Sport leader. "Rick, I have something important to discuss with you," I said. "I want to meet you in person, but not in your office or mine. Are you willing to meet?" Rick said, "Sounds interesting. Where?" It was all very cloak and dagger. We agreed to meet in the United Red Carpet Club at Denver Airport. Denver was between our offices in San Francisco and Kansas City, plus it was neutral territory.

When Rick and I met in Denver I got right to the point. "Rick, it's not working," I said. "HOK Sport doesn't want to be part of HOK, and we're not happy with that. Let's find a mutually agreeable way for your group to exit and go your own way." Rick said he agreed and was sure his Sport partners would too. We discussed how to reach agreement to unwind HOK Sport from HOK and agreed it would be impossible to discuss this between a dozen Sport partners and seven ExCom members. I proposed that just the two of us would sort through options, and each be responsible for keeping our colleagues up to date. Rick agreed, then smiled. "You have the easiest job," he said. You only have to convince the ExCom. I have to convince my 12 Sport partners—and they will have 15 different opinions!"

Rick and I met in Denver several more times over the next 60 days, and between meetings, kept our mutual colleagues informed. Together, we developed a strategy to sell HOK Sport to its leaders. Our final draft agreement was fair, with pluses and minuses for both sides, the hallmark of any good negotiation. It was also simple enough to fit on a single piece of paper. Have I repeated this theme enough? Once again, I found beauty in simplicity.

I discussed the one-page outline with my ExCom colleagues and gained their agreement, and Rick did the same with his colleagues. Then we turned our simple plan over to attorneys who would convert it into a formal legal agreement. The lawyers had their own ideas, and things proceeded more slowly. I understood the necessity, but it was frustrating—and suspenseful. However, Rick Martin and I stayed involved, and six months after that first secret meeting in Denver, we finalized our agreement to spin off HOK Sport.

The ExCom shared the job of informing the board of directors, shareholders, and individual offices around the firm. There were lots of questions, and we answered each fully and honestly. We finalized the sale of HOK Sport in December 2008. Rick and his colleagues named their new firm Populous, and we kept the name HOK.

The third big relationship problem was resolved. We had paid off our line of credit with our original bank and were making regular deposits to a strategic cash account. We had bought back the Kajima stock to once again become 100% employee-owned. And now we had dodged what could have been a knockout punch by selling HOK Sport. From that day forward, confidence grew across HOK. Fixing the Big Three meant freedom. It meant we could be ourselves. It meant we could chart our own destiny. As a result, HOK was more unified—and more optimistic—than at any time since our founding.

> *Fixing the Big Three meant freedom. It meant we could be ourselves. It meant we could chart our own destiny.*

Chapter 27: To Design a World-Class Firm

1. Prioritize paying down your debts when you have the cash flow to do it.
2. Look for a relationship with a bank that will treat you as a valued client and partner, not a deadbeat.
3. Build up a strategic cash reserve, by continuing to make payments to your bank once any debts are paid.
4. Keep in mind the concept of "saving face" when you negotiate with people who value that concept. Compromise, if you can, so that both sides save face.
5. Conduct sensitive discussions on neutral turf.
6. Negotiate difficult deals one-on-one with another person, rather than trying to negotiate by committee.
7. Negotiate the big picture first; then work out the details.
8. Strive for balance in your negotiations. If there are pluses and minuses for both parties, it's probably a fair deal.

CHAPTER 28

Transitions: The Third Generation

The founders were the first generation of HOK leaders. Jerry Sincoff was the second generation leader, followed by Bill Valentine for a brief time. I consider myself a third generation leader, although the passage of time has a way of compressing the years. Leadership generations overlap just as they do in families, where a child may have cousins more the age of aunts and uncles. This blend of leadership generations benefitted HOK, with older leaders sharing their institutional knowledge and passing down HOK culture, and younger employees sharing their technological prowess and bringing in new energy.

Susan Williams Joins the OpsCom, ExCom

I recruited Susan Williams to the OpsCom in 2015 to help Tom Robson handle the intense workload. Susan began her career with HOK Washington, DC in 1983 as a production architect, but soon became a top project manager. Susan is medium in height with medium brown hair—but she's a giant to her employees and clients. She is determined, focused on her projects, and speaks forcefully when things do not meet her high standards. Susan is passionate about her work and expects the best of every member of her team.

Susan was born in New Jersey and earned a Bachelor of Landscape Architecture degree from the University of Georgia. By graduation she had decided to become an architect and worked for several small firms as a draftsman. She moved to Washington, DC to be close to family and became a registered architect the hard way: working under the supervision of a registered architect for eight years, then passing the rigorous DC architectural registration exam.

Susan wanted to work for a large firm and arranged interviews with SOM and HOK. Her reactions were just like mine when I interviewed at the two firms years before. She did not like the rigid look and feel of the SOM office, but immediately liked the people and felt at home at HOK. We have something else in common: Susan met her husband, Morgan Williams, at the office. That led to yet another HOK marriage and two sons.

FIGURE 28.1 Susan Williams at her desk in HOK, Washington, DC.
Source: Photo courtesy of HOK.

Bill Hellmuth selected Susan as the newest member of the ExCom in 2017. She had heard this inner circle of top leaders was a difficult group of high-powered individuals and wondered how she would fit in. "I fit in well from the beginning," she told me with surprise. "Everyone is supportive. HOK is the same firm of really good people I joined in 1983, where people help each other to succeed. Our challenge is to get better and better."

General Counsel Promotion

Bob Staed loved his general counsel role at HOK, but constant travel kept him away from his young children when they needed him most. He reluctantly submitted his resignation in the Spring of 2005 to spend more time with his family. Later he became a specialized insurance broker serving design professionals. Bob was grateful to gain HOK as a client and remains a friend to the firm.

After a brief search for a new general counsel, we realized the best candidate was inside the firm. Don't always assume some impressive-on-paper outside hire is the answer. We promoted Lisa Green to general counsel in July 2005. Fortunately, Lisa thrived on travel. "I had never been outside the US before accepting a job offer from Bob and Paul," Lisa exclaimed. "HOK completely changed the course of my life—like being hit by a meteor. I have been around the world and visited many places—the Great Wall of China (twice), the Middle East, Europe . . . fantastic!" HOK also brought Lisa together with Tom Robson, the man who would become her husband. They were perfect for each other and Lisa was the perfect general counsel for HOK.

Lisa had joined the HOK legal department in 2000 and earned high praise from Paul Watson and Bob Staed. She was a dedicated, loyal, hard-working person, and established high standards for herself and others around her. She had represented HOK with distinction on every occasion, including the sale of HOK Sport. Under her leadership, the legal staff grew to six attorneys, arguably the best, most effective legal team in the design profession. A shining example of HOK culture occurred when Donovan Oliff, one of Lisa's top attorneys, resigned to take a high position in another firm, but returned to HOK after only 13 weeks at his new firm. As George Kassabaum always said, HOK people were often disappointed by what they found elsewhere. Donovan currently serves as assistant general counsel at HOK.

Paul Watson retired as senior counsel, in 2008, after a 45-year career at HOK. I'm proud that HOK is still the kind of company where people can enjoy long, fruitful careers, something that's now rare in the American workplace. Paul remained in touch with old HOK friends and hosted monthly lunches for former colleagues for many years. He passed away in 2014 at age 85, and we celebrated him for a life well-lived, and for his humor, friendship, and dedication to HOK.

Human Resources Changes

John Mahon had a 23-year career at HOK, first as director of human resources and later as a member of the ExCom. He died in October 2008, at his home in St. Louis, following a battle with cancer. John was a friend to all, as an HR pro should be, and we felt his passing across the firm. HOK established "The John F. Mahon, Sr. Scholarship Fund" at St. Louis University High School, where John graduated and later served on the board of trustees.

We appointed Jan Harmon as director of human resources in 2011. She was a native of Los Angeles and a graduate of Whittier College, who joined HOK LA in 1985 as office manager. She rose to become the HR leader in Los Angeles and impressed everyone with her deep regard for people. Her hard work and ability to work well with others are hallmarks of her character. Jan continues to live in Los Angeles, although much of her HR team is still based in St. Louis.

Because HOK invested in technology early, arrangements like this are common at HOK. One of the benefits of having multiple branches is that recruiting is easier because you can give people a choice of locations, rather than forcing them to move. Happy employees are better employees. Bill Valentine and I had been the first beneficiaries of this revelation, when we opted to fulfill firm-wide roles from San Francisco. We came to believe that when you are designing a world-class architecture firm, it's better not to have a central headquarters. Instead we evolved as a virtual firm with talented people located where they best fit or where they wanted to be. Today we are glued together with technology—and, of course, a lot of plane rides.

> *. . . it's better not to have a central headquarters. Instead we evolved as a virtual firm with talented people located where they best fit . . .*

Riccardo Mascia Heads Home

HOK elected Riccardo Mascia to the ExCom in 2010. He was just 46 years old but with a 15-year career at HOK as our "fixer." Riccardo earned widespread admiration for organizing the successful firm-wide retreat at Puerto Vallarta, and had served as managing principal in Mexico City, San Francisco, Los Angeles, and Hong Kong.

Shortly after Riccardo joined the ExCom, I asked him to move from Hong Kong to Chicago to fill a vacant managing principal position there. This time he knew about his new destination because Chicago was his hometown. Riccardo was born and raised there, and his entire extended family still lived there, including six sisters. Riccardo did his usual good job of building HOK Chicago up into a large, successful office. As a member of the HOK ExCom, he will have a voice in whether he ever moves again.

I interviewed Riccardo as I wrote this book, and he said, "From the beginning, I've been struck by how limitless HOK is, with endless experiences and opportunities. I run into old friends in Chicago, and when they ask me where I have been, I wonder how to tell them that I've literally been around the world. When HOK work takes me past Tiananmen Square or the Sydney Opera House or to Myanmar or Mongolia, I have to force myself to stop and remember how incredible it all is and how improbable it all once seemed."

Bill Valentine Retires

Bill Valentine retired in 2012, after 50 years with HOK. I had worked with Bill for 45 of those 50 years, first as his assistant, then as his partner. It had been nearly a decade since I had surprised Bill with my suggestion that he name a successor. Bill Hellmuth had long since proved himself and succeeded Bill Valentine as HOK president and design leader.

We hosted a big party for Bill V. on the grounds of Levi Strauss Plaza in San Francisco, a project he conceived and that in many ways defined his career. Bill was always proud of how perfectly the Levi headquarters fit the company he designed it for. And it occurred to me that the project was also a perfect reflection of Bill himself: warm and open and a people magnet. HOK colleagues, clients, and Bill's family listened as Gyo Obata gave a summary of Bill's accomplishments, in particular his leadership of sustainable design. Many others spoke of Bill's warmth and compassion and his commitment to clients.

Bill had the last word, saying what he had said so often over the years, "Our mission, our single mission, is to enrich people's lives." As Bill concluded his remarks, he removed his outer shirt to reveal a T-shirt with the HOK logo right over his heart. His message was clear: he loved HOK and the people in the HOK family. "The three founders were different in so many ways but shared a common regard for HOK people," Bill told me later, while reflecting on his 50-year career. "I could never have imagined having an opportunity like the one I had at HOK. Gyo gave me the encouragement and support to be my best as a designer, and my life was transformed as a result."

FIGURE 28.2 Bill Valentine in HOK shirt at his retirement party, 2012.
Source: Photo courtesy of HOK.

Financial Team Changes

Bob Pratzel also retired from HOK in 2012 after serving as CFO for 26 years. I will always be grateful for the great advice Bob gave me about the business side of HOK and how he helped us restore positive cash flow and pay off the bank. Bob also helped create the 50 Percent Rule for salaries, the 10-Month Rule for backlog, and the 90-Day Rule for converting accrual to cash. Bob continues to live near St. Louis with his wife and stays in touch with friends from HOK.

Tim Tynan, who had been so instrumental in helping clean up HOK's finances as controller, moved into the role of assistant treasurer of HOK for several years while I was CEO. He was a great partner in fixing the financial side of HOK, and I particularly enjoyed the clean, clear spreadsheets he created to help me motivate our board members to do better. Once Tim saw that less was more with these financial reports, he really got into it. Tim left HOK in 2012 to become CFO of another St. Louis-based company.

Carl Galioto Joins the ExCom

We elected Carl Galioto to the ExCom in 2012, just three years after he joined HOK as our chief technical architect. In that short time, he had turned HOK New York into a vibrant, successful office and provided new leadership and vision for the HOK buildingSMART group. Carl also raised the level of HOK technical architecture, beginning in New York, then at other HOK offices across the firm by recruiting other skilled technical architects.

As our newest ExCom member, Carl's clear thinking helped us with a long-term dilemma. The HOK network of offices had grown to 29 by 2014, primarily due to the establishment of branch offices in Canada and Asia. The mix of offices and branches had become unwieldy and ungovernable. Something needed to change. Carl suggested, "We need to shorten our lines." Carl was a student of history, including military history, and explained that shortening the lines meant concentrating troops for greater strength. For us it meant consolidating our network of offices for greater effectiveness. When Carl explained it that way, everyone understood at once.

Consolidating Offices

The ExCom developed a plan to organize HOK around large, strategic offices. Those larger offices would then maintain branch offices, and be held strictly accountable for their performance, including financial results. The large offices included New York and Washington, DC, on the east coast; Chicago, St. Louis, and Houston in the middle of the country; and San Francisco and Los Angeles on the west coast. Three large international offices in London, Toronto, and Hong Kong brought the total of large offices to 10. Naturally, we named the new network of 10 large offices the Big Ten.

Attaching branches to large offices took more work. Dallas became a branch of HOK Texas led by Houston. Atlanta and Tampa became branches of Washington, DC. New York had no branch at first, but eventually established a successful branch in Philadelphia. Hong Kong initially had four branches in Beijing, Shanghai, Viet Nam, and Singapore—but closed the Southeast Asia offices to become profitable. Toronto initially had branches across Canada, but eventually closed two to consolidate and achieve profitability. In other words, HOK shortened its lines—and then our Hong Kong and Toronto offices shortened theirs.

Other benefits of consolidation emerged. It was easier to oversee 10 key offices than it was to try to wrangle 29 far-flung ones. Branch offices became the sole responsibility of a Big Ten office, so the ExCom didn't have to spread itself so thin. Promoting and recruiting leaders was simpler too. We could place our strongest pros in the key strategic offices and groom up-and-coming leaders in the branch offices. None of this would have worked if we hadn't gotten our pyramid priorities in place first. Members of our strong board were leading the Big Ten offices. Good operations were assuring that we made money. And Big Ten and branch offices were able to interact and support each other through true collaboration.

Chapter 28: To Design a World-Class Firm

1. Embrace multiple generations at your firm. Seasoned employees will share their institutional knowledge and your company culture. Younger employees will share their energy and cutting edge knowledge.
2. Look for talent inside your firm first before recruiting people from outside.
3. Create a virtual firm, rather than having a central headquarters, and use technology to glue people together.
4. "Shorten your lines" if your firm gets too spread out and unwieldy. Put large, strategic offices or departments in charge of smaller offices or departments..

CHAPTER 29

The Right to Dream

Putting your house in order not only secures your financial future, it clears your mind and liberates your creativity. When you're constantly worried about making a profit, collecting fees, or making payroll, it's hard to marshal the mental energy to do great work. Many architects are not great businesspeople, and some may even feel that spending time on the operations side of their business is a waste. On the contrary, putting the fundamentals in place frees your mind to create—and to dream. It is a key step in designing a world-class architecture firm.

At HOK, we had empowered our strong board of directors, cleaned up our finances to achieve great operations, and set aside our petty rivalries to engage in true collaboration. The quest and striving to get to that point took years. I remember feeling startled to discover that we had arrived. By 2013, we had done it, not just talked about it. We had gotten to the place where I wanted us to go. We were at the top of the pyramid. The view was beautiful. We finally had the right to dream.

Pressing Sustainable Design

Bill Hellmuth had adopted Bill Valentine's dream of sustainable design. Bill V. had embraced green building goals in the early 1990s, and his advocacy had led HOK to become a leading sustainable design firm. However, Bill H. recognized that adoption was uneven across the firm. Some offices practiced sustainable design and others did not. Many offices pursued sustainable design for buildings, but not for interiors or other disciplines. A few provided sustainable design services only at the request of clients.

Bill Hellmuth dreamed that HOK could do better—and make the world a better place. "The building of buildings and the operation of buildings is 50% of the carbon emissions on the planet," Bill H. explained. "We can eliminate every single automobile, and that's only 20%. When you go through each of the things that affect carbon emissions, we are the biggest chunk of it, so we have the biggest responsibility." Bill wants HOK to design net-zero energy buildings that generate as much energy as they consume. He believes we can achieve this if we work in interdisciplinary teams and consider carbon emissions from the very start of a project.

In 2006, the American Institute of Architects (AIA) created the "2030 Commitment," a national strategy for reducing energy consumption and achieving carbon neutrality in the built environment by 2030. At Bill's urging, HOK became one of the first firms to adopt AIA 2030. Then Bill worked to assure every single office, market practice, and discipline followed through on it. I believe healthy firms, like HOK, have a responsibility to take a leading role in making the world a better place, just as Kassabaum did. Whether it's to pursue interoperability or to elevate sustainable design, we can and should work to make a difference.

Embracing AIA 2030 brought a new rigor to every project, requiring measurements of energy and carbon reduction at each milestone. Bill also insisted we share AIA 2030 metrics for every office side-by-side at board meetings, once again using positive peer pressure to spur lagging offices to improve. HOK's large size and diversity made compliance with AIA 2030 a special challenge, but the results are impressive. Today, HOK tracks the projected energy performance of every project and remains committed to achieving a carbon-neutral design portfolio by 2030. In addition, HOK has won 10 awards from the AIA Committee on the Environment and in 2019 was ranked the number-one green architecture firm by *Engineering News-Record*.

Case Study: Abu Dhabi National Oil Company

What does an innovative sustainable design look like at HOK? It looks like a dream. Here's the story of one HOK-designed building that is incredibly efficient, but also incredibly beautiful. The Abu Dhabi National Oil Company, or ADNOC, wanted a new headquarters in the United Arab Emirates, its home. ADNOC's executives envisioned something sleek and elegant, but also wanted the new building to be as energy efficient and sustainable as possible. In a desert city where the temperature can easily climb to 110°F, that is a tall order. The solution turned out to be a very tall building.

An ADNOC representative approached senior HOK consultant Steve Parshall about the headquarters project in Abu Dhabi. Subsequently, ADNOC invited HOK and two other regional firms to compete for the design commission. After HOK was selected, Parshall proposed engaging three different HOK offices in a friendly competition to enhance the creative effort.

For once, HOK wanted its offices to compete with each other! Steve said HOK would be happy to organize and run this blind design competition at no extra cost. The ADNOC representative was intrigued, and within a few weeks had agreed to Steve's suggestion. As HOK design leader, Bill Hellmuth would organize and run the competition. He selected three HOK offices—Houston, Atlanta, and Washington, DC—to compete. By the terms of the competition, Bill was neutral and did not assist any of the offices, including Washington.

The three teams worked feverishly to develop their visions for the headquarters, then presented their schemes to ADNOC's decision makers, who selected the winning design. However, two weeks later, our main ADNOC liaison sent us a magazine article featuring a photo of a new building. It looked eerily like the winning design. It was just a coincidence, but it would not do. I have noticed that Middle Eastern clients, even more than others, want their buildings to be bigger, better, and truly original. "We cannot allow our building to look like a copy of another building," the client told Bill Hellmuth. Bill had developed a good working relationship with the ADNOC representative, and agreed saying, "You're right, that would not be acceptable." The customer is always right.

How was Bill going to keep this incredible opportunity from slipping away from HOK? Instead of another long competition, Bill suggested HOK hold a week-long charrette in the London office, and pick the winner from three brand new designs. Every architect knows the term charrette, but for those who don't, charrette is a French word for a small wagon. In the nineteenth century, architecture students at the École des Beaux-Arts in Paris would work all night to finish their drawings, then a charrette would pick up their designs and bring them to the faculty for judging. Some students were not quite finished and would jump on the small wagon, called "*en charrette*" in French, and continue to work on their designs as the wagon rolled through the streets of Paris. Over the years, charrette has come to mean working around the clock to conceive designs or finish drawings for a client.

Fortunately, the ADNOC client agreed, and HOK held the charrette, this time with Bill as a design participant rather than coordinator. At the end of a week, HOK presented the three schemes to the ADNOC chairman, who said, "Mr. Hellmuth, I like your design the best, but it looks too short. Can you add more floors to make it taller?" Bill replied, "Of course! I know of no high-rise building that does not look better as it gets taller." The customer is always right! The ADNOC headquarters ended up topping out at 75 stories and 1,122 feet tall. Sometimes the best designs come from second chances, just as we had seen with the National Air and Space Museum decades before.

Bill's design for ADNOC is contemporary, elegant, and restrained. The most distinctive feature of this high rise is the top, where the two sides soar beyond the rest of the building to form an open, squared-off arch. The building's simple yet dramatic silhouette made it an instant icon on the

FIGURE 29.1 Abu Dhabi National Oil Company Headquarters, Abu Dhabi, United Arab Emirates.
Source: Photo by Tim Griffith. Photo courtesy of HOK.

Abu Dhabi skyline. Of course, this being an HOK design, the dramatic top of the building is not just beautiful but also functional. The opening houses the executive dining and barbecue areas and the modern architrave across the top contains mechanical equipment, topped off by a helipad.

Better yet, Bill's ADNOC Headquarters earned Leadership in Energy Efficient Design (LEED) Gold certification. How did he do it? All four sides of most buildings are the same, but Bill designed this skyscraper with different sides to respond to the hot Middle Eastern sun. The long north side always faces away from the sun, so it is clad in clear glass from floor to ceiling. Bill was lucky: The best views of the Arabian Gulf and Abu Dhabi's sweeping Corniche Road lie to the north. The long south side of the building is exposed to midday sun, which he managed by using fretted glass with an embedded pattern that reduces light and heat. Bill made the shorter east and west sides of the building windowless and clad them in white stone to admit no sun at all.

Nearly a quarter of the building's materials are recycled, energy-saving LED lighting is used throughout, and a gray-water system uses air conditioning condensate water to flush toilets. As a result of all this meticulous, BIM-tested design, the building's energy use has been even lower than planned.

The ADNOC headquarters established a new benchmark for HOK. This is the dream of sustainable design: environmentally friendly, energy-efficient buildings that are spectacular—and sacrifice nothing. Clients are most likely to embrace sustainability when they don't have to give anything up. This building will stand the test of time for both design and sustainability.

HOK Product Design

Thanks to the two Bills, sustainable design became a mainstream dream at HOK, but we also entertained more fanciful ones. We wanted to imagine, discover, or create new markets for HOK design services. Our discussions were ambitious and far-ranging—exactly how dreams should be. Could we design attractive, efficient modular housing? How about new designs for freeways? Another idea was to design the products we routinely specified in our architecture, engineering, landscape, and interiors work. An important part of the design process for a building—or anything inside or outside of a building—is the selection of manufactured products like windows and doors, furniture, light fixtures, carpets, and so on. For large projects, we literally choose thousands of products. The selection process was frequently frustrating because so often the perfect product did not seem to exist. Anyone who has built a new house or remodeled their kitchen will understand this tale of woe.

More than one HOK designer thought, "I wish I could design my own product instead of picking it out of a catalog. Then it would be perfect." That's why there was instant support for HOK to enter the product design business. But how would it work? Who would manufacture our designs? Would other architects be able to specify our products? How would we get paid? We eventually turned these questions and more over to a task force led by Riccardo Mascia, who seemed to specialize in our thorniest challenges. Riccardo vowed to seek out ideas that were, in his words, "ambitious, far-reaching, and creative." He later said, "HOK needed to be a firm that was continuously searching for new ideas to transform our business."

We launched HOK Product Design in 2009. Initially, any HOK employee with an idea for a new product design could submit it to a product review panel made up of HOK and outside advisors. We gave priority to products that filled a gap in the market. If the review panel selected a product, we refined it. We hired a small team of product designers to refine product *ideas* into product *designs*, ready for manufacture—sort of the way technical architects translate the designers' work into something buildable. Finally, a small HOK team marketed our product designs to manufacturers, who could make and sell them under a license agreement.

HOK product designers have won the best of Neocon Gold award, the Nightingale Medal, and were recognized by *Architectural Record* magazine for product distinction, among other honors.[1]

HOK Product Design has continued to evolve, and even began contracting directly with manufacturers to create entire lines of products. We did this because we realized it is more efficient, but also more cohesive, to design a line of products rather than one product at a time. The manufacturers pay HOK to develop the line, and, depending on the contract, we may also get a commission on each product sold.

Here are some examples of the most successful HOK product designs. Fittingly, HOK designed two of them to encourage collaboration. HOK came up with a commercial office furniture collection that encourages people to work together, rather than separating them as so much office furniture does. HOK designers also created a series of artisan-quality furniture pieces meant to nurture maker spaces, places with tools and components supporting people who want to turn ideas into projects. And finally, HOK Product Design invented a lab bench system for laboratories that is unique because it's incredibly flexible and adaptable—with adjustable heights, moveable shelving, and more.

HOK Product Design was something entirely new for us. For the first time, HOK was not paid for the current month's design effort. Instead we were paid again and again for the same design. Riccardo called this "making money while we sleep." And, of course, that's perfect, because when you sleep is when you dream.

Expanding Again

As you have seen, when I became CEO of HOK, my focus was on fixing the firm—not on growth. I wanted to use the pyramid strategy to rebuild a world-class architecture firm in which people helped one another to succeed. I wanted to make us better, not bigger. But a funny thing happened: By making HOK better, we did get bigger. Even though restoration was my primary goal, our fees grew by 57% during my tenure as CEO. Profits soared even more, causing HOK stock to go up 550%.

---

[1] https://www.molteni.it/en/designer/h-o-k-product-design

Ten years after I became CEO, we were ready to grow again. HOK was profitable and debt-free with a strategic cash reserve to tap for opportunities. The ExCom began to dream of expanding. We had many discussions about how to proceed that would be wise, not wasteful. We had fought hard for our cash and wanted to be smart with it. We considered adding offices in underserved parts of the world, like South America, but decided that was not the best way forward for us. In the end, the ExCom returned to one of HOK's core values: diversification. If we could invest in talented people or firms who brought a new market practice to HOK, we would go for it.

BBG: Hospitality Design

The first big market practice opportunity came to us from HOK New York. In 2013, Carl Galioto told the ExCom that BBG, a well-regarded New York hospitality design practice, had begun to struggle financially and wanted to be acquired. David Beer, Henry Brennan, and Peter Gorman founded BBG in 1984. The firm developed a hospitality specialty, designing hotels, hotel interiors, and conference centers. Later, BBG expanded to Shanghai to serve the growing Asia hospitality marketplace.

The ExCom met the current BBG leaders in New York and liked them. HOK had designed hotels but had not developed a specialized hospitality practice. This was a grand opportunity for us to master a new specialty. Better, yet, we could do it without adding a new office. Remember, we were interested in consolidating offices, not creating new ones. Within six months, BBG became part of HOK. The people of BBG New York moved from their downtown Manhattan offices to our midtown office soon after.

We were able to fold in BBG's Asia office too. Julia Monk, the BBG leader for hospitality interiors, was based in Shanghai, to serve Asian clients. For those who don't know, hospitality interiors is a highly specialized and detailed practice in which designers develop an overall interior theme, then select all finish materials—from crown moldings in the guest rooms to the dinnerware in the hotel restaurant. After the merger, Julia relocated to HOK Hong Kong. The ExCom elected her to the HOK board of directors, and today Julia continues as the director of the HOK hospitality practice.

Back in the Game

One of my personal dreams was to get back into the sports design business. It had really stung me when we had to give up HOK Sport, because we hadn't set it up right the first time. This fit well with the ExCom's vision, because sports architecture is a big market practice and arguably the most prominent. Not everyone knows about the new hospital in town, or the new university building—but everyone knows about the new stadium. The five-year term restricting HOK from doing sports design had expired at the end of 2013. The ExCom launched a hunt for talented sports architecture firms.

First Larry Malcic, of HOK London, recruited John Rhodes, a talented designer from the Populous London office. Since the five years were up, we were now allowed to woo people away from our former colleagues at what used to be HOK Sport. John and two other Populous colleagues joined HOK London a short time after the five-year restriction lifted. But we wanted to do more.

360 Architecture: Sports Design

A short time later, we learned 360 Architecture, another Kansas City sports practice, was interested in being acquired. Kansas City had become the center of sports architecture over the years. Why? Ironically, it happened as sports specialists split off from HOK Sport and formed their own firms. Brad Schrock and George Heinlein had left HOK Sport in 1995 and started up Heinlein Schrock. In 2004, they merged with another Kansas City design firm, and took the name 360 Architecture.

I called George Heinlein in Kansas City, and learned his partner Brad Schrock was working in a new 360 Architecture branch office in San Francisco just a few blocks from HOK San Francisco. Could this be a sign? Next, I called Brad and he agreed to meet. He was thin and athletic, with a shock of gray hair and a friendly demeanor. I liked him instantly. Brad confirmed 360 wanted to be acquired. When I asked why, he said, "We're growing, but not fast enough to provide good opportunities for our next generation of leaders. We need to be part of a big, international design firm like HOK to grow faster."

Brad told me 360 was already in negotiations with another firm but would be a better fit with HOK. He wondered how HOK would place a value on his firm. I was determined to learn from the mistakes of the past, and said price was only one of three important factors we wanted to understand about 360. A successful merger would depend on an evaluation of all three:

Price: This was the most straightforward part of our evaluation, based on an audit and review of 360 Architecture's backlog of work.

Operations: Having worked so hard to improve our own operations, we wanted to know how 360 was organized. How were their project teams structured? What accounting system did they use? What software did 360 use for design work? Getting the answers to these questions and many more would take some work.

Culture: This essential characteristic was the most difficult part of our analysis. Did both firms share the same culture? We had finally reclaimed HOK's culture of collaboration, based on people treating each other like family and helping each other to succeed. We wanted our new sport practice to become fully integrated into our firm, the opposite of our experience with HOK Sport.

I arranged for Brad, George, and the rest of 360's leadership group to meet the HOK ExCom at our upcoming quarterly retreat. The meeting was positive from the beginning, and both sides could imagine the others as future partners. Our cultures were similar. We began our operations analysis and identified adjustments that would be necessary for our merged firm. Finally, we developed a price based on a financial analysis and the 360 leaders eventually agreed. Thanks to regular deposits into our Wells Fargo strategic reserve account, we had the cash on hand to cover the cost.

360 Architecture was rebranded HOK Sports + Recreation + Entertainment in December 2015. We were back in the game after a gap of seven years. We were lucky. Finding the right firm could have taken a lot longer. With the addition of the sports practice in Kansas City, HOK now had 11 large offices. "The Big 11." We invited the 360 San Francisco branch office staff to move into the HOK San Francisco office.

One reason architects love designing stadiums and arenas is that people recognize them. Often, the general public doesn't pay any attention to the design of an office building, school, or hospital. Sports facilities are different. They're on TV. Millions of people visit them to attend games. HOK Sports + Recreation + Entertainment has already made a name for itself with dramatic sports designs such as Mercedes-Benz Stadium, home of the Atlanta Falcons.

Our merger with 360 Architecture was the final step in remaking HOK as the firm of our dreams. I remained CEO for another year to get 360 fully integrated into our culture, but I was thinking ahead to stepping down.

Finding the Next CEO

When we reached the top of the HOK pyramid, I thought, "my work here is finished." I had enjoyed the journey. I didn't need to hang around the destination. HOK had chosen me as CEO at a time when I might have had other dreams, but I had to fix the firm. Scaling that pyramid became my dream. I wanted to restructure, rebuild, and reunify HOK so it functioned as the family I had joined when I first arrived. Thirteen years later, we had done it—together—and it was time for others to take it from there. My last big job was to name a successor CEO, as was HOK tradition. I wanted this person to continue the work I had begun, keeping HOK strong and united, a place where people can reach for their dreams.

Whoever I chose would partner with HOK design leader and President Bill Hellmuth, so I asked Bill to work with me to identify the ideal new CEO. It sounds like a no-brainer to have people help pick their own partners, but I know some executives don't do it this way. I flew to Washington, DC regularly to visit the HOK office in Georgetown, and always stayed with my daughter, Elisabeth, and her family at their home near National Cathedral. I suggested to Bill that we discuss CEO candidates after work, over drinks—scotch, of course. We met several times in a sunny, private room at my daughter's house. After a few meetings, Bill began calling our room the "Scotchenarium."

HOK had chosen me as CEO at a time when I might have had other dreams, but I had to fix the firm. Scaling that pyramid became my dream.

At each meeting, we talked and talked about CEO candidates, but never felt like we had found exactly the right person for the job. After several meetings, I began to think Bill Hellmuth himself would be a great CEO. Even though he was our design leader, Bill understood finance, operations, and the importance of profits. Plus, he was a quick study. He always seemed to be the first to understand when others were struggling to digest information. His Washington, DC branch office was the best run and most profitable year after year due to his leadership and some great partners.

I was also impressed by Bill's innate leadership ability. He led rather than managed. Bill had overseen the tricky task of revising our bonus program, which was so important to restoring HOK culture. Bill had also recognized the emerging importance of green design and transformed HOK into a leading sustainable design firm. Bill Valentine had said many times, "Leaders have followers." Bill Hellmuth had emerged as a leader HOK people would follow.

At our next Scotchenarium meeting, I told Bill what was on my mind. "I think the right CEO candidate is sitting right in front of me," I announced. Bill was surprised, and said, "But I already have a cool job as president and head of design, and I would never give up the design role." I told him that every good leader shapes his role around his strengths. "You have a passion for design and the capacity to lead HOK as a designer," I explained. "After all, Gyo led HOK for 10 years after George K. died."

I could see Bill becoming more interested. "I need to think about how to do this," he replied. We met again a few weeks later, and Bill gave me his answer. "I will keep the firm-wide design leader role. That is the most important to me and I will not give it up," he said. "But I believe I can also handle the CEO responsibilities by focusing on strategy and delegating most of the work to the rest of the ExCom." I was delighted—and relieved. Bill was an inspired choice.

In April of 2016, Bill Hellmuth became the new chief executive officer of HOK at our annual shareholders' meeting. He was 62 years old and had been with HOK for 26 years. HOK was once again led by a Hellmuth. But remember, his uncle hadn't recruited him; Gyo Obata had. In fact, Obata had hired all four people who ended up leading HOK after the founders: Jerry Sincoff, Bill Valentine, me, and now Bill. Obata had a great eye for design, but also a great eye for who could help HOK design a great firm.

I moved into the role of HOK chairman when Bill Hellmuth became CEO—one last job at the same firm. I wanted to be able to keep an eye on things and offer advice to Bill and the ExCom. If there is a gracious way to help, without getting in the way, a transition role like this can be helpful—but not for long. It was time to move on with my life.

I decided to step down as chairman of HOK as of June 7, 2017, exactly 50 years after Gyo Obata had hired me in St. Louis. Bill Hellmuth asked me how I wanted to celebrate,

FIGURE 29.2 Bill Hellmuth became CEO of HOK in 2016.
Source: Photo by Stephen Voss. Photo courtesy of HOK.

and I suggested a party at the City Club a few blocks from our San Francisco office. I planned to remain active and engaged with buildingSMART International, writing this book, and other activities, and asked that my event be called a repurposing party—not a retirement party. It may sound like semantics, but I believe words and intentions matter. For this same reason, when people ask me the standard question, "How are you?" I don't say "fine." I always answer, "Excellent!" HOK was doing well and I really was excellent.

My "Repurposing"

About 100 people attended my repurposing party, including ExCom colleagues, past and present HOK friends, and my family. A surprise guest was Richard Petrie, chief executive of buildingSMART International, who flew all the way from London. Bill Hellmuth acted as emcee, and Bill Valentine and others gave short speeches thanking me for my contributions to HOK. When it was my turn to speak, I set them straight, pointing out that it was me who needed to thank HOK. After all, this great firm had given me a vibrant career where I got to have many jobs at one firm, growing from junior designer to CEO. HOK had offered me the opportunity to travel around the world and work on exciting projects. I had made lifelong friends and even found my wife, Jeanne, at HOK. Thank goodness I never left HOK.

Chapter 29: To Design a World-Class Firm

1. Put your house in order and secure your financial future to clear your head and marshal the mental energy to do great work.
2. Remember that buildings are the number one source of carbon emissions and make a commitment to improve your sustainable design practice—and the planet.
3. Work in interdisciplinary teams and consider carbon emissions from the very start of a project in order to achieve the most sustainable result.
4. Support lofty outside goals, once your firm is healthy on the inside.
5. Know that clients are most likely to embrace sustainability if they don't have to give up anything, so design clean, green buildings that are also beautiful and sacrifice nothing.
6. Find ways to get paid for your designs over and over again, so you can "make money while you sleep."
7. Work to make your firm better, and it may well grow bigger too.
8. Evaluate not just price, but also operations and culture, when considering acquiring a firm.
9. Shape your role around your strengths, as every great leader does. Then gather smart people around you and delegate the other aspects of the job to them.
10. Transition to an advisory role, and offer advice to your firm's new leaders—but don't do it for too long.

Afterword: HOK Today

As I stepped down, HOK was far different from the firm I joined 50 years before. And that progress has continued since I left. The founders laid out a long-term vision, intending for HOK to outlast them. And each CEO since has contributed additional ideas that have shaped the firm.

The State of HOK

Founder George Hellmuth wanted specialized leaders to find and keep talented people. Today the number of HOK people has soared from less than 30 at the founding to more than 1,700. In the course of that growth, HOK has evolved from mostly male to 52% men and 48% women. Specialized leaders continue to focus on design, technical architecture, management, or, of course, full-time marketing.

Hellmuth also knew that diversity of locations and disciplines would help HOK weather any storm. Sure enough, HOK has grown from one office in St. Louis to 11 large offices and many branch offices totaling 27 locations around the world. Architecture remains the dominant field, with almost 60% of the total work, but now interior design makes up 21% of HOK's revenue. Engineering, planning, consulting, graphics, on-site services and sustainability consulting contribute the remaining 19%.

Gyo Obata focused on developing expertise in specialized building types while he led HOK. Now nearly 60% of HOK's total work falls into six market practice areas: aviation and transportation; healthcare; science and technology; sports and recreation; justice; and hospitality. Of those specialties, healthcare and aviation are the biggest of all. Yes, HOK is still designing airports, after landing that very first signature project to design a new terminal for Lambert Airport.

Jerry Sincoff pushed for growth above all. Today, HOK's geographic reach is nothing short of amazing. In a recent year, HOK designed more than 4,000 projects in 87 different countries on six continents. Work in the United States made up about 80% of the total, followed by Canada at 6%, Europe and the Middle East at 5% apiece, and Asia at 4%. The ratios vary every year depending on the size of projects in each region.

I worked to implement great operations, which have put HOK in robust good health. In one recent year, HOK had the highest revenue of any US architecture and engineering firm.[1] What a contrast to 1955, the year of HOK's founding, when the little Midwestern upstart brought in less than 200 thousand bucks. As for modern times, in 2000, the turn

---
[1] "ENR 2018 Top 500 Design Firms," *Engineering News Record*.

242 Afterword: HOK Today

FIGURE A.1 World map showing HOK work in 87 countries in 2017.
Source: Image courtesy of HOK.

of the twenty-first century, HOK enjoyed revenue of $206 million. In 2020, HOK will earn around twice that amount. The firm's stock value has grown along with its revenue, and that stock is now wholly owned by HOK employees—employees who have earned the right to dream.

I also worked to restore true collaboration to the firm I loved. HOK has become a fully digital firm, with projects shared among offices through a cloud-based network. Every office makes use of what HOK calls "advance collaboration rooms" to hold videoconferences and share work efforts with other offices. It's the high-tech version of helping each other to succeed. The HOK board of directors also uses the rooms and remains strong by meeting monthly and sharing metrics of success.

Looking to the Future

HOK CEO Bill Hellmuth is now putting his own stamp on the firm. When Bill took over, he told me, "My dream is for HOK to become the best design firm in the world." It has turned out to be a benefit that HOK's leaders have come from different disciplines. Since Bill is a designer, that is his proper focus. He has built on HOK's past to prepare for the future he wants for the firm. Bill recognizes that certain core values embedded in HOK will help him achieve his design dreams for the firm.

"There is a sense of family," Bill told me. "I know that sounds corny, and maybe it's Midwestern, but heck, that's where our roots are, and I think it's heartfelt." Family members may argue, but when push comes to shove, they are aligned. "Aligned doesn't mean you agree on everything. Aligned means you agree on the basic principles," Bill explained. "It's important to have those heated discussions. It just means we agree on the general principles and we're going to work through how to achieve them." One thing Bill and his team always agree on is that strong financial underpinnings put HOK in a position to take risks and reach for dreams.

As Bill dreams of shaping HOK into the best design firm in the world, he is building on the firm's legacy rather than discarding it. The founders had lived through the Great Depression, so they wanted to make sure HOK would survive by taking on a wide variety of projects. Remember, there are no bad projects! "I want us to never lose our roots in terms of a good backlog of projects," Bill said. "These may not necessarily be the most glamorous projects, but are all about client service and keeping us going and training young professionals."

"I also want us to use that as the backlog—literally like a log in the fireplace—that then allows us to go after the really terrific, poetic projects that I think we should have more of," Bill added. In other words, Bill believes it's time for HOK to go after more signature projects, layering those on top of the diverse projects the firm has always pursued. "There are great moments, when a firm that has the legacy of HOK can really use that as a stepping stone to some of these other projects," he said.

None of this would be possible without pushing the envelope of technical architecture, a goal Bill is pursuing in partnership with Carl Galioto, the technical leader who was elected HOK president in 2017. Bill explained it eloquently: "The technical work at HOK never rose to be the art that it could have, and that's something we want to push now. The art and science of putting things together in the most beautiful ways imaginable—not just in ways that won't leak, but ways that are exquisite. If we can conquer that, and combine it with everything else we're doing, it's very powerful."

The Hellmuth Strategy

Bill, too, wanted to convey his vision for HOK in a clear, compelling graphic, which he first sketched by hand. What can I say? Architects are visual people. I had my pyramid. For Bill, the ideal graphical shape was a stylized square cross, which he says reminds him of a Swiss cross. Bill recognized that for HOK to do the world's best design, its work needs to be at the very center of the firm. Bill calls this work the "artifact," since HOK does much more than just design buildings these days. Yes, an artifact can be a building, but it can also be an urban plan, a product design, or a sustainability strategy—just to name a few. Bill placed this all-important artifact at the heart of his cross diagram, with key HOK departments supporting it.

FIGURE A.2 Bill Hellmuth strategy sketch for HOK, 2017.
Source: Image courtesy of HOK.

Design and Technical Architecture

On the vertical bar, design and technical architecture are the two interlinked disciplines directly responsible for HOK's work. Pure design is at the top, led by Bill himself. Technical architecture is below, the natural partner to great design, with Carl Galioto in charge. Bill envisions these two specialties, "leveraging the best minds in the HOK orchestra to achieve the best design outcome, all linked together in the best digital model."

Operations and Business Strategy

The other two elements depicted in Bill's diagram lie on the horizontal bars to the sides, supporting HOK's design work without dominating it.

The OpsCom is on one side of the cross, assuring that the teams who do the design work are well supported and well organized. Tom Robson is HOK's Chief Operating Officer and leads the OpsCom, along with Susan Klumpp Williams, the other operations maestro, who joined the ExCom in 2017. "The OpsCom supports our work by a focus on the metrics to support great work," Bill said. "Are we signing good contracts, billing and collecting our fees, and all of the other things necessary to support great work?"

On the other side of the cross is business strategy, called BizCom, which includes HOK's signature focus on marketing—and much more. Riccardo Mascia, as BizCom Chair, leads this effort to make sure HOK project teams have access to the best clients and project opportunities around the globe. Hellmuth described the business strategy mission this way: "Are we going after things that only we can do? Where is that great next project? How do we lash different offices together to achieve it?"

Sixty-five years on, a Hellmuth once again leads HOK, but in new directions and to new levels. Bill is following the HOK tradition of visiting every office and holding "Ask Me Anything" talks where he uses his cross-shaped strategy graphic to describe his vision. I no longer worry that the firm will fall apart. HOK is as solid as any of the buildings we've created. Future leaders will add new insights and strategies. HOK has designed and completed more than 34,000 projects. Of course, the work of designing a world-class architecture firm continues—and always will.

HOK is as solid as any of the buildings we've created.

Acknowledgments

This book would not have been possible without the help of many people, and I want to acknowledge and thank them all.

First, I am grateful to George Hellmuth, Gyo Obata, and George Kassabaum for beginning the great adventure called HOK. A special thank you to Gyo Obata for hiring me—and altering the course of my life. I also thank Gyo, the only living founder, for providing valuable insights about HOK by videoconference, his very first.

Gerry Gilmore, my colleague from early HOK days, first proposed, "These are great stories about HOK . . . someone should write them down!" I ran with his idea and I'm so glad I did. I hope the lessons we learned along the way will benefit people both inside and outside of the firm.

The families of the founders were another rich resource of information and insight. George W. Hellmuth and Daniel Hellmuth shared recollections of their father, HOK founder George Hellmuth. George Kassabaum's daughter, Karen Kassabaum Ivory, provided important information, photos, and news items about her father. She also reviewed and corrected early versions of the manuscript. Gyo Obata's wife Mary and daughter Kiku also added important details about Gyo's life before and during his HOK career.

Amy Graf Becker shared stories about her father, King Graf, during his tenure at HOK. Ron Labinski's wife, Lee, confirmed important details about the creation and growth of HOK Sport.

I am especially grateful to my long-term colleague and good friend Bill Valentine, who contributed information as I was writing the book, then served as a reviewer, improving and correcting early versions of the manuscript. Jerry Sincoff was also generous with his time, providing needed insights and revisions to the manuscript. I am also grateful for observations provided by HOK ExCom members Bill Hellmuth, Tom Robson, Riccardo Mascia, Carl Galioto, and Susan Williams.

Other HOK people provided critical information to fill in the blanks in my HOK timeline. Bob Barr shared key memories from his days at HOK in St. Louis and HOK Washington, DC, where he worked for many years. Jan DeWeer provided a wealth of statistical information. John Gilmore gave generously of his time to help with the timing of key HOK events. Lori Moran worked diligently to retrieve and provide photos from the HOK archives and helped with the last-minute rush to find the right images

I am grateful to my good friend Ian Howell for getting me engaged in buildingSMART. Ian also encouraged me as I began to write this book, especially by urging me to find an editor to help assemble the content. I want to thank Karen Newcombe, my first editor, for getting me started as an author and helping to organize my many HOK stories.

Friend and former CFO Bob Pratzel was invaluable in helping me sort through the sequence of events that occurred during my tenure as COO and CEO. Bob also reviewed the manuscript and provided helpful comments and corrections. HOK CIO Ken Young provided recollections of the HOK transformation from a paper-based practice to a digital practice.

Susie Becker, my former executive assistant, helped in countless ways during the preparation of this book, including acting as a reviewer, securing dates when events occurred, and tracking down detailed bits of information from others at HOK. Susie also reviewed the final manuscript and provided a detailed list of comments and corrections.

I owe a very special thanks to my daughter, Elisabeth Leamy, an author of two books of her own, who began reviewing the manuscript and, in the process, was moved to become my full-fledged editor. Elisabeth helped turn this book into a good book, then introduced me to John Wiley & Sons, who became my publishers. It was a rare and special privilege to have a father-daughter working relationship, one she and I treasure. Speaking of Wiley, the team there has made completing this book a smooth and exciting process and I thank them.

I want to express love and appreciation to my grandfather, Andrew Jackson "Pop" Hogue, who taught me to "measure twice, cut once" and kindled my interest in architecture; to my parents, who gave me the best start in life by setting high standards and encouraging me to do my best. I also owe a debt of gratitude to Mary Legate, my favorite high school English teacher, who instilled in me a love of writing. Thanks also to the Coffee Shop Gang for cheering me on as I wrote.

Finally, I want to thank my wife Jeanne, who provided support and encouragement as I researched and wrote this book. She is the love of my life—and HOK's greatest gift.

About the Author

Patrick MacLeamy spent 50 years at HOK, rising from junior designer to CEO and witnessing the firm's growth from a single Midwestern office to 27 locations across the globe offering architecture, interiors, engineering, planning and more. MacLeamy joined HOK St. Louis in 1967, then helped establish the firm's San Francisco outpost in 1970, later becoming managing principal of that office. He joined HOK's executive committee in 1995 and was named COO five years later. In 2003, HOK shareholders elected MacLeamy chief executive officer. He led the firm for 13 years. In 2016, MacLeamy chose a new CEO for HOK, remaining as chairman for one more year before retiring—or, as he likes to say, "repurposing."

MacLeamy led many signature projects at HOK, including the Moscone Center in San Francisco and the King Khalid International Airport in Saudi Arabia. Over the years, he worked as a designer, project manager, and even marketer at HOK, soaking up knowledge of all three disciplines. Trained as an architect, MacLeamy is a self-taught executive, who attributes his success to his ability to communicate clearly and his interest in "boring" things like financial metrics and digital standards, that architects often ignore.

MacLeamy believes in getting involved to help improve the building industry, and has served in many roles and received multiple honors for this work. He was a member of the Architecture and Engineering Productivity Committee of the Construction Users Round Table, convened by the General Services Administration, in 2003. The National Institute for Building Sciences honored him with its President's Award in 2005. MacLeamy served on the American Institute of Architects' Large Firm Roundtable for many years, and, in 2006, the AIA named him a Fellow in recognition of his service to the profession. MacLeamy was also chairman of the Construction Industry Round Table from 2012 to 2013. Recently he

Patrick MacLeamy at his desk in HOK San Francisco, California.
Source: Image courtesy of HOK.

was elected to membership in the National Academy of Construction in recognition of his many contributions to the building industry.

MacLeamy's proudest association is with buildingSMART International, which works to achieve open standards for the exchange of digital information in the building and infrastructure industries. He was a founding member of buildingSMART in 1994; elected a fellow for his service to the organization in 2018; and currently serves as international chairman.

MacLeamy is a recognized thought leader who advocates leveraging technology to improve design. He has been a featured speaker at many industry events, authored numerous national and international articles, and testified before Congress about the need for digital standards in the building industry. He is perhaps best known for the MacLeamy Curve," which advocates assigning ample resources early in the design process, optimizing the design and correcting mistakes early when it is easy and cheap—instead of during construction when it is difficult and expensive.

MacLeamy earned his Bachelor of Architecture and Master of Architecture in Urban Design degrees at the University of Illinois at Urbana. In 1965, he won the coveted Paris Prize administered by the Van Alen Institute, allowing him to attend the École Nationale Supérieure des Beaux-Arts in Paris and the American Academy in Rome.

MacLeamy lives in Novato, California, outside of San Francisco, where he practices what he preaches by serving on the city's Design Review Commission, which he has done for decades. He is married to Jeanne MacLeamy, also an architect, who he met at HOK. They have two children and three grandchildren.

Connect with him at MacLeamy.com.

Index

NOTE: Page references in *italics* refer to figures and photos.

A

Abu Dhabi National Oil Company (ADNOC), 232–234, *233*
accounting. *See* finances
Adams, Ansel, 10
Advance Technology Group (ATG), 195, 206–207
Alcoa building (Los Angeles), 72
Allen, Michael, 18
American Institute of Architects (AIA)
    2030 Commitment in energy use reduction, 232
    effort curve presentation, 193
    Kassabaum as Council of Fellow chancellor, 75
    Kassabaum as president of, xxi, 28
Anchorage Federal Office Building project, 52
Apple headquarters (Cupertino, California), 128, *129*
Architect's Journal, 150
Architectural Record magazine, 235
Arctic Design, 51
Arizona prison system study, 55
Asian expansion, 98–99, 101–107, 127. *See also* growth and expansion
Ask Me Anything meetings, 209–210, 212, 244
ATG (Advance Technology Group), 195, 206–207
AT&T, 140
AutoDesk, 135, 140–142, 189, 193, 206
aviation specialty
    Asia projects, 107
    dispute over, 171
    firm-wide market practices and, 120
    as major HOK specialty, 241
    Saudi Arabia projects, 81, 87, 90–91, 127, 131–132
    teams form in, 80
    "unbroken chain" of work in, 81

B

Baillargeon, Pierre, 100
Bank of America credit line, 166, 171, 186, 219–220
Bartolomi, John, 206
Bartz, Ed, 96–97
Bath, Toby, 199
BBG (Beer, Brennan and Gorman), 236
Becker, Susie, 129–130, 139, 180, 184
Beer, David, 236
Bennett, Michael, 151
Bernstein, Phil, 189, 193
BIM. *See* Building Information Modeling
BizCom, 244
board of directors. *See* HOK board of directors
Boas, Roger, 60–62
Boatmen's Bank (St. Louis), 32, 83–85, 166
bonuses
    ExCom and, 133
    HOK Sport provision on, 95–96, 166–167
    investor concern about, 166
    90-Day Rule and, 156
    restructuring of, 202–204, 239
Boulder County jail project, 54–55
Breitkopf, Gertraud, 189
Brennan, Henry, 236
Building Information Modeling (BIM)
    in collaborative design and construction, 192
    HOK implementation of, 193–194
    innovation with, 27
    in King Saud University project, 195–196
    technical architects and mastery of, 200
    transitioning to, 142–143
    value of computerized systems, 58
buildingSMART@HOK, 193–194, 195, 201, 229
buildingSMART International, 140–143, *142*, 194, 240

C

CAD. *See* computer-aided design
Cannon, Ken, 51
Carrier, 140
Carver, Chris, 95
Cassetta, Lou, 51–52
Caudill, Bill, 145
Caudill, Rowlett & Scott. *See* CRS/CRSS
Cauthen, Jerry, 53–54
CCWC. *See* Crittenden, Cassetta, Wirum & Cannon
Cecil, Denny, Highton (CDH, London), 148–149
Cecil, Ray, 148
change orders, 189–190
Charles Luckman Architects, 72
Chicas, Robert, 200
chief financial officer (CFO), 85. *See also* Pratzel, Bob
chief operating officer (COO), 154. *See also* operations
Church of England commissioners, 99–100
Cirangle, Ernest, 107
Citicorp headquarters (New York), 25
clients
   change orders and, 190
     (*See also* effort curve)
   listening to, importance of, 24
   meeting needs of, 22–23
   problem-seeking technique, 145, 147
   production integrity and, 25, 28
   pyramid strategy and, 175
   sincerity with, 55, 88
   Sincoff focus on quality service, 118–119
collaboration
   company culture grounded in, 33, 82–83, 167
     (*See also* company culture)
   with engineers, 25
   financial metrics in fostering, 155–156
   in reducing change orders, 190
     (*See also* effort curve)
   "true collaboration" in pyramid strategy, 173, *175*, 202, 207, 209, 216, 242
Collins, Michael, 43, 61
Comeau, Terri, 149
company culture
   "Ask Me Anything" talks, 209–210, 212, 244
   considerate communication as, 34, 124
   employees cared for, 34–35
   erosion of, amid growth, 82–83, 121–124, 136, 172
   family atmosphere of HOK, 35–36
   firm-wide market practices effect on, 124
   HOK name and humor about, 37–38, 39
   HR director as advocate, 85
   MacLeamy's focus on reclaiming, 209–218
   in merger with 360 Architecture, 237–238
   mutual respect key in, 33–34
   pyramid strategy as part of, 210
   St. Louis fire and, 38–40
   staff photos, posting on intranet, 211–212
   storytelling as bonding, 36–37
Compensation Committee (CompCom), 203
computer-aided design (CAD)
   3D CAD, 142
   BIM vs., 193
   customized software by HOK, 135
   in reviewing design versions, 25
   upgrades, 206
   See also Building Information Modeling
Construction Users Round Table (CURT), 189–193
contractors and effort curve, 190–193
Conversations with Myself, an Interpretation (Kassabaum), 75
Cope, Beverly, 106–107
Cope, Dennis, 106–107
core boards, 29, 213–214
corporation vs. partnership, 30–31
Courtenay, Ralph, 148, 198
Cranbrook Academy (Michigan), 11–12
Crittenden, Cassetta, Wirum & Cannon (CCWC, Anchorage), 42, 50–52
Crittenden, Edward, 42, 51
CRS/CRSS (Houston), 145–147, 149, 182
C-suite. *See* HOK Executive Committee (ExCom); HOK office of chairman (OOC)
CURT (Construction Users Round Table), 189–193

D

Dallas-Fort Worth International Airport (DFW), 44–46, *45*, *81*
Davis, Clark, 110, 148, 173, 179
Demick, Pat, 68
Denny, John, 148
"The Depression-Proof Firm" (Hellmuth), 8

Index

depression-proof strategy, 7–8, 9, 15, 23, 47, 88, 156
design
   innovation and, 23–25
   Obata as principal designer, 15
   specialized leadership in, 8
   successors in, 70–71, 181–182
   in traditional effort curve, 190–191 (*See also* effort curve)
   See also Hellmuth, Bill; Obata, Gyo; sustainable design; Valentine, Bill
Design Core Board, 214
DesignIntelligence magazine, 207
detail drawings, 26, 27
Devine, James, Labinski & Myers (Kansas City), 94
DeWeer, Jan, 85
digital images, 137, 138
Dinkeloo, John, 10
diversification, 7–8, 9, 23–24, 236, 241
Drury, Charles, 4
Dubai Marina project, 151

E

Eads, James B., 3–4
effort curve. *See also* MacLeamy Curve
   controlling cost, 191–192
   CURT problems and, 189–190
   design change costs, 192
   at HOK, 193–194
   KAUST case study, 194–196, *195*
   as "MacLeamy Curve," 198
   smart effort curve, 191, *192*–193
   traditional, 191, *191*
Eichler, Joseph, 64
Eisenhower, Dwight, 58, 134
e-mail system, 137, 138
employees
   diversity goals for, 208, 241
   MacLeamy's visits with, 209–210
   recruitment program, 207–208
   shareholder benefits, explaining system to, 210–212
   stock options for, 31–32
   talent, retaining, 7, 9, 107, 197
   See also bonuses; company culture; human resources
Engineering News-Record, 232
engineers, collaboration with, 25, 190–191

European expansion, 99–100, 103, 150–151. *See also* growth and expansion
ExCom. *See* HOK Executive Committee
Executive Committee (ExCom). *See* HOK Executive Committee

F

Fallingwater (Pittsburgh), 48
Feinstein, Dianne, 62–63
50 Percent Rule, 155, 186
finances
   accounting consolidation, 205–206
   bonuses, 133, 156, 166–167, 202–204, 239 (*See also* bonuses)
   cash flow troubles, 83–84, 134, 171
   CFO addition, 85
   collecting overdue bill in Malaysia, 89–90
   crises amid low profits, 165–167
   enforcing financial metrics, MacLeamy on, 174–175
   50 Percent Rule on salaries, 155, 186
   HOK Sport, selling off, 222–223
   Kajima, buying out, 221–222
   leadership changes in team, 229
   MacLeamy's COO appointment and, 154
   90-Day Rule, 155–156, 205
   paying off bank credit line, 219–220
   robust and record revenue for HOK, 241–242
   scrutiny of reports by board of directors, 186
   simplified accounting practices, 157–158
   10-Month Backlog Rule, 156–157
   See also stock
Flambert, Richard, 42
Forrest, Dorothy, 22, 74
founders. *See* HOK founders (Hellmuth, Obata & Kassabaum); *individual names of founders*
The Fountainhead (Rand), 34–35
Fur Exchange Building (St. Louis), 4, *5*
furniture design, 235
"The Futurity of HOK" (Sincoff), 120

G

Gale, Dan, 23, 42, 49–50, 53, 54
Galioto, Carl, 189, 193, 200, *200*–202, 229–230, 243–244

Geisel, Vernon, 38
General Services Administration (GSA), 189–190
Gerstner, Lou, 172
Gilmore, Gerry, 23, 44–45, 72–73, 95
Golden Gate Bridge, 49
Gollins Melvin Ward (GMW), 100
Gorman, Peter, 236
Graf, King
    background of, 68, 99
    Dallas office establishment and, 45
    as Hellmuth's marketing assistant, 23
    Hong Kong office establishment and, 98–99
    leadership transition and, 79
    as marketing leader, 68–69, 69, 117
    on "New Marketing," 83
    Pittsburgh project office and, 47–48
    retirement of, 161
    storytelling by, 36–37
    Valentine's first impression of, 70–71
    See also HOK Executive Committee; HOK office of chairman
Great High Schools project (Pittsburgh), xxi–xxii, 23, 25, 47–48, 69, 71
Green, Lisa, 163, 226–227
growth and expansion
    in Asia, 98–99, 101–107, 127
    crises resulting from, 171–173
    in Europe, 99–100, 103, 150–151
    geographic reach of HOK, 241, 242
    lessons learned from, 93–94, 96–97
    in Middle East, 90–92, 149, 151
    in Obata era, 93–100
    project offices, 41–46
    purchases and mergers in Sincoff era, 145–152
    Sincoff focus on, 118, 164, 167, 241
    See also innovation
GSA (General Services Administration), 189–190

H

Hagee, George, 72
Hajjar, Daniel, 151
Haldeman Associates, 147
Harmon, Jan, 227
Heinlein, George, 237–238
Hellmuth, Bill
    Abu Dhabi oil company sustainable design by, 232–234, 233
    on adding designers to board of directors, 187
    on bonus program restructuring, 203, 239
    building on HOK's foundation, 242–243
    as CEO successor to MacLeamy, 238–240, 239
    design competition and, 232
    on HOK's 50th anniversary, 214
    on HOK vs. SOM as workplace, 201
    as HOK Washington design director, 110–112, 111
    on leadership retreat, 215
    Obata's hiring of, 110
    peer recognition as "dream" of, 176
    strategy of, 243, 243–244
    sustainable design goals of, 231–232
    as Valentine's successor, 181–182, 228
    Williams' selection to ExCom by, 226
    See also HOK Executive Committee
Hellmuth, George F.
    background and early career of, xiii, 3, 5–7, 9–10
    death and legacy of, 161–162
    depression-proof strategy of, 7–8, 9, 15, 23, 47, 88, 156
    generosity to employees by, 35–36
    on geographic expansion, 41–42, 45
    HOK founding and, 14–17
    as international subsidiary president, 73–74
    legacy of, 36–37
    MacLeamy's first impressions of, xx–xxi
    marketing changes after, 80–81
    marketing innovations by, 21–23
        (See also marketing)
    marketing successor for, 67–69, 69
    mutual respect demonstrated by, 34
    nephew's hiring at HOK, 110
    New York office opening and, 72–73
    photos of, 6, 7, 16, 69, 162
    Priory School project and, 19
    on public relations value, 30
    on sincerity with clients, 55
    stock ownership and, 30–31, 67, 74
    Washington, DC, office and, 43
    See also HOK founders

Hellmuth, George (founder's father), 4–5
Hellmuth, George W. (founder's son), 73, 109, 111
Hellmuth, Harry, 4
Hellmuth, Mimi, 214
Hellmuth, Nancy, 111
Hellmuth, Nick, 9
Hellmuth, Obata & Kassabaum. See HOK founders
Hellmuth, Ted, 110
Hellmuth, Yamasaki & Leinweber (HYL, St. Louis), 9–10, 12, 14–15, 17–19
Hellmuth & Hellmuth (St. Louis), 4
Herold, Ken, 136, 138, 140–142
Herold, Mary, 142
Highton, Michael, 148, 151
Hines, Gerald, 97, 118, 129
HNTB (Howard, Needles, Tammen & Bergendoff), 95–96
Hogue, Andrew Jackson "Pop," 192, 196
HOK + 4 (consortium), 74, 90, 91, 100
HOK board of directors
  advance collaboration rooms use by, 242
  BIM implementation and, 193–194
  on central services consolidations, 205–206
  core boards reports to, 213
  empowering, 185
  establishment of, 31
  expansion and revamped structure, 158, 163
  Galioto addition to, 201
  Kajima, two board seats for, 102
  MacLeamy's address on resolving crisis, 173–176
  replacing members of underperforming offices, 186–187
  scrutiny of financial reports by, 186
  "strong board" in pyramid strategy, 173, 174, 175, 186–187
  sustainable design retreat, 107–108
HOK Canada (Toronto)
  Ask Me Anything meeting in, 210
  Big Ten office consolidation and, 230
  company unrest and, 171
  Dubai Marina as project of, 151
  establishment of, 149
  percentage of company's projects by, 241

HOK Construction, 133
Hok Design Annuals, 214
HOK DRAW and DrawVision, 135
HOK Entertainment, 133
HOK Executive Committee (ExCom)
  Big Ten office consolidation by, 230
  board expansion and, 158
  board member replacements by, 186–187
  on bonus program restructuring, 203–204
  celebrations for 50th anniversary, 214–215
  on central services consolidations, 206–207
  CEO vacancy post-Sincoff, 165
  company in crisis and focus on, 172
  core boards restoration and, 213–214
  on diversification, 236
  establishment of, 117
  expanding, 180–181
  on financial problems, 134
  on firm-wide market practices and reorganization, 122
  on fiscal year changes, 157
  Galioto hiring and addition to, 201, 229–230
  Hellmuth's (Bill) addition to, 182, 185
  HR and CFO additions to, 163
  invigorating, 179–180
  leadership retreats and goals of, 122–123, 215
  MacLeamy's appointment to, 133–134
  MacLeamy's CEO appointment, 167
  MacLeamy's COO appointment, 154
  Mascia addition to, 228
  office leader dismissals and, 183–185
  on paying off bank credit line, 220
  on push-back over market practices, 124
  pyramid strategy, role in, 176
    (See also pyramid strategy)
  recruitment program with HR, 208
  Robson as COO on, 182, 185
  on selling off HOK Sport, 222–223
  staffing of Mexico City office, 147
  on technology advances and costs, 136–138
  Williams' addition to, 225–226

Index

HOK founders (Hellmuth, Obata & Kassabaum), 1–75
  "collaboration inside" as foundation, 33–40
    (*See also* company culture)
  company name, humor about, 37–38, 39
  early years of, 17–19
  formation of, 15–17
  founders' history, 9–15
    (*See also* Hellmuth, George F.; Kassabaum, George E.; Obata, Gyo)
  growth and project offices, 41–46
  innovations by, 21–32
    (*See also* innovation)
  logo, 17, *17*, *50*
  MacLeamy's arrival at, xvii–xxii
  overview, xiii–xv
  project management, 57–58
    (*See also* leadership and management)
  succession planning by, 67–75
    (*See also* succession planning)
  See also MacLeamy era (2003–2016); Obata era (1982–1,993); Sincoff era (1993–2002); *specific HOK offices*
HOK (international office locations)
  Berlin, 151
  Dubai, 151
  Hong Kong, 98–99, 107, 199, 230, 236
  Mexico City, 147–148, 198
  Moscow, 151
  percentage of company's projects in, 241
  Prague, 151
  Tokyo, 103–107
  Warsaw, 149, 151
  See also HOK Canada; HOK London
HOK International (subsidiary), 74
HOK London
  accounting procedures at, 205
  Big Ten office consolidation and, 230
  company unrest and, 171
  establishment of, 99–100
  firm-wide market-practices, reaction to, 124
  HOK Sport and, 150
  merger with CDH, 148–149
  Telefónica project and, 198
HOK Matrix, 81–82, 118–120
HOK office of chairman (OOC)
  establishment by Obata, 79
  on expansion to L.A., 93
  on Kajima's investment, 101–102
  on Kansas City office opening, 95–96
  Obata as consultant, 112–113
  Stauder on, 84, 109
  on Tampa office, 97
  See also HOK Executive Committee
HOK OneFirm User Guide, 123
HOK operations committee (OpsCom), 181, 182, 225, 244. *See also* operations
HOK Product Design, 234–235
HOK San Francisco
  Big Ten office consolidation and, 230
  firm-wide market-practices, reaction to, 124
  MacLeamy as managing principal, 84, 87–92, 127
  MacLeamy's move to, 48–50, *49*
  management of, 199
  market practices at, 82
  Moscone Center project, 60–63, *62*, *84*, 87, 88, 128, 190
  as project office, 41–42
  in sports design merger, 237–238
  Stauder at, 50, 57, 84
  sustaining company culture at, 82
  transportation projects through, 53–55
  Valentine at, 42, 48–50
HOK Sport (Kansas City)
  company crisis and, 172
  establishment of, 94–96
  financial crisis at, 166–167
  London merger, 150
  new sports design ventures after, 237–238
  selling off, 222–223, 227
  sport specialization, strength of, 119
HOK Sports + Recreation + Entertainment, 238
HOK St. Louis (headquarters)
  Big Ten office consolidation and, 230
  cash flow troubles and, 83–84
  Chicago office opening and, 148
  Davis at helm, 110
  fire at, xiii, 38–40
  firm-wide market-practices, reaction to, 124
  Graf's marketing leadership at, 68–69
  Kajima staff at, 102
  leadership teams (*See* HOK Executive Committee; HOK office of chairman)

market practices at, 82
Sincoff as Kassabaum's assistant at, 72
Stauder operations promotion at, 84
sustaining company culture at, 82
talent drain from, 48
transfers to international offices, 99, 100

HOK (U.S. offices)
Atlanta, 147, 230, 232
Chicago, 148, 228, 230
Dallas, 44–46, 69, 103, 124, 230
Houston, 145–147, 173, 182, 194–196, 230, 232
Kansas City (See HOK Sport (Kansas City))
Los Angeles, 93–94, 107, 124, 182, 199, 227, 230
New York, 42, 72–73, 124, 201–202, 202, 229, 230, 236
Tampa, 96–97, 133, 230
Washington, DC, 43, 82, 110–112, 151, 225, 230, 232
See also HOK San Francisco; HOK St. Louis (headquarters)

Honeywell, 140
Hong Kong airport, 107
hospitality design, 236, 241
Houston Galleria, 97, 98, 99, 146–147
Howard, Needles, Tammen & Bergendoff (HNTB), 95–96
Howell, Ian, 140–142

human resources
in bonus program restructuring, 203
ExCom and, 133, 163
innovation and staffing, 29–30
leadership change in, 227
Mahon at helm of, 84–85
office leader dismissals and, 184
staffing for Mexico City office, 147
streamlining, 207–208
See also Mahon, John

HYL. See Hellmuth, Yamasaki & Leinweber
Hysell, Anne, 91
Hysell, Bob, 91–92

I

IAI (International Alliance for Interoperability), 142
IBM, 118, 172
IECO (International Engineering Company), 53–54
Indian Health Service hospital (Bethel, Alaska), 51–52

innovation
core boards, 29, 213–214
CRS firm and, 145–146
design, 23–25
founders and, 16
marketing, 21–23
production, 25–28
start-to-finish, 28–29
stock ownership, 30–32
for sustainable design, 231–232

Integrated Project Delivery (IPD), 193
interior design, 30, 241
International Alliance for Interoperability (IAI), 142
International Engineering Company (IECO), 53–54
International Standardization Organization (ISO), 143
internship program, 207
interoperability, 141
intranet and website (HOK), 137, 138, 211–212
IPD (Integrated Project Delivery), 193
ISO (International Standardization Organization), 143
Ivory, Karen Kassabaum, 12–13

J

Jacobs, Bob, 72–74
James S. McDonnell Planetarium. See McDonnell Planetarium
Jaros, Baum & Bolles (New York), 140
J.E. Sirrine firm, 145
Jeddah airport project (Saudi Arabia), 90–91, 131–132
Jen, Chi Chen, 37, 43, 72
Jobs, Steve, 63, 128
"The John F. Mahon, Sr. Scholarship Fund," 229

K

Kahn & Jacobs (New York), 72–74, 149
Kajima, Shoichi, investment by, 101–104, 107, 118, 221–222
Kajima Corporation (Tokyo), 101–107, 165–166, 171
Kamphoefner, Henry, 70
Kantner, Hal, 136, 146

Kassabaum, Dorothy Gaston, 12
Kassabaum, George Alexander, 12
Kassabaum, George E.
    as AIA president, xxi, 28
    background and early career of, xiii, 3, 10, 12–14, 112
    cash flow management and, 83, 84
    community involvement of, 75
    company name, humor about, 37–38, 39
    death of, 74–75
    dual roles of, 200
    efficient workload management by, 28
    on geographic expansion, 41
    as Graf's mentor, 68
    HOK founding and, 14–17
    L.A. office opening and, 93
    MacLeamy's first impressions of, xxi
    mutual respect demonstrated by, 34
    photos of, 14, *16*, 75
    production innovations by, 25–28
    production successor for, 71, *71*–72
    on St. Louis office fire, 38
    on stock ownership, 30–31
    See also HOK founders
Kaufman, Edgar, 48
King Abdullah University of Science and Technology (KAUST), 194–196, *195*
King Khalid airport (Riyadh), 81, 87
King Saud University project (Riyadh), 73–74, 81, 91, 194
Kodiak Island High School (Alaska), 42, 50
Koopman, Herb, 26
Koshijima, K. C., 221

L

Labinski, Ron, 94–96, 121, 150, 222
laboratories market practice, 82
laboratory bench system design, 235
LaGuardia Airport project, 201–202, *202*
Lam, Juliette, 172
Lambert Airport terminal (St. Louis), 9, 14, 17, *18*–19, 81
Lawrence Berkeley National Laboratory, 140
leadership and management
    fixing offices with new leaders, 197–202
    leadership retreats, 122–123, 215–217, *216*–*217*
    leading vs. managing, 58–60, *59*
    MacLeamy era transitions, 225–230
    Moscone Center case study, 60–63, *62*
    Obata era transitions, 109–113
    project managers, 25–26, 29, 57–58
    Sincoff era transitions, 161–164
    See also HOK board of directors; HOK Executive Committee; HOK founders; MacLeamy era; Obata era; Sincoff era; succession planning
Leamy, Elisabeth, 64, 109, 154, 238
Leamy, Patrick. *See* MacLeamy, Patrick
LEED (Leadership in Environmental Energy and Design), 196, 234
legal issues, 30, 37, 84, 162–163, 203, 226–227
Leinweber, Hellmuth & Yamasaki (LHY, Detroit), 9, 12, 14
Leinweber, Joe, 9, 15
LeMessurier, Bill, 25
Levi Strauss & Co. headquarters (San Francisco), 87, 228
Lin, T. Y., 60–61
Lobb Partnership (London), 150
logos (HOK), 17, *17*, *50*, 214, *215*
Los Angeles County teaching hospital, 182
Luckman, Charles, 61, 72

M

Mackey, Eugene, 14
MacLeamy Curve. *See also* Effort Curve
    controlling cost, 191–192
    CURT problems and, 189–190
    design change costs, 192
    at HOK, 193–194
    KAUST case study, 194–196, *195*
    smart effort curve, *191*, *192*–193
    traditional, *191*, 191
MacLeamy, Jeanne MacArthur, 63–64, 131, 167, 208, 240
MacLeamy, Patrick
    AIA presentation on effort curve, 193
    Alaska projects and, 50–53
    arrest in Saudi Arabia, 131–133
    Asian expansion and travel experiences, 103–107, *106*, *127*, 130–131
    on board expansion and revamped structure, 158
    in buildingSMART development, 140–142, *142*
    CEO, appointment and election of, 167, 173 (*See also* MacLeamy era)

as chief operating officer, 153–158, 165–167
  (*See also* finances)
on collecting overdue bill in Malaysia, 89–90
on "doodling," 185–184, 184–*185*
on European expansion, 151
ExCom, appointment to, 133–134
executive assistant for, 129–130
on executive coaching lessons, 153–154, 172
first impressions of HOK, xx–xxi
on generosity to employees, 34–36
on Graf's leadership, 69
on growth and health of HOK today, 241–244, *242*
on hiring of HR director and CFO, 85
on HOK 50th anniversary, 214
as HOK chairman, 239–240
on HOK impact, xiii–xv
on joining HOK, xviii–xx, 22–23
on Kajima's investment, 102
on leadership retreats, 123
on leading vs. managing, 58–60, *59*
on Los Angeles expansion, 93–94
as managing principal in San Francisco, 84, 87–92
at market-practice workshop, 120–122
marriage of, 63–64
on Mexico City office, 147–148
on Middle East work and travel, 90–92
on paperless office, 139–140
in Pittsburgh, 47–48
on planning, 29
on playground build in Mexico, 216–217
on positive peer pressure value, 186
retirement of, 238–240
on "running toward trouble," 90–89
in San Francisco, 48–50, *49*, 53–55
on stock ownership, 32
Tech 2000 development and implementation by, 136–138
on "toilet seat lesson," 59–58
on Valentine's influence, 71
See also Moscone Convention Center
MacLeamy, Patrick (son), 64
MacLeamy era (2003–2,014), 169–240
  Big Ten office consolidation during, 230
  bonus program restructuring, 202–204
  celebrating HOK's 50 years, 214, *214*–215
  central services restructuring, 205–208
  company culture, reclaiming, 172, 209–218
    (*See also* company culture)
  company in crisis, 171–173
  effort curve, 189–196
    (*See also* effort curve)
  election in 2003, 173
  expanding into new markets during, 235–238
  finding new leaders, 197–202
  fixing offices during, 197–204
  launching product design, 234–235
  leadership during, 179–187, 225–230
    (*See also* HOK Executive Committee)
  naming next CEO, 238–240
  pyramid strategy, 172–176, 173
    (*See also* pyramid strategy)
  retreat for leaders, 215–217, *216*–*217*
  securing financial freedom, 219–223
  sustainable design, fulfilling dream for, 231–234
Mahon, John
  as adviser to ExCom, 133
  death of, 227
  on executive coaching for MacLeamy, 153–154
  as head of human resources, 84–85
  on HOK Sport value, 222
  invigorating ExCom and, 179
  as new ExCom member, 163, *163*
  recruitment program by, 207
  re-election of, 173
Malcic, Larry, 100, 148, 236
management. *See* leadership and management
Management Core Board, 213
Managing vs. Leading, 57–59, *59*
Mancinelli, Lou, 149
Marcus, Stanley, 97
Marin County Civic Center, 49, 64
marketing
  BizCom and, 244
  Dallas airport project and, 44–45
  full time, need for, 7
  Hellmuth's legacy in, 15, 118
  innovation and, 21–23
  Pareto Principle in, 199
  project offices and, 42
  specialized leadership in, 8
  with specialized teams, 80–81

marketing *(continued)*
  succession in, 68–69
  in Washington, DC, office, 43
  See also Graf, King; Hellmuth, George F.; market practices and specialization
Marketing Core Board, 213
market practices and specialization
  building type teams and project specialists, 80–81
  corporate services specialty, 163–164
  firm-wide market practices, 119–122
  healthcare specialty, 80, 82, 124, 171, 176, 241
  higher education specialty, 81, 82, 194–196
  HOK Matrix and, 81–82
  justice system specialty, 54–55, 63, 80, 82, 120, 241
  New Marketing and, 80–81
  push-back over firm-wide market practices, 124
  retail design specialty, 97–100, 98
  retreat focus on firm-wide strategy, 122–123
  science and technology specialty, 241
  sports design specialty, 94–96, 119, 150, 236–238, 241
    (*See also* HOK Sport)
  See also aviation specialty
Martin, Rick, 222–223
Mascia, Riccardo
  as BizCom chairman, 244
  firm-wide retreat, organizer for, 215, 216
  at helm of Chicago office, 228
  hired as Mexico City leader, 147–148
  in HOK Product Design launch, 234–235
  as "the fixer" in Hong Kong office, 198, *198*–199
Mascia, Sofia, 148, 198
Mascia, Sofia-Marie, 198
McCrary, Ed, 199
McDonnell Planetarium (St. Louis), xvii–xviii, *xviii*, 19
McIntire, Bob, 128
Meditations (Marcus Aurelius), 75
Mercedes-Benz Stadium (Atlanta), 238
Meunter, Rolf, 50
Miami Dolphins stadium project, 96
Microsoft Excel, 139, 157
Microsoft Windows, 136–137
Missouri Council of Architects, 75
Monk, Julia, 236
Moscone, George, 62–63
Moscone Convention Center (San Francisco)
  Apple announcements in, 128
  MacLeamy as project manager for, 61–62, 84
  management lessons of, 88, 190
  as San Francisco office accomplishment, 87
  winning challenging project, 60–61, 62
MUNI (San Francisco Municipal Railway), 53–54
Murphy, Joseph, 14
Murphy and Mackey (St. Louis), 14
Mylar use, 26

N
National Air and Space Museum, 43, 44, *61*, 111–112, *112*
Neiman-Marcus store (Houston), 97
Nervi, Pier Luigi, 19, 25
Netsch, Walter, xvii
net-zero energy buildings, 231
Nightingale Medal (Neocon Gold award), 235
90-Day Rule, 155–156, 205
Nortel (Canada), 149
Northwest Council of Governments (Washington state), 63

O
Oakland County courthouse (California), 57–58
Obata, Chiura, 10, 11
Obata, Gen, 109
Obata, Gyo
  Air and Space Museum design by, 43, 44
  airport terminal design and, 19
  amusing story about, 37
  background and early career of, xiii, 3, 10–12, *11, 14*
  in choosing future leaders, 239
  as consultant, 112–113
  Dallas airport design by, 44–46, *45*
  design successor for, *70*, 70–71
  digital images use by, 138
  on geographic expansion, 41
  "get the job" focus of, 118
  Graf and confidence in, 68
  graphic designer and, 30
  HOK founding and, 14–17

at HOK's 50th anniversary party, 214–215
Houston Galleria design by, 97, 98
innovation of, 23–25, 28–29
MacLeamy's first impressions of, xix–xxii
on MacLeamy's move to San Francisco, 48
McDonnell Planetarium design by, xvii–xviii, *xviii*
as Moscone Center designer, 60–61, 62
mutual respect demonstrated by, 34
office of chairman establishment by, 79 (*See also* Obata era)
photos of, 11–*13*, *16*, *111*, *113*
Priory School Chapel design by, 18, *19*
San Francisco office and, 41–42, 48, 50
Sincoff hiring by, 71–72
on St. Louis office fire, 40
stock ownership and, 30–31, 101–102
on "unbroken chain" of work, 97, 128
on Valentine's retirement, 228
wartime internment, 10–11
in winning over clients, 22
as Xerox center designer, 127–128
See also HOK founders
Obata, Haruko, 10, 11
Obata, Yuri, 11
Obata era (1982–1,991), 77–113
designer as chairman, 79–86
financial troubles, 83–85
growing pains, 82–83
growth and specialization, 93–100 (*See also* growth and expansion)
New Marketing in, 80–81
project specialties begin in, 80–82
San Francisco office during, 87–92
stock sale to investors, 101–108
sustainable design emergence, 107–108
transitions and hiring of family, 109–113
See also HOK office of chairman
office locations. *See* HOK (international office locations); HOK (U.S. offices)
office of chairman (OOC). *See* HOK office of chairman
O'Leary, Dennis, 163
Oliff, Donovan, 227
operations
companywide crisis and, 171–172
COO successor, need for, 181
ExCom "action items" in improving, 179–180
"great" operations in pyramid strategy, 173, *174*–175, 207, 214, 215, 241
Kassabaum's expertise in, 84
MacLeamy's COO appointment, 154
Robson's COO appointment, 182, 183, *185*
See also MacLeamy, Patrick; Stauder, Bob
OpsCom. *See* HOK operations committee
organizational culture. *See* company culture
Our Lady of the Snows (Belleville, Illinois), 28
ownership innovation, 30–32

P

Pac Bell Park (San Francisco), 63
Pareto Principle, 199
Parshall, Steve, 232
Peace Shield (Saudi Arabia), 146, 147
Peña, Willie, 145
Petrie, Richard, 240
Petticord and Mills (Washington, DC), 43
philanthropy, 214, 216–217, *217*
pin-bar drafting system, 26
Pittsburgh project office, 47–48
Plaza Indonesia (Jakarta), 99
Populous architects (London), 236
Port Authority of New York and New Jersey, 202
Porterfield, Neil, 29
Pratzel, Bob
on buying back Kajima stock, 221–222
as CFO, adviser to ExCom, 133
establishing financial metrics with MacLeamy, 154–157
financial accountability by, 186
financial crises, confronting, 165–167
hiring as chief financial officer, 85
HOK financial security as "dream" of, 176
on HOK London finances, 205
invigorating ExCom and, 179
as new ExCom member, 163, *163*
on Obata's stock buy-back, 101
on paying off bank credit line, 219–220
on purchase of CRS firm, 146, 147
re-election as CFO, 173
retirement of, 229
on stock shareholder system, 211
predesign services, 28

Priory School Chapel (St. Louis), 18, *19*, 25
production
   innovation and, 25–28
   Kassabaum as principal, 15
   specialized leadership in, 8
   successor in, 71–72
   See also Kassabaum, George E.; operations; Sincoff, Jerry
project architects, 26, 29
project managers, 25–26, 29, 57–58. *See also* leadership and management
project offices, 41–46
   Anchorage, 42, 50–53
   in Belleville, Illinois, 72, 96
   Dallas, 44–46
   in East St. Louis, 96
   local architects, sharing workload with, 23
   Madrid, 198–199
   Pittsburgh, 47–48
   San Francisco, 41–42, 48–50, *49*, 53–55
   Washington, DC, 43
Providence Hospital (Anchorage), 42
public relations, 30
Purvis, Paul, 148
pyramid strategy
   board member replacements and, 186–187
   central services restructuring, 205–208
   chief operating officer importance in, 181, 182
   core boards effectiveness in, 213–214
   dreams in, 175–176, 216, 231–238
   empowering board of directors for, 185
   finding new leaders, 197–202
   as focus of leadership retreat, 215–216, 216
   MacLeamy's retirement and, 238
   office leader removals and, 183–185
   overview, 172–176, *173*

Q
Quality Improvement Project Management Initiative, 213

R
Ralston-Purina headquarters project (St. Louis), 71
Rand, Ayn, 34–35
Raven, Peter, 107–108
Reagan, Ronald, 79
Reay, Chip, 30, 38
Remington, Bill, 30
Rhodes, John, 236
Richert, Terry, 52–53, 63
Robbie, Joe, 96
Robson, Tom
   coming to HOK in merger with CRS, 146–147
   COO appointment, 182, 183, *185*
   Hellmuth's (Bill) strategy and, 244
   on MacLeamy's Houston visit during crisis, 172
   marriage of, 226
   OpsCom assistance for, 225
   Saudi university project and, 194–195
Roebling, John A., 3–4
Roemer, Chester, 72
Rouse Company, 120
Rowlett, John, 145
Run toward Trouble, xiv, 87–89, 92

S
Saarinen, Eliel, 11–12
St. Sylvester's Church (Missouri), 161
San Bernardino County Courthouse (California), 88–89, 190
San Francisco Board of Supervisors, 62
San Francisco Municipal Railway (MUNI), 53–54
San Francisco Redevelopment Agency, 60, 63
Saud, Abdullah bin Abdulaziz Al (king), 194–195
Saudi Aramco, 194–195
Sauer, Larry, 39
Schrock, Brad, 237–238
Scott, Wally, 145
Self, Larry, 103, 133–134, 150–151
Sendai Airport (Japan), 107
Sheard, Rod, 150
Shell, 189–190, 193
SHG (Smith, Hinchman & Grylls, Detroit), 6–7
Siconolfi, Chuck, 176
Silicon Valley projects, 127–128, 129
Sincoff, Jerry
   background of, 71
   as CEO (*See* Sincoff era)
   at HOK's 50th anniversary party, 214

on Kajima's investment, 101–102
on MacLeamy's need for coaching, 153–154
market practices tallying and, 82
Obata's leadership transition and, 79
as production leader, 71, 72
retirement of, 163–164
See also HOK Executive Committee; HOK office of chairman
Sincoff era (1993–2,000), 115–168
board of directors, revamped structure to, 158
client focus, 118–119, 164
financial crises during CEO vacancy, 165–167
financial metrics, enforcing, 153–158 (See also finances)
firm purchases and mergers, 145–152
firm-wide market practices and reorganization, 119–123, 164
growth and expansion as priority, 118, 164, 167, 241
leadership during, 117, 161–164
MacLeamy's firm-wide role, 127–134 (See also MacLeamy, Patrick)
push-back over reorganization, 124
retreats and team-building, 122–123
technology transition, 135–143 (See also technology)
three-pronged strategy, 117–122
SIU. See Southern Illinois University
Skidmore, Owings & Merrill (SOM)
Galioto work at, 189
hajj terminal design by, 132
Hellmuth's (Bill) early work at, 110
HOK Chicago building and, 148
HOK recruits from, 199–201
MacLeamy's job offer at, xvii
Moscone Center proposals and, 61
Obata's early work at, 10, 12
smart effort curve, 191, 192–193, 195
Smith, Hinchman & Grylls (SHG, Detroit), 6–7, 9
Smithsonian, 43, 44
SOM. See Skidmore, Owings & Merrill
Soto, Roger, 147, 194
Southern Illinois University (SIU), 19, 72, 81, 96
Spear, Joe, 95

specialization. See market practices and specialization
Spivey Building (East St. Louis), 72
sports design specialty, 94–96, 119, 150, 236–238, 241. See also HOK Sport
St. Enoch Centre (Glasgow, Scotland), 99–100
St. Louis (city), 3–4, 9–10
St. Louis Dispatch, on office fire, 38–40
St. Louis Magazine, 18
Staed, Bob, 162–163, 173, 226–227
Stanford University library project, 41–42, 50, 81
State University of New York, 81
Stauder, Bob
on collecting overdue bill, 89
freehand detailing by, 26
promotion to operations post and OOC, 84
resignation of, 109
in San Francisco office, 50, 57
in tackling financial troubles, 84–85
See also HOK office of chairman
Stinger, Bill, 100, 148
stock
employee options, 31–32
employees, explaining system to, 210–212
increase in value of during MacLeamy's tenure, 211–212, 235
Kajima, buying out, 221–222
Kajima dissatisfaction with value, 165–166, 171
Kajima's investments and stock sale, 101–108
ownership, 30–32, 67, 79
shareholder meeting in 2003, 173
Stratford, Gordon, 149
study models, 24
succession planning, 67–75
for CEOs, 165, 238–240, 239
design successor, 70, 70–71, 181–182
importance of, 4, 67
international subsidiary, 73–74
Kassabaum's death, 74–75, 75
marketing successor, 68–69, 69
production successor, 71, 71–72
Sullivan, Thomas, 44–45
sustainable design
Abu Dhabi oil company case study, 232–234, 233
BIM and, 143

sustainable design *(continued)*
  energy-efficient buildings, HOK's interest in, 107–108
  Hellmuth's (Bill) goals for, 231–232
  innovations in, 231–232
  Valentine as leader in, 108, 117, 176, 231

T
Tatum, Jay, 194
Tech 2000, 136–138, 206
technical architecture, 200–201, 229, 243–244
Technical Core Board, 214
technology, 135–143
  in advance collaboration rooms, 242
  Advance Technology Group, 195, 206–207
  buildingSMART development, 140–142, 142
  digital workplace, benefits of, 139–140
  early CAD, 135
  firm-wide roles accommodated by, 227
  interoperability and, 141
  for project tracking, 58
  recruitment benefits and, 227
  Silicon Valley projects, 127–128, 129
  See also Building Information Modeling
Telefónica project (Madrid), 198–199
10-Month Backlog Rule, 156–157
Terrazas, Eduardo, 147
Thompson, Ron, 131–133
360 Architecture, 237–238
Tishman Construction (New York), 140
Tokyo Telecom headquarters, 107
Truman, Harry, 54, 75
Tucker, Tad, 100, 148
Turner Construction Company, 61–62, 190
TWA, 37
Tynan, Tim, 85, 154–157, 205, 211–212, 229

U
Udvar-Hazy Center (National Air and Space Museum), 111–112, 112
Union Station (St. Louis), 120
University of Alaska Fairbanks housing, 42
University of Wisconsin, 81
Urbana Architects (Toronto), 149

V
Valentine, Bill
  Alaska work and, 42, 48, 50
  Asian expansion and, 103–106, 127
  background of, 70, 72
  on celebrating HOK's 50th anniversary, 214
  as design leader, 70, *70*–71
  digital images resistance by, 138
  on "dream" for sustainable design, 176
  financial crises and, 165–167
  on Graf as "peacemaker," 71
  leadership retreats and, 123, 215
  on leader's qualities, 239
  as Levi Strauss project designer, 87, 228
  Los Angeles expansion and, 93–94
  MacArthur hiring by, 63
  MacLeamy's injury and, 131
  MacLeamy's leadership and, 57, 84, 87, 153–154, 167
  MacLeamy's move to Pittsburgh and, 47–48
  MacLeamy's retirement party and, 240
  as MacLeamy's team leader, xxii
  at market-practice workshop, 120–122
  Moscone Center project and, 61
  MUNI project and, 53
  naming design successor for, 181–182
  Obata's leadership transition and, 79
  on office leader dismissals, 184
  as president, 165, 167, 173, 179
  retirement of, 228, 229
  in San Francisco office, 42, 48–50
  in securing Apple project, 128
  on selling off HOK Sport, 222
  as sustainable design leader, 108, 117, 231
  on sustaining company culture, 82
  Tokyo travel experiences, 103–106, 106
  as vice chairman for design, 117 (*See also* HOK Executive Committee)
  as Xerox center designer, 127–128
Valentine, Jane, 70
Verser, Marjory, 14
videoconferencing, 242
Voelker, Bill, xix, xx, 33

W
Washington University (St. Louis), 6, 10–11, 13, 14, 28, 71, 75, 100
Watson, Paul
  as ExCom adviser, 133
  at HOK's 50th anniversary party, 214
  as in-house attorney, 30

    legal department growth and, 162–163
    Obata's friendship with, 37
    retirement of, 227
    workload of, 84
website and intranet (HOK), 137, 138, 211–212
Wellner, Dennis, 95
Wells Fargo (San Francisco), 220, 221
Wembley Stadium (London), 150
Whitcomb, Frank, 131
White House (Houston), 146
Who Says Elephants Can't Dance? (Gerstner, Lou), 172
Wilkinson, Bruce, 146
Williams, Morgan, 225
Williams, Susan Klumpp, 225–226, *226*, *244*
Wirum, Harold, 51
World Trade Center, 15, 201
Wright, Frank Lloyd, 48, 49, 64

X

Xerox Palo Alto Research Center (PARC), 127–128

Y

Yamasaki, Minoru, 6, 7, 9–10, 12, 13, *14*–15, 18–19, 201
Young, Ken, 136, 138, 139, 176, 206